Welcome to Paranormal Perspectives

It was important for me to develop Paranormal Perspectives for those seeking a deeper understanding of the paranormal world. This series is intended for sceptics, believers, and those who have unfathomable experiences and are often frightened by them. These books will help their understanding of what is happening to them.

The Paranormal Perspectives series will explore, in-depth, the encounters, theories, and research into incomprehensible events and how these experiences motivated remarkable individuals to delve deeper and share their extraordinary relationships of the paranormal with the world.

Paranormal Perspectives begins with five books exploring the spectrum of metaphysical events, with insight from the UK's top ghost detective, a licensed clinical psychologist, a retired English professor, a prolific UFO investigator, and a writer specialising in first-hand, personal paranormal encounters.

You, too, may have had a lifetime of unearthly experiences and may wish to add to the series. Please visit 6th-books.com for further information. We look forward to hearing from you.

I hope you enjoy this series as it guides you on your quest and pulls back the veil to shine light into the unknown.

Sleep w

G L Davi

Author of *Haunted: Horror of Haverfordwest*

Paranormal Perspectives

One Big Box of 'Paranormal Tricks': From Ghosts to Poltergeists to the Theory of Just One Paranormal Power
by John Fraser

A Jungian Understanding of Transcendent Experiences
by Susan Plunket

Hauntings, Attachments and Ghouls
by G L Davies

Portraits of Alien Encounters Revisited
by Nigel Harry Watson

Where the Spirit Led
by Brad Burkholder

What People Are Saying About

Paranormal Perspectives: Portraits of Alien Encounters

This admirable study plunges promptly into the darkest psychological regions behind the jolly mythology of aliens and UFOs peddled universally by the entertainment media. To the uninitiated it will be scary, certainly, but an eye-opener well worth the effort.
Robert Rickard, *Fortean Times*

Part of the value of Nigel's book is in showing how these "extreme" reports shade into the generality of UFO cases and other anomalous personal experiences.
Peter Rogerson, *Magonia*

Nigel is never one to shirk a challenge and simply thrives upon situations which would make less broad-minded imaginations warp, creek and eventually collapse in utter despair! Certainly, he was tested in the case of Paul Bennett, then a 13-year-old schoolboy from Shipley, West Yorkshire. For Paul claimed the most remarkable track record for seeing UFOs, entities, ghosts, robots and so on. Not for him occasional glimpses of these other worlds. They impinged directly upon his reality, and he lived with them.
Jenny Randles, *Northern UFO News*

UFO Investigations Manual
As with all Haynes manuals the quality and content is great, the subject is well covered and just my cup of tea.
Trevtron, *Amazon* review

This book is a must read for anyone who claims to be a ufologist, as it puts us on the trail of what could be the solution to the most common cases of sighting among the uninformed population. I recommend it 100%.
Leopoldo Zambrano Enríquez, *Amazon* review

This is a fascinating book by Nigel Watson which has been well researched and presented. It explains the history of UFO sightings with lots of facts and photographs. The thing I like is that it is balanced, for example, it covers the faking and misidentification of UFOs as well as credible sightings. There is also speculation about the possible propulsion of UFOs etc. In addition, it contains a section devoted to UFOs making a UFO report etc. There's very comprehensive coverage of a challenging and fascinating subject – I cannot think how anyone with an interest in the subject would not find this a worthy addition to their bookshelf.
Nimbus, *Amazon* review

The author has no axe to grind, which is refreshing, and he writes in a very objective as well as informative manner.
R.E. Cox, *Amazon* review

Ideal present for anyone interested in UFOs.
Antony, *Amazon* review

This is probably as good and comprehensive an analysis of the UFO phenomenon as one is likely to find in such a compact format. Nigel Watson knows ufology from the grassroots; he's done the investigatory legwork and could never be described as an 'armchair ufologist'.
John Rimmer, *Magonia*

UFOs of the First World War
I would recommend this book. It's very scholarly and entertaining. The amount of information can be a little overwhelming at times, though.
OE, *Amazon* review

This book was an excellent read and in my opinion an unbiased account and analysis of reports of aerial phenomena straddling the WWI period. I especially enjoyed the de-bunking of myths.
Oscar, *Amazon* review

It has some great World War I information and we get to see how these UFO sightings occurred around the world right before the war. There is also some mention of the UFO that the Red Baron shot down. Possibly a hoax, so the book doesn't spend time trying to convince you that these were actual aliens, but it does lay out the facts with documentation that something was seen that could not be explained for the most part. It's a fun read.
William R. Schlichter, *Amazon* review

Captured by Aliens?
This is an important book and one which I recommend.
Peter Rogerson

The backbone of the book is the Barney and Betty Hill abductions in 1961, which seem to have started the phenomenon in its modern form, though there were earlier equivalent instances. The Hills crop up in most chapters, but along the way we also discover Victorian "airship" sightings, the "contactees" of the 1950s – who rather than being abducted claim to have had a more voluntary exchange of information with aliens and visits to their ships (who were almost all like ordinary humans and tended to come from Mars or Venus) – and the evolution of

the key parts of abduction stories, from intrusive medical examinations to lost time.
Brian Clegg, *Amazon* review

Although his conclusions support the view that the abduction phenomenon, and indeed a large part of the entire UFO story, is of psycho-social origin, this is without the hard-line dogmatism that mars much of the "sceptical" writing on the topic. He is careful to note that there are many instances where we have to simply admit that we do not know.
John Rimmer, *Magonia*

Paranormal Perspectives: Portraits of Alien Encounters Revisited

High Strangeness British UFO Cases

Previous Books

Portraits of Alien Encounters, VALIS Books, London, 1990.
ISBN: 978-0951625101

UFO Investigations Manual: UFO Investigations from 1892 to the Present Day, Haynes, Yeovil, UK, 2013.
ISBN: 978-0857334008

UFOs of the First World War: Phantom Airships, Balloons, Aircraft and Other Mysterious Aerial Phenomena, History Press, Stroud, Gloucestershire, 2015.
ISBN: 978-0750959148

Captured by Aliens? A History and Analysis of American Abduction Claims, McFarland, Jefferson, North Carolina, 2020.
ISBN: 978-1476681412

Paranormal Perspectives: Portraits of Alien Encounters Revisited

High Strangeness British UFO Cases

Nigel Watson

6TH BOOKS

London, UK
Washington, DC, USA

First published by Sixth Books, 2025
Sixth Books is an imprint of Collective Ink Ltd.,
Unit 11, Shepperton House, 89 Shepperton Road, London, N1 3DF
office@collectiveinkbooks.com
www.collectiveinkbooks.com
www.6th-books.com

For distributor details and how to order please visit the 'Ordering' section on our website.

Text copyright: Nigel Watson 2024

ISBN: 978 1 80341 745 5
978 1 80341 876 6 (ebook)
Library of Congress Control Number: 2024938649

All rights reserved. Except for brief quotations in critical articles or reviews, no part of this book may be reproduced in any manner without prior written permission from the publishers.

The rights of Nigel Watson as author have been asserted in accordance with the Copyright, Designs and Patents Act 1988.

A CIP catalogue record for this book is available from the British Library.

Design: Lapiz Digital Services

UK: Printed and bound by CPI Group (UK) Ltd, Croydon, CR0 4YY
Printed in North America by CPI GPS partners

We operate a distinctive and ethical publishing philosophy in all areas of our business, from our global network of authors to production and worldwide distribution.

Contents

Chapter 1	A Portrait of a Percipient: Paul Bennett	21
Chapter 2	Close Encounters and Children	90
Chapter 3	The Liverpool Leprechauns	109
Chapter 4	Shadowlands of Ufology: Mrs Trench	125
Chapter 5	"We Are Here": Josephine Elissah	135
Chapter 6	Alien Messages and Impressions: Norman Harrison	150
Chapter 7	Contemplating Cosmic Questions: Martin Bolton	165
Chapter 8	Aliens in the Family ... and the Pink Panther Abduction: Stefan Lobuczek	183
Chapter 9	Taken Elsewhere: Paula Green	190
Chapter 10	Nocturnal Invaders	208
Chapter 11	Angelic Visions	220
Chapter 12	A Combination of Factors	228

Author Biography	238
Previous Titles	239
Note to the Reader	241
Appendices	243
Appendix 1 A Safe Home for UFO Files	245
Appendix 2 UFO Databases	247
Appendix 3 The Great British UFO Learning Centre	249
Magazines and Websites	250
Bibliography	253
Glossary	256
Index	259

To the UFO enigma.

Acknowledgements

I am indebted to all the people I interviewed for this book who gave me their valuable time and hospitality. And, to everybody who has given me their advice (whether I took it or not), information and support, I offer my grateful thanks.

For their encouragement and ideas, special thanks go to: Martin Kottmeyer, Jenny Randles, Robert Rickard, John Rimmer, Peter Rogerson, Roger Sandell and David Sutton.

My thanks are due to the following UFO investigators who have, through their own investigations and reports, aided mine: Brian Allan, Chris Aubeck, Graham and Mark Birdsall, Peter Brookesmith, Eileen Buckle, David Clarke, Andrew Collins, Mike Covell, Ian Cresswell, Geoffrey Doel, Tony Dodd, Hilary Evans, Chris Evers, Carl Grove, Kevin Goodman, John Hanson, John Harney, Leslie Harris, John Hind, Richard Holland, Ted Horton, Philip Hudson, Miles Johnson, Martin Keatman, Barry King, Isaac Koi, Philip Mantle, Shirley McIver, Steve Mera, Robert Morrell, Richard Nash, Norman Oliver, Granville Oldroyd, Graham Phillips, Mark Pilkington, David Rees, Andy Roberts, Malcolm Robinson, Paul Screeton, Terry Shotton, John Spencer, Susan Stead, Clas Svahn, Tim Swartz, David Sydeserff, Alan Walsh, Peter Warrington, John Watson, Dirk van der Werff, Paul Whetnall, Trevor Whitaker, Nigel Wright.

Thanks to Charles Bowen, Jerome Clark, Gordon Creighton, Charles Fort, John Keel, and Jacques Vallée whose writings have all been very helpful and thought provoking.

Thanks also go to, John Croft, Alan Drinkell, Clive Potter, Rob Waugh and Robin Witting.

To all the membership of UFOIN, and to SUFORS members: Dennis and Keith Beacroft, Graham, Roger Hebb, David Johnson, Perry, and Ray & Liz.

The ideas expressed in this text are solely my own and do not necessarily reflect those of the people mentioned above.

Abbreviations

APRO: Aerial Phenomena Research Organization.
ASC: Altered State of Consciousness.
ASSAP: The Association for the Scientific Study of Anomalous Phenomena.
BRUFORP: Bradfordian Research into Unidentified Flying Objects and Related Phenomenon.
BSRA: Borderland Sciences Research Association.
BUFOG: Birmingham UFO Group.
BUFORA: British UFO Research Association.
CAS: Classic Abduction Syndrome (or scenario).
CAUS: Citizens Against UFO Secrecy.
CIA: Central Intelligence Agency.
CSICOP: Committee for the Scientific Investigation of Phenomenon.
CUFOS: Center for UFO Studies.
ESP: Extra Sensory Perception.
ETH: Extraterrestrial Hypothesis.
FBI: Federal Bureau of Investigation.
FOIA: Freedom of Information Act.
FSR: Flying Saucer Review.
GSW: Ground Saucer Watch.
IFO: Identified Flying Object.
IUR: International UFO Reporter, journal published by CUFOS.
LAPIS: Lancashire Anomalous Phenomena Investigation Society
LITS: Lights in the Sky.
JASON: July, August, September, October, November. Peak periods of UFO activity according to Paul Bennett.
Majestic 12: See MJ-12.
MJ-12: Alleged secret US Government agency that deals with UFOs and aliens.
MIB: Men In Black.
MT: Metro Triangle.

MUFOB: Merseyside UFO Bulletin.
MUFON: Mutual UFO Network.
NUFOR: National UFO Research.
NDE: Near Death Experience.
NICAP: National Investigations Committee on Aerial Phenomena.
NUFON: Northern UFO Network.
OLM: Outer Limits Magazine.
PSH: Psychosocial Hypothesis.
SETI: Search for Extraterrestrial Intelligence.
SUFORS: Scunthorpe UFO Research Society.
SP: Sleep Paralysis.
UAP: Unidentified Aerial Phenomena.
UAP: Unidentified Anomalous Phenomena.
UAV: Unidentified Anomalous Vehicle.
UFO: Unidentified Flying Object.
UFOIN: UFO Investigators Network.
USAF: United States Air Force.
WUFOS: Wirral UFO Society.
YUFOS: Yorkshire UFO Society.

Preface

The UFO enigma is here to stay. Every now and again there are mutterings that the subject is a dead duck, but it only takes a new sighting, a video or a photograph to revive interest in the topic.

The revelation in 2017 that the US had funded a secret Advanced Aerospace Threat Identification Program (AATIP) to the tune of 22 million dollars, along with videos taken by US Navy pilots, brought UFOs back into the headlines.

Now retitled as Unidentified Anomalous Phenomena (UAP), the storm of publicity brought about US Congress hearings where the idea that UAPs are of a non-terrestrial origin was strongly endorsed. Another consequence was that the Pentagon set up an All-domain Anomaly Resolution Office (AARO) to collect, record, investigate and evaluate UAP reports and is mandated to provide Congress with an annual report of their findings, whilst NASA has set up an independent UAP study that will concentrate on "aerial" phenomena.

Kevin Knuth, Robert Powell and Peter Reali, members of the Scientific Coalition for UAP Studies, in a 2019 paper note that reliable witnesses have seen structured craft that exhibit "impossible" flight characteristics. They state: "Estimated accelerations range from almost 100g to 1000s of gs with no observed air disturbance, no sonic booms, and no evidence of excessive heat commensurate with even the minimal estimated energies. In accordance with observations, the estimated parameters describing the behavior of these craft are both anomalous and surprising. The extreme estimated flight characteristics reveal that these observations are either fabricated or seriously in error, or that these craft exhibit technology far more advanced than any known craft on Earth."

Their belief is that: "The observed flight characteristics of these craft are consistent with the flight characteristics required for interstellar travel."

Other serious supporters of UAPs have agreed with such views and have speculated that these non-terrestrial craft are from other dimensions.

We should wind the clock back to 1947 when Kenneth Arnold's sighting of flying saucers, initiated fears that they were some kind of Soviet super weapon or extraterrestrial visitors preparing to invade our planet.

At that time the United States Air Force quickly established Project Sign to investigate sightings and in an unreleased "Estimate of the Situation" it was claimed that after filtering out cases that could be identified as misidentifications, the remaining cases might be of interplanetary vehicles.

An article in *Life* magazine in April 1952 supported such an outlook. Reviewing hundreds of reports from the Air Force files, it concluded that UFOs "cannot be explained by present science as natural phenomena – but solely as artificial devices, created and operated by a high intelligence." And "no power plant known or projected on earth could account for the performance of these devices."

Long before Kevin Knuth, Robert Powell and Peter Reali, the *Life* article quotes from Dr Walther Riedel, who had worked on rocket technology at Peenemunde in World War Two:

> First, the skin temperatures of structures operating under the observed conditions would make it impossible for any terrestrial structure to survive. The skin friction of the missile at those speeds at those altitudes would melt any metals or nonmetals available.
>
> Second, consider the high acceleration at which they fly and maneuver ... In some descriptions the beast spirals straight up. If you think of the fact that the centrifugal

force in a few minutes of such a maneuver would press the crew against the outside, and do likewise to the blood, you see what I mean.

Third ...There are many occurrences where they have done things that only a pilot could perform but that no human pilot could stand.

Fourth, in most of the reports there is a lack of visible jets. Most observers report units without visible flame, and no trail. If it would be any known type of jet, rocket, piston engine, or chain-reaction motor, there would, be a very clear trail at high altitude ... It is from no power unit we know of...

Project Sign was superseded by Project Grudge and Project Blue Book that sought to explain all sightings and dismissed any exotic explanations or theories. This was done to prevent military communications being clogged up by flying saucer reports that could be initiated by a foreign power to camouflage a real missile attack.

Civilians like Donald E. Keyhoe and his National Investigations Committee on Aerial Phenomena (NICAP) organisation took up the challenge to thoroughly investigate UFO sightings and to get the Government to admit that they were hiding evidence of interplanetary visitations.

Whilst Keyhoe took a scientific approach to the subject, he was concerned about "the crackpots who claim to have ridden saucers and talked with spacemen or women. Unfortunately I have laid the groundwork for these phonies to succeed; I think I have built up a fairly logical case for an interplanetary answer... you have to be stronger than the fakers."

Keyhoe was frustratingly stuck between the rock of the Air Force's extreme scepticism and the hardcore contactee "crackpots" who thrived on telling wild stories with no evidence to back up their claims.

The physical sciences do have their place in the study of the UFO phenomenon, but the tendency has been for other aspects of the phenomenon to be ignored or excluded for the sake of what is regarded as scientific objectivity. For example, the late Charles Bowen who edited *Flying Saucer Review*, related the story of a well-known UFO investigator who interviewed a UFO witness whose story was so improbable that he listened to the person in an ultra-sceptical vein. Several years later the same investigator was staggered to read a report of a case that was very similar to the old case he had cast aside for fear that it was a romantic fabrication. In the process of UFO investigation, this kind of censoring of evidence is not uncommon.

When Project Blue Book was closed in 1969, it concluded that:

1. No UFO reported, investigated, and evaluated by the Air Force was ever an indication of threat to our national security;
2. There was no evidence submitted to or discovered by the Air Force that sightings categorized as "unidentified" represented technological developments or principles beyond the range of modern scientific knowledge; and
3. There was no evidence indicating that sightings categorized as "unidentified" were extraterrestrial vehicles.

That was a pretty damning conclusion, one that the British Ministry of Defence has always concurred with. It does make you wonder if the latest NASA and AARO studies will come to similar findings, or will they find the truth (whatever that is) that ufologists lust for?

Going back to the 1970s, civilian groups and individuals carried on with a gritty determination to continue their work. It was in this decade stories of alien abductions slowly became accepted by ufologists. These told of people being forcefully zapped inside spaceships and intimately examined. They presented a sharp contrast to the friendly space rides given to the contactees, yet the abductees like the contactees often passed on the message that the aliens will save us from inevitable doom if we do not change our ways.

Flying saucers dominated classic science fiction films of the 1950s, but with a few exceptions they had cheesy plotlines and pathetic special effects. The release of Steven Spielberg's *Close Encounters of the Third Kind* in 1978 changed all that. His big budget homage to those films and to the subject of UFOs, powerfully showing Government secrecy, abductions, all types of impressive looking UFOs and the aliens' ability to contact chosen people through telepathic images. It all culminates with the release of human abductees and the appearance of enigmatic spindly grey aliens emerging from their gigantic mothership. The fanfare of publicity surrounding it in Britain certainly gave interest in the subject a big boost.

That film and the stream of imitators helped establish the image of the alien greys, that Keyhoe would have dismissed as the imaginings of crackpots.

Close Encounters shows they are from outer space and have far superior technology to our own. The extraterrestrial hypothesis (ETH) scores over so many of the ideas advanced to replace it, in that it is a natural explanation. Paranormal and parapsychological theories try to explain the elusive quality of alien encounters, but they are unsatisfactory because they use one set of mysteries to explain another.

The ETH supporters seek spaceships, the paranormal enthusiasts and contactees chase "space ghosts" whilst the so-called "new ufologists" of the 1970s sought relevance, context and understanding of the UFO experience by embracing the psychosocial hypothesis (PSH).

The PSH regards UFO experiences as the outcome of personal psychology in the context of the cultural and sociological setting. Peter Rogerson, one of the pioneers of new ufology noted:

"We should perhaps think of separate social panics, rumours, folklore and contemporary mythologies, all organised around a common structure of the flying saucer."

Whatever theory you support there is no simple and all-embracing answer to the UFO phenomenon.

My *Portraits of Alien Encounters* book was written with the excitement of the release of *Star Wars, Close Encounters* and the boom in science fiction films in the background. My aim in that book, and this revised update, was to collect, investigate and record the reports that came my way.

I discovered a massive underbelly of reports that even ufologists were likely to reject as too weird or unbelievable, by people who might be cruelly branded as crackpots. UFO and paranormal scholar Hilary Evans notes that calling people crackpots or labelling their accounts as "figments of the imagination" offers no help to the percipient or to our understanding their experiences. He goes on to say that, "in neglecting the investigation of such reports, science is passing over a wealth of case-material which could tell us more about how the human mind works."

Portraits was a snapshot of ufology, mainly in northern England, of that period, and finally published in 1990. Now many decades later this is an extensively revised version and some of the chapters have been deleted and replaced with newer and more relevant cases and reports that supplement the older ones.

The cases here show the sheer variety of UFO experiences, and I have tried to present them as best as possible in the words of the percipients without trying to force them into any explanatory box.

Notes and References

Knuth, Kevin H. et al. "Estimating Flight Characteristics of Anomalous Unidentified Aerial Vehicles," *Entropy*, Vol. 21, 10 939. 25 Sep. 2019, at: https://www.mdpi.com/1099-4300/21/10/939

Darrach Jr., H.B. and Ginna, Robert. "Have we Visitors from Space?" *Life*, 7 April 1952, p. 81 and p. 97.

Bowen, Charles. "Vexed Questions," *Flying Saucer Review*, Vol. 24, No. 2., August 1978, p. 2.

Rogerson, Peter. "Towards a Revisionist History of Ufology," *MUFOB*, New Series 13, Winter 1978/79, p. 14.

Powell, Linda. *Against the Odds. Major Donald E. Keyhoe and His Battle to End UFO Secrecy*, Anomalist Books, Charlottesville, Virginia, 2023, pp. 113–114.

Evans, Hilary. *Visions. Apparitions. Alien Visitors*, Book Club Associates, London, 1984, p. 15.

Introduction

1970s Ufology

To me the 1970s was the Golden Age of ufology, it was a time when local, national and international groups were having regular meetings and cases were reported and discussed in a growing number of magazines. We hammered out letters and articles on typewriters and used landline telephones. Abduction and high-strangeness reports were just about being accepted by ufologists, Roswell was just a footnote in history and Rendlesham was yet to come.

The Apollo moon-landing missions led to my interest in UFOs. I started by collecting newspaper clippings that mentioned anything related to space exploration and at the local library, I got any book available on the subject. On the same shelves were books about UFOs and I inevitably gravitated towards them. Some featured sober stories of "respectable" people seeing strange things in the sky and the USAF investigations into the matter, written by the likes of Donald Keyhoe.

There were as many contactee books, by George Adamski and George Hunt Williamson who said they met the space people on Earth and were taken on trips inside the saucers. *The Scoriton Mystery* by Eileen Buckle impressed me because it related to events in England, and it had connections with Adamski. Later, I was disappointed to read Norman Oliver's criticism of the case in his *Sequel to Scoriton* and his conclusion that it was a hoax.

At the time I was open to the idea that spaceships might be visiting us. Erich von Daniken's *Chariots of the Gods?* seemed to confirm that they had been visiting us for thousands of years.

The Apollo missions had made it logical to think that if we could leave our "cradle" then alien intelligences could have done so long ago. This type of reasoning was certainly used in Stanley Kubrick's *2001: A Space Odyssey*. I saw this in the early 1970s and was really knocked out by the special effects and its use of the black monolith(s) that represented an alien intelligence.

From one of the UFO books, I got the address of *Flying Saucer Review*, and I started subscribing to it straight away. In this the writings of John Keel indicated that the ETH theory when applied to UFO reports was found wanting. Not much later I started getting the *Merseyside UFO Bulletin* (*MUFOB*) that was later renamed *Magonia*, which maintained a sceptical outlook towards the ETH and promoted other aspects of the "new ufology".

Another big influence on me was Robert Rickard's *The News* that became the great *Fortean Times*. Since I had already begun cutting out "space" stories in the newspapers it wasn't a big leap to start sending any Fortean-type clippings and articles to *The News*.

In the meantime, I collected reports of UFO and paranormal events in my hometown of Scunthorpe and the surrounding county of Lincolnshire. Using this material, I wrote a few short articles about UFO sightings in the area for the local newspapers. These put me in contact with a couple of other people interested in the subject.

SUFORS

One day I met the manager of the Grange Farm Hobbies Centre, and he suggested setting up a group. He put an announcement in the local press asking for people to come to an introductory meeting. I didn't expect much of a turn-out but was shocked and pleased to find a room full of people who wanted to start a group. After much deliberation we called ourselves the Scunthorpe UFO Research Society (SUFORS). Our first official meeting was held on 24 May 1972, and our rather ambitious aims were to:

1. Collect, evaluate and disseminate information on UFOs and allied phenomena.
2. To promote free speech and open-minded conversation on UFOs and allied subjects.
3. To promote interest locally, and later, internationally, liaising with other organisations, allied to our own.
4. To combine conversation and debate with practical fieldwork, including regular skywatches, and to liaise with suitable authorities.

For two years we had weekly meetings at the Hobbies Centre. Here we would bring the latest UFO books and magazines and discuss the various theories to account for UFO reports. John Keel and his view that UFOs were some kind of inter-dimensional force that could come in and out of our time frame/dimension was much in favour.

One or two members were staunch supporters of George Adamski, but the rest of us were sceptical. Our group established a small library of books, but it was mainly a social group. To gain funds to pay for the hire of the room we even ran a few "UFO Discos" in the main hall of the Centre. They were so popular that the Centre started running their own discos.

Not long after forming, about six of us piled into a Bedford Workabus and spent a week visiting Warminster, Stonehenge, Silbury Hill, West Kennet Long Barrow and Glastonbury. We visited Cradle Hill and did a bit of skywatching, but we only saw a few other UFO seekers. Indeed, it would have been hard to guess that Warminster had been a hotbed of UFO activity in the 1960s. To relieve the boredom, some members of our group hid behind a bush when some American ufologists came up Cradle Hill one night. Using a metal detector, they blasted eerie electronic sounds into the air, not surprisingly the visitors were excited and delighted by this alien activity. After a cursory walk round, the Americans went home thinking they had encountered the notorious "thing". The only spooky thing we saw were the staring eyes of sheep in a nearby field.

On the same trip we met Molly Carey who had taken hundreds of photos of Stonehenge; they indicated that all forms of figures and illustrations had been chiselled into the rock faces. Unfortunately, these could have been created by the effects of shadows upon the rough surface of the rocks and a dose of imagination – just like the structures "seen" in Mars space probe pictures.

Later in the 1970s, I made two more visits to Frome and Warminster. These again involved visits to local pubs and Cradle Hill. The only sign of a UFO came one night when a car full of us were driving to Frome. Along with two other cars, we stopped at the side of the road to watch a group of lights slowly flying towards us, but after several minutes we heard engines and saw that the object was an airship with lights attached to it. If it had not got closer, we would have been convinced that we had seen a flying saucer.

Another trip involved meeting an old and distinguished Lincolnshire folklorist, Ethel Rudkin. Many years earlier she had written a detailed account of phantom black dog reports in Lincolnshire for the Folklore Society. Over a fine spread of tea and scones she said she had thought about sending up a kite before we arrived to make us think it was a UFO. She obviously had a good sense of humour and was intrigued to learn how the folklore of black dogs had a link with UFOs.

During the 1970s, I became more interested in collecting evidence and interviewing witnesses. One of the earliest reports I collected was taken from the *Scunthorpe Evening Telegraph* that tells of how busman Melvyn Batty and his two children saw a silver UFO, going from west to east. They were walking home along Frodingham Road, Scunthorpe, on the morning of 20 November, and Melvyn said: "I thought it might have been a jet plane but then I noticed that it had no wings. It was dome-shaped and was going across the sky faster than an ordinary aeroplane without leaving a trail. It was a perfectly clear sky and I'm sure I was not mistaken." When nearby RAF Manby and RAF Scampton were contacted, they said that nothing unusual was seen or reported to them. It was possible they saw an aircraft or even a bird reflecting the morning sun.

There was a bright blue flash and sparks associated with a muffled bang, over parkland near Bottesford Lane, Scunthorpe, in the early hours of 05 August 1971. Between 25 and 29 October 1971 there was a spate of sightings over Scunthorpe. Whilst walking up Mary Street, which is in the town centre, at about 7 p.m. on 27 October, my grandmother saw a brilliant red light which looked like a balloon, go up and then go down changing to orange as it did so. An hour later, ten-year-old Paul Richardson of Dewsbury Avenue, saw a "bright red light that seemed to come down, changed to an orange light and moved off terribly fast". Two other separate sightings were made by Richard and David Langton, and Linda Robinson. The next day at teatime, two women saw what they described as a sun coloured "double-saucer" move slowly from the southeast to northwest. It stopped for a few minutes then went out of sight leaving a reddish-gold line in the sky. There were other sightings of a "red oval object", a "red pulsating light", a flashing red light associated with the buzzing sound of a refrigerator, a UFO with green, red and blue lights around it, a UFO chasing two geese that split into six silver objects with black patches on them, and an oval object with two long exhaust pipes. This mini-flap ended with the sighting by Mr Hills of a hovering port-holed craft, which seemed to be tubular in shape, as he was driving towards Crowle Crossroads at 8.45 a.m.

Through contact with David Rees and Jenny Randles, in 1974 SUFORS joined their regional collective of UFO groups, which eventually became the Northern UFO Network (NUFON).

This helped cement relations between groups and individuals scattered throughout the north of England and was intended to facilitate the communication of UFO reports and data. Most of this information was diligently collected and published by Jenny Randles in the monthly *Northern UFO News*.

By the end of 1976, SUFORS was virtually a spent force. Two of our most charismatic members had gone on a quest to India, but via a nasty traffic accident in Turkey, they ended up moving to Sheffield.

A few of us did meet informally, and SUFORS was officially revived in 1977, after some local UFO sightings created a renewed interest in the subject. We held monthly meetings at the Central Community Centre, but it did not have the same friendly environment as the Grange Farm Hobbies Centre. In 1978 we invited a variety of guest speakers, including Rex Dutta the publisher of *Viewpoint Aquarius* magazine, who visited us twice. He was well dressed and well spoken, and I recall he drove an E-Type Jaguar. On one of these occasions, he hypnotised a few people in the audience. He was a promoter of Adamski and other contactee cases and was into New Age topics. It was his view that:

> Space Mind/Full Mind/Manas being the technical term, can make a body at will; whether the body is the "Space Man, Space Woman," or is a UFO, Mother Ship, etc. Any form, at will. That's why the Space Peoples take the shape the earthling wants/fears/expects; if our own personal aura stinks, we see monsters; if we are conceited, we see imitations of ourselves (but, of course, not quite as good as ourselves) i.e. humanoids; if we want/fear/expect golden-haired messiahs, we see those.
>
> Space Mind/Full Mind/Manas can make landed Saucers dense-physical enough for the French Government to estimate from the ground depressions their weights to be

up to 100 tons. All these are real, are dense, are seen on radar, are responsive to our five-only senses.

Of course, Space Mind/Full Mind/Manas does not grub around with light-years, but travels with the instantaneous speed of thought. How long does it take your mind to think of getting to the Star Sirius? You're there already.

In contrast, in March, John Croft of the Cleethorpes Astronomical Society gave a talk on interplanetary spaceflight and how we might contact extraterrestrials, using our own less superior technology.

We ran the Fourth NUFON conference at the Scunthorpe Film Theatre on 24 June 1978, where Gary Heseltine, now a well-known ufologist, who lived in Scunthorpe at that time, made an appearance. Tickets for a full day of talks cost an astonishing £1.50. In the *Checkpoint* science fiction fanzine (No. 90, July 1978) Darroll Pardoe wrote:

> We went to the "4th Northern UFO Network Conference" in Scunthorpe on the last Saturday in June: it was organised by a group of the "New" UFOlogists: i.e., those who regard the phenomenon as subjective rather than objective. The audience was less than might be hoped (about 40), but the audience did include a number of vocal old-guard UFOlogists who provided a bit of verbal confrontation (including one amazing person who dragged in Ur of the Chaldees and the *Protocols of the Elders of Zion*).
>
> In the morning we saw some movie film of UFOs, which wouldn't have convinced anybody, but apparently is the best available, UFOs being notoriously shy of cine-cameras. And as a change from the serious stuff, the evening was devoted to a two-hour show of clips from

sf films given by Philip Jenkinson, including a complete version of Melies' 1903 trip to the moon film.

After the conference SUFORS officially died away as we did not have enough core members to keep up a monthly schedule, and we again resorted to informal meetings in local pubs.

As NUFON and Jenny Randles's UFO career progressed she was able to pass on to me what were then called "high strangeness" cases. Many of these were reported after the release of Steven Spielberg's *Close Encounters of the Third Kind*. I was lucky enough to attend a preview screening of the film in London in March 1978, but it wasn't what I expected. Nonetheless it was a visually striking movie that brought to life the weird world of ufology (as seen through American eyes) even if you had never heard of Hynek or Vallee. On reflection, it is surprising the release of this film did not help sustain SUFORS during 1978.

High Strangeness

My high strangeness investigation reports were supplied to the UFO Investigators Network (UFOIN) and published in *MUFOB* and were eventually collected and expanded in my original version of this book: *Portraits of Alien Encounters*. Even these close encounters contained as many ambiguities and lack of solid evidence as sightings of lights in the sky. Shirley McIver, who was writing a thesis about ufology as part of her degree course in Behavioural Science attended several of the interviews I conducted with UFO witnesses.

Another important publication was *UFO Brigantia* that started life in 1983 as the *West Yorkshire UFO Research Group Newsletter*, edited by Paul Bennett. Issue No. 15, January 1986 of *UFO Brigantia* saw the editorship pass over to Andy Roberts. He continued its chronicle of local UFO cases and reported, often in a sceptical and humorous vein, the many highs and lows of ufology in general. Top writers in the field often wrote for *Brigantia* and it was a busy period when alien abductions were hotly debated here and in *Magonia*.

Phantom Airships

Back in the 1970s, I started going through old newspaper files to collect historical UFO or Fortean reports. This was mainly inspired by articles in *FSR* by Carl Grove, Jerome Clark, John Keel and Roger Sandell that discussed phantom airship and Spring Heeled Jack sightings in the nineteenth and early twentieth centuries. Granville Oldroyd conducted intensive research into these areas and passed on most of his findings.

Granville was a prolific visitor to newspaper and library archives in the 1970s and 1980s in search of pre-1947 UFO stories. His prime interest was in collecting data about the British airship scares of 1909 and 1913, and this gradually spread to include anything related to rumours, legends and Fortean phenomena. Most of this material he had to transcribe by hand and then he typed it out to provide a presentable copy of his notes. Once he had gathered enough data to fill a large envelope, he posted copies to me and other researchers like David Clarke in Sheffield.

And it was Granville's painstaking research that was the foundation for many of our (Oldroyd/Watson) co-authored articles in *Magonia*, *Flying Saucer Review*, the *Fortean Tomes* journal series and was the basis for several chapters in *The Scareship Mystery* (Domra, 2000). Granville was the co-author in 1985 of David Clarke's very first booklet, *Spooklights: A British Survey*, that gathered many archive accounts of what are known today as "Unidentified Aerial Phenomena" abbreviated as UAP. The material in the booklet was later used in Paul Devereux's book *Earthlights Revelation* (1989).

But by far the largest collection of our (Oldroyd, Clarke and Watson) data appeared in *The 1912–1913 British Phantom Airship Scare Catalogue* published by the Fund for UFO Research in 1988.

In our correspondence the main topics concerned short discussions about the validity or credibility of pre-1947 "phantom airship" flaps and how they compared with modern-day UFO reports, and the new lines of research Granville was planning to embark on. Although we corresponded for many years, he never revealed much about himself or his out-of-ufology activities or life. The most he revealed was that he worked as a gardener and owned a ten-ton road roller! I only met him once in the car park of a service station midway between his home in Heysham, Lancashire, and mine in Scunthorpe, where we exchanged a load of bulky documents. He seemed to be a very reserved person who chose his words carefully and this reflected his general approach to his research, he was never one to embrace wild theories or speculate beyond the given facts of a case. Granville enjoyed submerging himself in the newspapers and public record office files of the early part of the twentieth century, where the world was a totally different place compared to the later part of that century.

Now in the twenty-first century the process of his research looks equally ancient. Research now consists of googling, and you can exchange information and comments in seconds via email and social networks, whereas in the old days we clattered away on typewriters and used a mail service that took several days to send letters and documents. As most UFO newsletters and magazines came out on a monthly or quarterly basis, often punctuated by delays, some debates could rumble on for years.

Alien Influences

Looking back, I think we were inclined to think that there was some form of paranormal and/or mental interface between us and the aliens. With the inspiration of Carl Jung in the 1950s and the outpourings of Keel it did seem likely that "they" could directly or indirectly influence our minds, culture and society.

For me ufology served on a social and educational level. I gained a circle of friends in Scunthorpe that increasingly included people who were not directly interested in UFOs, and I regularly corresponded with ufologists and witnesses throughout Britain. One unknown consequence of my communications was revealed by Malcolm Jenson many years later:

> Nigel Watson came into my life circa 1979 when I related to him my 1975 sighting. Years later he was responsible for introducing me, through common interests, to a lady who was to become my wife. 34 years later, still is! Avril and her mum had a close encounter of the first kind in 1969 at Washingborough, Lincs, and the object was picked up on radar and reported in the press. My wife has an alternative brain-wiring with her high-functioning autism/Aspergers, and therefore is a stickler for the smallest of detail. It could also be that this alternative brain-wiring is a key factor in the amazing amount of experiences she has had both before our union and during.

As I noted earlier, the psychological aspects of ufology finally encouraged me to take a degree in the subject and made me even more sceptical of the ETH and UFO theories in general. In addition, I went off to study Film and Literature at the University of Warwick which helped me look at how UFOs are represented in popular entertainment and how such cultural influences have had an impact on real ufology.

Since then, ufology has changed for good and bad, but I still find it a fascinating subject that has taken me from Scunthorpe to the wildest frontiers of Magonia.

Notes and References

Buckle, Eileen. *The Scoriton Mystery*, Neville Spearman, London, 1967.

Oliver, Norman. *Sequel to Scoriton*, privately published, London, 1968.

UFO Warminster website at: http://www.ufo-warminster.co.uk/index.html

"Ethel Rudkin (1893–1984)," *North Lincolnshire Museum*, at: https://northlincolnshiremuseum.co.uk/discover/ethel-rudkin-1893-1984/

"Dome-shaped Scunthorpe UFO," *Scunthorpe Evening Telegraph*, 25 November 1970. Cited in *South Lincs UFO Study Group Newsletter*, No. 32, Jun. Jul.Aug., 1971, p. 1.

"Birthday boys got all lit up," *Scunthorpe Star*, 13 August 1971. Cited in *South Lincs UFO Study Group Newsletter*, No. 32, Jun. Jul. Aug., 1971, p. 1.

Watson, Nigel. "Scunthorpe Wave of UFO Sightings," *South Lincs UFO Study Group Newsletter*, No. 36, December 1971.

Dutta, Rex. *Flying Saucer Viewpoint*, Pelham, London, 1970.

Coulsting, Jean. "Flying Saucer Contacts," *Earthlink*, Vol. 2, No. 3, Summer 1978, pp. 23–25.

"Northern UFO News: The Story," by Jenny Randles, *Oz Factor Books* website, at: http://www.ozfactorbooks.com/northern-ufo-news-january-2019.html

Watson, Nigel. "People, Communication & Names," *Northern UFO News*, No. 33, February 1977, pp. 3–4.

Watson, Nigel. "Group Biography: SUFORS," *Northern UFO News*, No. 44, January 1978, p. 4.

Pardoe, Darroll. *Checkpoint*, No. 90, July 1978, at: https://checkpoint.ansible.uk/cp090.html

Chapter One

A Portrait of a Percipient

Paul Bennett

Jenny Randles put me in touch with Paul Bennett to find out more about his prolific UFO experiences. Paul was born on 13 September 1963, and from the age of eight onwards he has seen many types of UFOs and paranormal phenomena. He lives in a pleasant home in Wrose, which is situated between Shipley and Bradford in West Yorkshire, and on meeting and talking with him he is articulate and intelligent.

The area where he lives is hilly and within only a few yards of his house are stretches of countryside which are ideal localities for observing the heavens or for encountering visitors from other planets. Paul enjoys being in easy reach of the surrounding countryside, and as we will see later, he cares deeply for the state of the environment, but of even more stimulation to him is his large collection of books.

Most of his books are about UFOs and represent the works of such authors as, Keel, Vallee, Daniken, Berlitz, Trench, Shuttlewood, Adamski, Steiger, Holiday, etc. As might be imagined this is a very comprehensive collection and almost every shade of UFO opinion can be discovered between their covers.

He also owns books on various aspects of Fortean phenomena, folklore and even one book about witchcraft. Paul has read all of the Bible, and he told me that, "Revelations is my favourite chapter, I keep reading that..."

He views the Bible as the source book for the events interpreted by Erich von Daniken, and other authors who leapt onto the Ancient Astronaut theory bandwagon after the publication of *Chariots of the Gods?* in 1969. In the past his "minority" viewpoint has brought him into conflict with some of his school friends and teachers. Paul claims:

> (John) Keel is the best ufologist around at this point in time, and almost all his theory work is accurate and logical to believe that some people find logical, I find it very hard to believe that some people find Keel's work preposterous and ridiculous.
>
> True, he does emit theories which are way out, but if you examine all the evidence Keel has looked at, and put two and two together, it becomes clear that his ideas of the superspectrum, the contactee hoax, MIB, and the UFO phenomenon's relationship to the paranormal, cannot be disputed. Like me, Keel does not connect UFOs with science, for the simple reason that there is no connection.

Keel's major and most influential book is *Operation Trojan Horse* in which he explains that he believes that the UFOs, or to be more precise the force (or forces) behind the UFO phenomenon, can "move" throughout the electromagnetic spectrum. Since the human sensory apparatus can only perceive certain very small areas of the spectrum (heat and light), the forces that manifest as UFOs and the paranormal can play havoc with our senses, and then swiftly retreat back into the "hidden" areas of the spectrum.

Keel also believes that the UFO entities are feeding us with false information in order to distract UFO investigators from the truth, and that sinister men in black (MIB) are out to suppress and destroy evidence for the existence of UFOs.

Since *Operation Trojan Horse,* Keel's books have dealt more and more with the sinister aspects of MIB encounters and the dangers of pursuing the subject too deeply. These elements of danger and the fear of the unknown probably draw Paul's attention to Keel, who has made scaring ufologists and UFO witnesses into a fine art!

Paul isn't a complete disciple of Keel, since he notes that:

> If the UFOs do come from a separate reality, then almost all the problems of the phenomenon can be explained. Only the question of how they jump from dimension to dimension is to be answered. More and more people are turning to the theory of the superspectrum. Clark and Coleman, authors of *The Unidentified* and *Creatures of the Outer Edge* call John Keel the pioneer of the fourth-dimension hypothesis. But Keel refers much of his work to the pioneer Charles Fort, who refers to the possibility of separate dimensions on many occasions.
>
> For some strange reason, I regard or compare myself to John Keel. His beliefs are mine. His style of writing is similar to some of my smaller work. His beliefs are outrageous at first glance, so are some of mine.

Although Paul counts the subjects of "astronomy, meteorology, nuclear physics and a little psychology" as being of interest to him and of relevance to his UFO studies it does seem odd that he believes that science is of little use towards the solving of the UFO riddle.

In an exasperated tone Paul wrote that:

> The number of times I have told people that UFOs are not extraterrestrial visitors, and that they have nothing to do with science is too innumerable to count. I have told ufologists – Nigel Watson for one – that UFOs have little relevance to science, and that science, as it is at the moment, will never be able to decipher the phenomenon. I still hold that view, and the evidence to this continues to accumulate.

From Paul's viewpoint, Establishment Science is too remote and dogmatic in its attitude towards ufology. In his area, two members of the Bradford Astronomical Society, Brian Jones and Phillip Clark, have expressed a sceptical attitude toward the subject of UFOs. In a local newspaper they claimed that alien visitors from outer space was a load of bunk, and that with enough time and sufficient data they could disprove every close encounter sighting ever reported.

"In a way I pity people like this," wrote Paul, explaining that:

> I could hand out several tens of cases which they wouldn't be able to explain. Clark and Jones are continually telling the public things which they say are facts, but just aren't. How can ufologists deal with idiots like these? Edward Condon gave ufologists hell for several years.
>
> James Randi and Phillip Klass are, at the moment, coming out with items of excrement, which just don't stand up as being good explanations. Klass and Randi are to ufologists, what locusts are to crops: some of the most horrible pests imaginable!

Paul is very keen on finding out about UFO sightings in his area, which he has dubbed the "Metro Triangle" (in emulation of Charles Berlitz's "Bermuda Triangle" and Charles Fort's "London Triangle"). These triangles are areas where UFO and paranormal events appear with more frequency than other parts of the world.

Paul's Metro Triangle has its base marked out by the towns of Skipton, Ilkley and Otley, and its apex reaches past Halifax.

John Keel calls such locations as "window areas". According to Paul's research,

> since the year 1960, the Metro Triangle has held host to something like 2,500 reports of unidentified flying objects.

A Portrait of a Percipient

"Why?" may you ask, "has not all of this been reported." The simple answer to that is "I do not know." It may be because there are not many dedicated ufologists in this area. But one reason I do know, is that three quarters of the UFOs reported to the newspapers in this area are not printed.

One basic characteristic of the Metro Triangle (MT) is that many towns within the triangle end in the word "LEY." There are for instance towns like Otley, Guisley, Shipley, Cottingley, Bingley, Keighley, Burley, Ukley, Morley, Stanley and Batley. There are several smaller suburban areas within the Triangle ending in "LEY."

The late great Alfred Watkins, the pioneer of the ley system gave the ley system several names. He called leys both "LEA" and "LAY". And all the towns in the Metro Triangle used to have endings of either "LEA" or "LAY" e.g. Shipley used to be Shiplea. Is there, I wonder a connection with the names of towns and UFO activity?

Another theory of Paul's is a phenomenon he calls JASON. From his research he found that UFOs appeared with more frequency during the months of July, August, September, October, November, the first letter of each month contributing to the abbreviation JASON.

In 1977, "the Metro Triangle had an extraordinary flap, the biggest since 1961. In the months of JASON, I collected over forty UFO reports, six poltergeist cases and five ghost accounts." Unfortunately, Paul only has a few brief details about these sightings because his collection of reports and newspaper clippings disappeared during 1978 when he was in hospital (this episode in his life will be related later in this chapter).

After Paul's first two UFO sightings he set up a small informal UFO group in late December 1974. He and a school friend, Darryl Tate, formed the group to cater for the interests of their school friends, and they called it BRUFORP, which is the abbreviation for Bradfordian Research into Unidentified Flying Objects and Related Phenomenon.

Paul visited Warminster (the centre of all UFO manifestations in England – if not the world – according to author, Arthur Shuttlewood) during the mid-1970s, he has been in contact with a group called National UFO Research, which is run by David Kay who lives in Brighton.

Members of National UFO Research have similar interests to Paul, and they,

> seem convinced that their region around Brighton is a window. Although they do get a fairly high flap concentration down there, it cannot be compared with a good window region. The "Brighton Triangle" as they have now tagged it, has about the same amount of UFO sightings as we in the Metro Triangle have.

Paul's grandmother is slightly psychic but otherwise he is the only member of his family who has a great deal of interest in the unknown. In Nigel Mortimer's account of "The Paul Bennett Story" in *Northern UFO News*, No. 101, he notes:

> It seems that most of his family had some kind of strange encounter or odd happening, but they tended to be somewhat more reserved. He claims his family are descended from true Romany stock and that his grandmother was a gypsy. He claims his Great-Grandmother was so "tuned-in" to the other world that she actually met Jesus Christ! His Grandfather even labelled Paul "the second coming". Although Paul recognises, he tends to go to extremes at times! But his grandfather does claim lifelong sightings of LITS (Lights in the Sky –

N.W.). Both Paul's brothers also claim encounters with "True UFOs".

Amongst his school friends who are interested in UFOs or who have seen UFOs, Paul is their natural leader. Of greater influence to him has been his friendship with a friend of the family, David Lawson, who is a local spiritualist. David has given Paul an awareness of the paranormal and this has probably coloured a great deal of his thinking and created an environment within which he can place his ideas.

I first visited Paul on 5 September 1977, and during my on-going interviews with him I tried to remain neutral and not attempt to unduly influence his thoughts on UFOs and the paranormal. However, just by being interested in his sighting, I might have influenced him to a certain extent, but a UFO investigator cannot help this unless he or she can render themselves invisible! The effect of the UFO investigator upon UFO witnesses and percipients would make a fascinating thesis, but for the time being we will ignore this digression.

Paul has discovered that:

Sometime in the early part of the 1960s, a UFO organisation calling itself Northern UFO Skywatch Organisation appeared in the triangle region. In 1967 the group had a ball. Reports flew in at an incredible rate during JASON, and their files no doubt grew at hell of a rate. The leader of this group, Mr Vincent O'Connell seemed a very highly rated individual in the UFO field at the time. I've seen his files, and one of them, about three hundred pages thick, is crammed full of UFO cases from this area, 98% of which I have never heard of.

O'Connell's file of sightings from this area contain reports of a woman who was pestered by an orange ball of light; of a typical Adamski-shaped saucer (sic) witnessed by three workmen; of a UFO with tripod-like legs which seemed to touch down in a field and of course, endless accounts of lights-in-the-sky. All of these reports occurred in the 1960s, as did the massive mothership which was seen by hundreds of people over Yeadon, then fly down near Eshott and back to Yeadon again. This UFO was admittedly tracked on radar and had several tens of photographs taken of it; but I wasn't even around to expose the case then. It seems that nobody ever got hold of any of these reports. Mr O'Connell seemed to keep all the reports to himself and let no other UFO organisations hear about them. Idiots in the newspapers tried to call him a cultist and a freak, but was he really...?

Early in the 1970s, O'Connell made his last report to the newspapers. Since then, O'Connell has become a recluse. He very rarely talks of the subject. His files are all he has left on the subject. All the rest of his equipment, books, etc., on UFOs were vandalised, many were stolen (but the culprits were never discovered), whilst other items of his just disappeared. His interest in the subject deteriorated to the extent that he only talks to other people with genuine interests in UFOs. He says that the subject is a dangerous thing to dabble with. It is this that reminds me of Keel's statement in his book *UFOs: Operation Trojan Horse*: "Dabbling with ufology is as dangerous as dabbling with black magic..." and I seem to agree with the statement. And if this statement is correct, then really I shouldn't be researching into the subject. Keel says in the same paragraph: "even suicide can result ... for this reason, I strongly suggest that parents FORBID their children from becoming involved. Schoolteachers and other adults should not encourage an interest in the subject."

Presumably Keel is immune from encouraging any interest in ufology, he just writes to warn others! This element of danger and mystery is, I think, the key to Paul's interest in UFOs and the paranormal. He is exploring territory that is feared by his elders, he has been warned of the dangers, but there is nothing more exciting than investigating forbidden territory.

On 6 October 1977, Paul and his friends had a shock when they were walking to school. Staring out of the fog which surrounded them, were a couple of eyes, looking directly at them. This apparition scared them considerably until they discovered that the staring eyes belonged to a friendly horse!

Fear is an emotion one must expect when exploring the unknown, but the following anecdote illustrates that Paul's curiosity grips his soul more firmly than fear. On this occasion Paul and his friends had been on the steps that go up to Idle Hill Reservoir, when they saw a UFO.

Paul immediately shouted, "Look, a UFO" and he ran up the steps for a better view, meanwhile all his friends ran down the steps in fear of the UFO! Fortunately, they soon discovered that the UFO was nothing more than the planet Venus.

This curiosity explains why he could write about what Elsie Wright told him, as follows: "her attitude regarding the occult is straight forward: 'Don't dabble with it!' She seems convinced that ghosts and poltergeists amongst other things, are very dangerous. Why she thinks this I don't know."

Paul's fascination with the unknown has led him to fill several exercise books with accounts of his own UFO sightings and paranormal experiences, along with accounts of local happenings. These books along with the information gleaned from interviewing him, and various other sources, have supplied me with a wealth of material regarding his dealings with the unknown. I've tried as much as possible to use Paul's own words in describing his encounters, which truly represent a vast slice of the superspectrum!

It is noteworthy that Paul has written that his ambition in ufology is "to become well known and get on in the field" and that in the next few years he would like the Bradford area to become the new Warminster. Having said that, I should point out that Paul is not utterly sensationalistic in his approach to ufology and the very existence of his exercise books on UFOs show that he is willing to invest a considerable amount of his time collecting and researching UFO reports. In fact, Paul derides members of such groups as the Aetherius Society, as cultists, since he has observed that members of the local branch will believe anything and are not rational in their approach to the subject.

First Sightings

The first UFO sighting by Paul Bennett was on Sunday, 13 May 1972. He saw a disc, the length of a taxicab. This phenomenon was glowing white and flew at a terrific speed past his bedroom window. Paul wrote: "This UFO was about three to four yards (2.7m to 3.6m) away from me when I saw it. I was about a yard from the window, and the UFO was about two and a half yards (2.3m) from the window when it flew past. I would give almost anything to get another good look at that UFO. The UFO made absolutely no audible noise at all, I think that's what scared me when I saw it."

According to Paul the UFO looked exactly like the one photographed over Holloman Air Force Base, Alamogordo, New Mexico, on the 10 October 1957. (This photograph is reproduced in *The Flying Saucer Story* by Brinsley Le Poer Trench.)

Paul on a later occasion wrote again about this sighting, and he added the following information:

"At about 10.30 10.45 p.m. on the given date I was lying awake in bed and simply gazing in the air. Then I heard a slight whistling noise and the next thing I knew a gleaming white disc went hurtling past the window at approximately 350mph.

This is all I saw of it, but it was real and no hallucination or hysteria."

Almost exactly twenty months later on Monday, 14 January 1974, Paul had his second UFO sighting. At 8.40 p.m. whilst looking out of his bedroom window at the Pleiades star cluster, he saw a flash of light in the direction of Aldebaran and the Hyades star cluster in the constellation of Taurus. This light flared to an exceedingly bright magnitude of -5.2 (the bright star Sirius only has a magnitude of -1.6) and went slowly past his field of vision. It continued moving in a westerly direction until it suddenly made a ninety degree turn and in a split second shot up towards the moon. After crossing the face of the moon, the light dimmed and then flared up to a magnitude of -6.0. After hovering at the zenith, it grew a little dimmer and then shot off to the horizon in about three seconds.

It was soon after these two sightings that Paul and his friend Darryl Tate formed the Bradfordian Research into Unidentified Flying Objects and Related Phenomenon group.

Idle Hill Reservoir

On Friday, 10 October 1975, Robert Hopkins, Andrew Callaghan and Paul were playing in a woodland area, near Paul's home. One of his friends looked up towards the Idle Hill reservoir, and shouted, "What the hell's that?" They all looked up and saw a "glowing red, cigar-shaped object" directly over the reservoir.

Later on Tuesday, 21 October 1975, Robert Hopkins and an anonymous witness saw a "glowing green object". This too was seen hovering over the reservoir, the exact time of this sighting was recorded as being 7.33 p.m.

11 days later, on Saturday, 1 November 1975, yet another red cigar-shaped UFO was seen hovering over the reservoir at 7.25 p.m. Paul spotted the fact that there was an 11-day cycle to these sightings, so, "on 12 November 1975, Jon Tilleard and myself went to the reservoir with a camera, binoculars, notebook, and a

pen and pencil. We were around and on the reservoir for almost an hour. It was as if the people within the saucers knew that Jon and I were going to observe the reservoir; no UFOs were sighted over there that night and to this day no UFOs have been seen above the Idle Hill Reservoir."

During this period of UFO activity over Idle Hill Reservoir, Paul, at a nearby spot saw a robot.

The Robot

"On the 12th of October 1975, (at 4.05 p.m.) Andrew Hammond and myself were slowly walking home from our school, and making our way up towards Carr Lane Cliffs.

"As we got to the top of Hope Avenue, we both split up. Andrew walked up another part of the field as I continued forward," wrote Paul.

During my first interview with him, he told me, "at first when I was (walking along) at the bottom of the field it was… up there I thought it was just a man, you know, it just looked like a person. So if anybody in them (nearby) flats ever saw it, it looked just like a person."

I asked him why he took a closer look at this "man", Paul said: "Er well, as I carried on walking home, well what happened, I'm always inquisitive at looking for things now, and I just looked up at him to see what he was doing, and he appeared to be just a man with a rather big body and real thin legs. And I thought 'men don't look like that' you know, so I walked up and looked up and he was in the shape of a, like two round circular balls and I carried on walking further up, and then I could see that it wasn't anything like a man."

Paul wrote:

After getting about five yards (4.6m) from the bottom of the cliffs I noted his definite shape, height, colour, and appearance.

What I could see was a monster-like thing, about 12 feet (3.6m) tall scooping up samples of dirt, with small charcoal deposits in it, (picking) up and placing (the deposits) in the side of his abdomen. The monster was, as well as 12 feet (3.6m) tall, a definite green colour. The arms which collected the dirt/charcoal samples, were exactly like a fly's leg. Two arms were observable and both were about four feet (1.2m) long. A remarkable thing about the monster was that he had two very thin stilt-like legs and two small plate-like feet. The head had no eyes, nose, mouth, ears or hair, but looked just like a thick, solid ball of green metal.

I threw some stones at the thing and only one of them hit. It made a "ping" sound, as if it had hit metal. Even though I hit the thing it did not retaliate in any way.

Roger Hebb and I interviewed Paul, and presented below is a transcription of our conversation, which has been re-arranged slightly for ease of continuity.

R.H. "You didn't imagine it?"

P.B. "Well there is physical evidence there. When I saw this, I only had two books on UFOs. It was just after the sighting that I really got interested in it."

N.W. "Had you heard about the Flatwoods monster before then?"

P.B. "No, I hadn't, not before it, it was after it, about three weeks after I got (the book) *Uninvited Visitors*."

N.W. "By Ivan Sanderson?"

P.B. "Yes, and there was something about Flatwoods in that, and I thought it just sounds like what I saw. Except the eyes."

N.W. "Why? What sort of eyes did you see?"

P.B. "It didn't have eyes, that had eyes, that one at Flatwoods, but this one didn't."

N.W. "What did it exactly have in the way of a head?"

P.B. "It had a kind of circular metallic ball; it didn't have eyes."

N.W. "It was all the same colour?"

P.B. "The top part was a darker shade."

N.W. "But you couldn't tell if it was green or brown?"

P.B. "Dark green or light brown."

N.W. "How high do you think it was?"

P.B. "Ten to twelve feet (3 to 3.6m)."

N.W. "So it was quite big."

P.B. "Yes it was."

N.W. "What colour was it?"

P.B. "It was green, well I'm colour blind, either green or brown. It looked green but it could have been brown."

N.W. "Could you see it in detail?"

P.B. "Not everything, but I could see the little pockets at its side, and it was putting like, gravel into them."

N.W. "How often did it scoop its arms; did they scoop in unison?"

P.B. "No, about once every ten seconds it went down."

N.W. "Both arms went down together to scoop up, did they?"

P.B. "No, one scooped up at one time and then there would be another one a few seconds later and would do exactly the same thing."

N.W. "Like a paddling motion?"

P.B. "Yeah, like a paddling motion, yeah."

N.W. "Did the arms swing around like a circle then?"

P.B. "It just, well now I think of it, its arms seemed to grow a bit longer, it seemed to scoop 'em down, bring 'em up and put them into like a little pocket in its side. It'd stay still, and the other one would dig exactly the same."

N.W. "It was doing that all the time?"

P.B. "Yes. Except for a couple of... it didn't do a thing for about twenty seconds, twenty or thirty seconds."

N.W. "Did it lift its feet?"

P.B. "It didn't look as if it was, it wasn't stepping, it was just floating."

N.W. "How did it move?"

P.B. "Well, when it moved it looked as if it were hovering. It didn't move its feet at all, it didn't move the position of its feet, it just seemed as if it hovered."

R.H. "How long did you see it for?"

P.B. "How long did I see it? About two minutes."

R.H. "Did you see it disappear?"

P.B. "No. I didn't see it disappear, no, because my friend (Andrew Hammond) was stood over by them cliffs over there and he was staring at me, and I saw him out of the corner of my eye, and looked over to him, shouted there was something up there, and as I looked back it had gone."

N.W. "Then you both ran up there, did you?"

P.B. "No. I walked up there."

N.W. "But before that you ran to your friend?"
P.B. "Yeah."
N.W. "And when you went up to the site, what did you exactly see?"
P.B. "Two impressions about the size of a dinner plate, in the ground and just little grooves in the ground, as if there had been some shovel or something smaller, a trowel digging it up, just around the site where it had stood."
N.W. "How long did the physical traces last for?"
P.B. "About one week, three or four days."
N.W. "You don't think anything else could have caused the physical traces then?"
P.B. "A friend at school said that Guides have campfires up the top of the cliffs, but three or four months ago I asked him where they were, and I asked him if there had ever been any Guide camps up there and he said not as far as he knew, and he goes to every single one." (Which seems unusual because the Guides are a group for young girls not boys – N.W.)
N.W. "Was the area scorched?"
P.B. "Well, the prints were warm, the ground around it was fairly warm but the actual imprints were very warm indeed."

In a letter in which Paul described his robot as the "Wrose Monster" he claimed that where the robot had been he "saw several things, a) a large burnt patch in the grass (17 feet by 9 feet, 5.2m x 2.7m); b) two perfectly circular impressions in the ground, about a centimetre (0.4 inches) deep, and each 'landing pad' – as I call them – were exactly a foot (0.3m) in diameter; c) there were lots of scoop marks in the ground and each mark was warm, so were the two landing pads."

On my second visit to Paul's home on 9 October 1977, I was able to obtain further information from him about this sighting. I was also able to talk to Andrew Hammond, who was in the vicinity during the sighting. The interview went as follows:

N.W. "You were with Paul when he saw that robot?"

A.H. "Well I was just opposite him actually, he were about a hundred yards (91m) away, and he went up the cliff and I went the other side of the cliffs, and I looked up and I thought I saw something and I thought it were Paul. And I shouted, no, it were you that shouted to me wasn't it?"

P.B. "Yeah, I shouted to you."

A.H. "You shouted to me, you said 'did you see something up there?' and I said 'yeah, what were it?' no I didn't believe you at first, did I?"

P.B. "No, he didn't, he didn't believe me."

A.H. "I thought I saw something, but I thought, 'oh it must have been you trying to make me think so,' he always does that. That's the reason I didn't believe him at first."

P.B. "Just when we were at the bottom (of the cliff), I says that there should, if there is anything, there should be two circular prints and there should be scoop marks, like claw marks in the soil, where it were digging up. And he didn't believe me, and he says, 'oh prove it,' you know."

A.H. "When we went back we saw the things, exactly what he described, you know, the two pads."

P.B. "And I showed them to people from school the next day."

N.W. "Was the whole area burnt as it is now?"

P.B. "No, I don't know whether it were burnt by that…"

A.H. "You said that it were Guides camping up there."

P.B. "Yeah, but even if it were Scouts, Girl Guides or whatever you call them up there, how did I know those prints were up there?"

N.W. "You didn't run straight up (the cliff), though, when you saw that robot, did you?"

P.B. "No, when I, I ran, I ran over to him (Andrew Hammond), he were stood at the step of the cliffs. Pity we didn't have a Geiger (counter) we could have measured for any radioactivity."

In one of his exercise books Paul wrote: "The case of this suspected robot was closed for several months as a hoax. But later re-opened by Andrew Hammond."

This statement seemed rather self-contradictory especially since Paul was the prime witness. So I asked him about this:

N.W. "How come you put a 'regarded hoax' in connection with your robot sighting?"

P.B. "Well there was this Guide camp up there, an annual Guide camp up there you know and er, when I heard that somebody said that they put... they had like a barbecue stand, like two stands and they stand it near top of (the) cliffs. Well, I thought they must have put the stand there and the imprints must have been from the barbecue stand, and that (the robot) must have been an hallucination or something, and I didn't bother with it."

Apparently, Paul's renewed interest in UFOs made him remember his robot sighting and after reading about the Flatwoods monster sightings recorded in *Uninvited Visitors* by Ivan Sanderson, he gave his observation more importance.

At our second meeting I asked for more specific details regarding the sequence of the robot's movements. I again asked about the movement of the robot's arms (or perhaps we ought to describe them as claws).

P.B. "It scooped up alternately, I think. One arm scooped up and then (the) other arm. And it put it in a little pouch. And the other arm did exactly the same thing, and it did this alternately.

"You know last time when you were tape recording me (and you asked) 'how did it get the claw up to there' (the pouch) you know, 'did they lengthen or not', they didn't lengthen. But they must have been rubber to do it. How... don't know, how it did it."

N.W. "How many times did it do that before it moved?"

P.B. "Ten or eleven times."

N.W. "Quite often then?"

P.B. "Yeah."

N.W. "How quickly do you think it did it then? Quite fast?"

P.B. "No slow, about..."

Paul demonstrated this motion with his own arm, and his arm took about five or six seconds to extend and retract.

N.W. "What colour were the claws?"

P.B. "They were black, I didn't mention that (before)."

N.W. "Anything else on it black?"

P.B. "No."

N.W. "How were you able to see the feet of this robot?"

P.B. "Well, when it moved it lifted off the ground and floated."

N.W. "And you saw the feet then, did you?"

P.B. "I saw the feet then, yeah."

N.W. "I wondered how it moved."

P.B. "It sort of rose up, in stages. First it went there then it went along a bit and then rise up a bit more, and then it went suddenly down again..."

N.W. "That was the whole motion?"

P.B. "Yeah."

N.W. "Was the motion very abrupt?"

P.B. "No, like a... bit like a swan gliding up in the air and coming back down again."

Once the robot started floating along it did not start scooping up again until it returned to the ground. The distance it travelled from (the observer's) right to left was a matter of a few feet. Once it started scooping up for the second time, it was observed by Paul for "not longer than thirty seconds. Then I turned around and saw him (Andrew Hammond) and it had disappeared when I looked again," said Paul. When I asked Paul how he thought the robot disappeared, I wondered if he thought it went off in a spaceship or some similar device, he just replied that he "didn't know".

A similar case of a soil sampling entity occurred in August 1976. Three young children were playing near the Reddish Vale golf club and Fir Tree School, Reddish, Great Manchester, when two of them, attracted by a flash of light, saw a humanoid figure in a silver suit. It had slanted eyes, a grey beard, yellow hair, and floated six inches (15cm) above the ground. After vanishing and reappearing at a nearby shed, it unhooked a square shovel from its waist and used it to dig up soil samples that it put into plastic bags. After it vanished and reappeared to take more samples, there was another flash of light and a gust of wind. All three children then saw a silver-grey object with a silver dome shoot into the sky, passing over the school (*Northern UFO News*, No. 47, April 1978, pp. 4–5).

Dreams

To shed a little light onto Paul's robot sighting and to illustrate the impact of the UFO subject on Paul, the following part of our interview with him on 5 September 1977, is of interest:

N.W. "What sort of dreams about UFOs do you have?"

P.B. "Sightings."

N.W. "Sightings?"

P.B. "Yeah. Sightings. All it is, it only lasts about 5 minutes all the dreams about UFOs I have (lost this period of time). All it is, I'm either playing or writing something and something will alert me. I'll turn around and there'll be a UFO hovering behind me or something silly, and that's literally all it is, it only lasts a couple of minutes."

N.W. "Do you ever have the same dream recurring about UFOs?"

P.B. "No, I don't think so, I might have done but you know you cannot always remember your dreams. Two of us had the same dream and we drew the objects that we saw in separate rooms and they both came out with the same thing on."

N.W. "Who was your friend?"

P.B. "Jon Tilleard."

N.W. "A school friend?"

P. B. "Yeah."

R.H. "What was the dream about?"

P.B. "Well, I once had a dream or semi-dream, I don't know whether it were a dream or not, of a (space) capsule flying past the (bedroom) window, he had exactly the same one."

N.W. "When was that exactly?"

P.B. "Last year (1976) or 1975, I think it was 1975, October or November 1975."

N.W. "About the time you saw the robot?"

P.B. "Similar to that time, yeah."

N.W. "How often do you go sleepwalking then?" (Paul mentioned that he sometimes walked in his sleep before I started recording our interview.)

P.B. "About once a month."

N.W. "Have they coincided with your UFO sightings?"

P.B. "I haven't noticed that; I haven't noticed."

Paul seemed very intrigued with this idea, and he said that in future he would check this if he had any more UFO sightings. Later, Paul wrote about this dream episode (which is reminiscent of his very first UFO sighting) and he revealed the following:

> October 17, 1975, I think that was the date. Asleep in bed, I remembered the most clear UFO dream I had ever had. A large group of objects, very similar to NASA's Mercury rockets, came down (I presumed from the Idle Hill reservoir), and shot past my bedroom window. I sat up and looked out of my window and watched them head down towards Bolton Wood quarries nearby.
>
> In the dream (I think) that I awoke at about 3.00 a.m. and looked at them. For all, I know, it could have been a sighting, it seemed so vivid and lifelike, but I'm almost certain that I dreamt it.
>
> The following day at school, Jon Tilleard happened to mention UFOs. On telling him that I had dreamt of

UFOs the previous night, he – to my amazement – said he too had dreamt of UFOs on the same night. Just out of interest I asked him to tell me what he had dreamt... he only got halfway through his story – I finished it off for him!

By some extraordinary coincidence, both of us had dreamt that we woke up in the middle of the night, saw UFOs flying past (both Jon and myself saw Mercury craft objects), and watched them veer over the local quarries.

What caused Jon and myself to have the same dream? Was it of a parapsychological nature, a ufological nature (both?), or just a coincidence? The idea used by Keel, that UFOs and the occult are of close relation, could come into mind in this case.

Paul fixed his attention on UFO dreams once again in 1979, but to maintain this chronology of his experiences, we will deal with this additional material later in the text.

Blackout

One night sometime during this period, Paul was in bed reading *Invisible Residents* by Ivan Sanderson, when his bedroom light went out. At first he thought it was his brother Andrew playing tricks on him, but when he saw that his bedroom door was shut, he knew this wasn't possible.

Also, he noticed the light switch had been clicked down to the off position, which made him conclude that the light must have been terminated via the switch rather than being due to an electrical failure or a power cut.

"Then I thought there was something weird," said Paul. At that moment Paul's alarm clock fell off the shelf and he sought protection beneath his bed covers. Surfacing a few minutes later, he found the light switched on and the alarm clock safely returned to its shelf.

Cigar

Late August 1976, Neil Edmundson, "D.L." and Paul were playing just to the west of some woods in Ravenscliffe. As all three of them ran towards Paul's grandmother's garden, Paul looked up towards the golf course which is located to the north of Ravenscliffe Woods. As he looked up, he "noticed a massive glowing silver object flying west at a very slow speed. The UFO was about a half mile away from us, but only several hundred yards away from some of the golfers (on the nearby golf course)."

"When we first saw the object only one end of it could be seen, and we all thought it was a plane. As it came up from behind the hill, we all noticed that the object was not a plane. It looked like a silver cigar-case on edge, but its overall size astounded us. At an estimate it was about 250 feet (76m) in diameter."

The cigar-shaped UFO which was at an angle of 45 degrees, moved higher into the sky at a speed of approximately 40mph. Eventually, it disappeared from view behind some clouds.

Paul was surprised that there was no article about this UFO in the local newspapers the day after the sighting, because "it flew directly above that group of golfers".

The Black Entity

"On the 15th of October, 1976, I was playing with some friends several yards from Westfield Grove when I turned around and saw a small black, two-year-old, child-sized humanoid thing run across the road and up Westfield Grove. At the time I saw the thing was between 7.30 and 8.30 p.m. About a minute or so later I ran to the area where I saw the thing and found nothing."

I discussed this sighting with Paul, and he told me:

P.B. "There were about six of us stood here (on the pavement near Paul's home). I was stood here, turned round, and I saw a little black creature, about two foot (0.6m) tall, standing on the road (it moved) to the edge (then onto the) path and up Westfield Grove."

N.W. "Only you saw it though?"

P.B. "Yeah."

N.W. "What did this black entity look like, this little humanoid?"

P.B. "Its head was squashed a bit like a tomato, you know what the top of a tomato looks like?"

N.W. "Indented slightly."

P.B. "Yeah. It's legs, it didn't have any toes or anything like that, only straight legs that ended, with flattened feet. It's arms, it had no fingers or no hands, it just came to an end just like its feet, and no nose, eyes, mouth or anything like that, that I could notice. And it had no ears. It was just like a deformed blackened body."

N.W. "How did it walk then, did it move quickly?"

P.B. "Just, you know how you see dwarfs at the circus, they run with little, short paces, just like that."

N.W. "Your mother said she thought it was a..."

P.B. "Dog."

N.W. "Yeah."

P.B. "She was only joking, but when I first saw it, she said it were imagination, (then) she said it were a dog or something."

N.W. "Don't you think it was a dog then?"

P.B. "It wasn't a dog, no, definitely not a dog."

R.H. "What time did you see that?"

P.B. "About 8 p.m."

R.H. "Wasn't your mum in the house, couldn't you have shouted to her?"

P.B. "No, because I only saw it for about two seconds, I turned around and saw it."

N.W. "What about your friends?"

P.B. "They all took it as absolute rubbish, except one of them, he agreed to look for some evidence, and we found little footprints."

N.W. "They looked like paw prints, did they?"

P.B. "No, they were just circular, and there were no little toe prints or anything like that. Whatever it were, it wasn't imagination."

This sighting whether it was real or not, certainly had an effect on Paul, and his friend, as can be seen from his first exercise book devoted to his UFO experiences:

With all my friends laughing about it, they all walked away. Everybody that is except Michael McDermott, he stayed behind to help. After about three minutes of searching for evidence, Michael found the most fantastic evidence; there on the pavement were two small circular footprints.

At the side of the road was a small puddle, the humanoid thing must have stepped into the water and ran up the dry path leaving altogether about thirty small prints finally leading to J.B.'s garden.

Then for about another quarter of an hour I was searching for even further evidence but found none.

Even later Michael claimed that he heard a faint whistling and a voice calling my name. I do not think I specified this evidence earlier and if I did not I am very sorry.

Michael claimed that he heard the voice come from behind our hedge and we both saw the hedge move. There was no wind to make the bush move.

This scared me a little and that night I attempted to block the case out of my mind, I could not, then when I was lying in bed the same night, I was more frightened than I had ever been before. As I was staring at my door a silhouette of a small man appeared against it. At this point I felt like screaming out but I managed to calm down. But that was not all, about eight minutes later a voice definitely said audibly or telepathically, "Paul, Paul, Paul." That night I could hardly sleep because of the incident.

If this was my imagination (which it wasn't), then why would anyone or anything do that?

Was it a practical joke?

Or did it have a serious basis behind it? If it did, it to me, seemed pointless.

The humanoid had no face and no hands from what I could notice. Almost a year and a half earlier Jon Tilleard witnessed the same experience. He is always telling me the story of a small black man about two feet (0.6m) tall with no face walking towards him.

He told me of this about eight months before I saw my humanoid. But Jon admits, if he had had my incident, "I'd have been damn terrified." This is still my best case, only with the exception of the robot.

Paul, in another of his books, mentions Jon Tilleard's encounter in more detail:

It was a calm night on October 15th, 1976, I saw a "midget-MIB" and it (tried to) scare the hell out of me. About two years before hand, Jon Tilleard claimed he had a similar experience, but it was a little more terrifying.

Before my "mid-MIB" event, Jon was always telling me of a small black humanoid which once appeared on his bed and walked towards him.

"It's almost identical to the one you saw," he tells me. With a height of about 18 inches (46cm), the little man "...

just appeared out of nowhere, and walked, on my bed, towards me," (said Jon). Just like my mid-MIB, he could see no facial features and its hands just ended without fingers. (He's never told me about its feet, I assume that's because it was covered with the bed sheets.)

Was it an hallucination? Jon says "No!" He is sure of this, because he felt the man actually walking on his bed! His reaction when he saw the man was obvious – he was terrified, letting out an immediate scream, he flew out of his bed terrified to turn on the bedroom light, and waking up everyone in the family. He is sure he was not dreaming.

After my mid-MIB sighting, I cannot but help think that my encounter was presustained (sic) into my mind: a type of autosuggestion. If it wasn't this – and I do not think it was – then why should Jon and myself see the same (?) man: what is the connection? Are these cases similar by chance or is it possible that something strange is going on? I think that, for the moment, I'll stick to the philosophy a friend (Dave Pendleton) of mine uses: "There's no such thing as coincidence."

Moon

At 6.35 p.m. on 27 December 1976, Paul and Andrew Hammond were looking through Paul's telescope. Observing the moon, Andrew noticed that it was speeding up and slowing down. Paul looked through the telescope and noticed the same thing happen. According to him the moon was definitely exceeding its orbital velocity of 10,000mph.

Obviously, they had seen the moon move quickly due to the magnification of the telescope. Any telescope, even a quite small one, has to be constantly moved in order to keep the moon – or any other celestial phenomena – in view. I put this point to both Paul and Andrew, but Paul replied:

"No... it wasn't that, no it was just going at a normal speed and then it would suddenly speed up, and it wasn't the telescope at all."

Andrew added:

"It was quite distinctive as well."

One interesting comment by Paul is that if he had (before this observation) "read Don Wilson's book *Our Mysterious Moon*, I would not have wondered."

"Then after that, a mysterious black object emanated from somewhere near the Hyginus crater/rille area and slowly moved up towards the massive crater Albategnius and then disappeared. At the date when we were observing the Moon it was in it's [sic] first half," wrote Paul.

"You also saw that moon phenomena with Paul, didn't you?" I asked Andrew. He said that they both thought that it was probably something on the eyepiece lens of Paul's four-inch reflector telescope.

"I wiped the lens about eight times," said Paul. Despite this they still observed this peculiar black object which seemed to be hovering above the surface of the moon. This phenomenon eventually disappeared into the night-side of the moon. When I interviewed Paul and Andrew, their statements compared well with Paul's written account, but quite obviously that doesn't discount the very subjective nature of these observations.

Ilkley Moor

Paul's opinion is that,: "Ilkley Moor has to be one of the most famous moors in the world, full of beauty and glamour, but also full of hidden mysticism – this 'mysticism' making it a utopian dreamscape."

Paul's interest in ley lines (invisible straight lines which link ancient archaeological sites) led him and his friends Andrew Callaghan and Jon Tilleard to visit one of the stone circles on Ilkley Moor, on 19 February 1977. Paul obtained a few chippings from one of the stones in order that he could run a few tests on them. In my original report on Paul Bennett's experiences (in *MUFOB*, New Series, No. 11, Summer 1978), I reported that he and his friends had managed to move the stones a few inches, and whilst doing this they had all felt a mild electric shock.

Paul says this is wrong and that they didn't feel any shock. Three weeks after their visit, Paul received a UFO report from Darryl Tate. According to this story a Mr T. and three other witnesses who were members of a "military group" (the Observer Corps., as a matter of fact) in the Bradford Metropolitan area, saw a UFO hovering directly above the stone circle on Ilkley Moor.

This UFO, which was observed by Mr T through binoculars for three minutes forty-one seconds, was seen on Wednesday, 23 February, 1977, at 10.30 p.m. It was described as disc-shaped, metallic-grey in colour and was estimated to have been about 50 feet (15.2m) in diameter.

The three "military men" said that the UFO had also been tracked on radar, but they refused to reveal their names and added that the case should not be made public. Paul, in one of his books, asked: "Was the UFO moving the stone back in place? Or was it just homing in on the ley lines?"

On one of my visits, Paul informed me that there are 82 cup and ring markings on Ilkley Moor. This had an interesting link with a dream I had a few days before, in which I vividly remembered obtaining a job which paid a weekly wage of £82.00. On waking I was puzzled as to why this was such a specific number.

These sorts of small coincidences might be considered trivial, but it is surprising how often they occur, and I can't remember any other dreams I've had in which a number has been prominent. As for cup and ring markings they are concentric rings and channels etched into rocks, their origin and meaning are enigmatic. In Great Britain they are usually found in Scotland, Ireland and Northern England. Many interpretations have been made of the meaning and purpose of the cup and ring markings, but it is intriguing to quote John Foster Forbes who writing in 1939, claimed: "There is an affinity between these cups and the nature of stars. A star is a generator and transmitter of Cosmic Energy in spiral form. These cups could be used as micro-cosmic examples of spiral staral energies."

F.W. Holiday in his book *The Dragon and the Disc* notes that a lot of cup markings have been found in Bronze Age archaeological sites in Scandinavia. He claims that one set of the cup markings in Bohuslan, northwest Sweden, depicts a disc-shaped object with landing legs extending from it.

This and other evidence made Holiday contend that the observation of the UFO phenomenon made mankind respond to these sightings by initiating Man's most ancient religions; and that is why the disc-shape (the symbol of the UFO phenomenon) is so prevalent throughout history.

However, since it has become the habit of writers to link UFOs and the activities of "ancient astronauts" to any biblical or ancient archaeological mystery, most of this evidence can only be regarded as anecdotal due to the very multitude of possible interpretations and theories that can be advocated with greater authority and likelihood.

Another distinctive feature of Ilkley Moor is the fylfot (swastika) stone, which Paul claims is the only one of its kind in Western Europe. Paul has drawn a ley line from Stonehenge to Boddam Castle in Scotland, it neatly intersects the fylfot stone and is 650 miles in length.

The ley line also intersects another locality Paul is interested in, namely the Cottingley Fairy Glen. Here, "IIn the early autumn of 1917, two young girls, Elsie Wright and her younger cousin Frances shocked the scientific world by producing the most amazing photographs of a group of fairies!" wrote Paul.

Indeed, these fairy photographs were greatly publicised by no less a person than Sir Arthur Conan Doyle who wrote a book on the subject titled *The Coming of the Fairies* in 1922. Recently they have come under critical fire, to the extent that James Randi (a professional magician) has stated: "They are some of the greatest fakes ever produced." The BBC made an excellent play called *Fairies* based on the activities surrounding the two cousins. An actor associated with the production commented that one of the cousins told him: "We photographed figments of our imagination." Which is a neat way of pleasing believers and sceptics alike.

Paul has written to Elsie Wright (now Mrs Elsie Hill) who gave him some fundamental facts on the subject. She told him in a letter: "They are something to do with flowers... and their home is somewhere under the Earth."

He links the idea that fairies live underground, with his idea that the fylfot indicates an entrance to the hollow Earth. He says the combination of these two ideas "could revolutionise modern ufological beliefs".

Certainly, many writers about UFOs have theorised that the UFOs and their crews inhabit the interior of our Earth, and this theory links the modern mythology of the UFO with the superstition and folklore surrounding such ancient enigmas as fairies, hobgoblins, brownies, bogies and the whole spectrum of supernatural creatures.

Paul contends that you can draw a straight ley line from the fylfot stone which intersects a fylfot at Mycene, Greece, and continue it, until it reaches the Giza Complex in Egypt. This ley line is in the region of between 4,000 and 5,000 miles in length.

Another connection is linked to the famous American contactee George Adamski, who first met a person from outer space on 20 November 1952. Paul links a photographic plate the spaceman returned to Adamski which depicts enigmatic swiggles and a swastika, and the strange swastika-like boot-markings the spaceman left in the Californian desert, to the Ilkley Moor fylfot stone. Paul wrote:

> The first time I set my eyes upon the Ilkley Moor Fylfot, I seemed bewildered, it was such a beautiful piece of art. Me being such a monomaniac on UFOs I immediately felt that it had some connection to the flying saucer phenomenon. My theories came out connecting the swastika stone at Ilkley with the Cottingley Fairies, and hollow Earth concept, UFOs and Stonehenge, and they seemed so preposterously correct that anyone could have taken the idea in immediately.
>
> Still today, I am more than certain that UFOs are closely related to Fylfot. Look at Adamski's strange findings etc.
>
> The swastikas which continually appear in UFO lore has had me thinking over it for about three years now. The swastika, if acted upon uniformly would give a wheel motion and possibly some type of self-perpetuating flying machine. There are thousands of reports of the UFOs spinning continually.
>
> In nature, the swastika seldom appears. It becomes apparent only on the petal appearances of some wild plants: but the one which most resembles the carving at Ilkley most, must be the cloud and pressure waves noted by satellite photographs over the polar ice caps – their appearances are identical.
>
> Although the supposed nature of the Fylfot is one of good luck, or a charm which averts the Evil Eye, I do not accept it. The figure is one of life.
>
> The (photographic) plate handed to Adamski supposedly told of how a UFO flies: why should it have a picture of a disc (which is most probably supposed to be a UFO) with a swastika at the centre?

The major problem which makes the Riddle of the Swastika harder to solve is that when you look at the original 5–6,000-year-old carving, it has a massive, hook-like protuberance which affects the uniform spinning motion greatly.

In my mind (and as far as I know, my mind alone), the complex model, and the riddle and answers of the whole UFO phenomenon has its heart deep inside the Swastika enigma. It's been lying there for six millennia, and only a small handful are working at it. There are pieces of a very strange jigsaw in the Swastika. Bit by bit, I keep finding pieces, and they fit; but the part which connects the Fairies, Fylfot, UFOs and X is missing. Speculation? I feel confident enough to give a blatant "no!" There is something in this phenomenon and there is a large part of the UFO-jigsaw in the Metro Region: a force (?) which only manifests itself so not to show that something "weird" actually does exist here.

It is for Paul a short step from the Ilkley Moor stones to the answer of the UFO riddle. These stones which are surrounded in ancient mystery and romance, offer clues for Paul's detective work and like Sir Arthur Conan Doyle's Sherlock Holmes, he stalks relentlessly every little scrap of information and moulds it into his overall concept of the UFO phenomenon.

UFOs

On Wednesday, November 16th, 1977, Jon Tilleard and I went down to a fifteenth-century graveyard, and on walking back up Westfield Lane at about 7.05 p.m. I noticed a very strange UFO in the shape of a two-headed sperm cell. At first, I thought it was a meteor, until it began "wobbling". Then it began acting erratically I alerted Jon and pointed the object out to him.

For the next five or six seconds it just kept flying in an unusual manner, and then a small, cube-like, black box dropped from the rear end of the object. When this happened the remaining part of the object moved like a rapid wave pulse on an oscilloscope, until it just faded out (disintegrated). The black box, however, could still be seen, and it slowly descended to the ground over Idle Moor. The cube seemed to be falling very slowly, somehow defying gravity.

At the beginning of 1978, Paul accidentally fell into a crater on Idle Moor near Clairmont. Paul attributed the crater to the box-like part of the UFO which had floated down to Earth. There was a sequel to this sighting which Paul described:

Sometime in November of 1978 (exact date not bothered to be recorded), Jon Tilleard saw what he described as an orange light in the evening sky, just as it was beginning to darken.... The object moved fairly slow all the time he was watching the UFO. How it moved out of view, Jon cannot recall.

The UFO was a cube-shaped object with slightly curved edges. It did not seem to be a solid object, it looked more like pure energy – it was not ball lightning, nor was it atmospheric plasma.

In 1977, Paul discovered several sightings made by witnesses who had seen a satellite cross the sky, and then a few seconds afterwards would see in the satellite's wake a meteor-like flash of light.

"One case involved six or seven friends of mine," wrote Paul, who continued, "I noticed a light in the sky and pointed it out to them. As it neared the horizon, the satellite faded and almost immediately after, it was accompanied by a very bright flash, very similar to sheet lightning. About thirty people came and told me of these sightings, each one almost identical."

The Thump

In August 1977, Paul was in his grandmother's house, "I was writing a letter about UFOs and halfway through writing something about the psychic, the psyche, you know. And suddenly... somebody definitely thumped me on the leg and there was nobody there. I thought 'God what was that?' I listened and there was nowt there and it wasn't the cat, it couldn't have been the cat it were sat next to me."

Mystery Man

When visiting Paul on 1 February 1978, he told me the following story which he said he had not told anyone else before. One night near the end of 1977 (perhaps late November), Paul was playing with a tennis ball in the living room of his home. The time was about 1 a.m. and his parents were out for the evening. His tennis ball rolled into the dining room, and when he looked through the door in order to collect it, he saw an apparition in the opposite corner of the dining room. He saw a man 5 feet 6 inches to 5 feet 8 inches (1.67m to 1.72m) tall, dressed in a greyish suit.

The face and hands of the man were a glowing white colour, and he was holding the telephone receiver in his right hand. Paul only saw this man for a second or so, and he admits he might have imagined it.

Telephone Trouble

During my first interview with Paul on 5 September 1977, the telephone rang, and when he returned from answering it, Paul claimed that a heavy breather had phoned him. This same type of telephone caller had plagued him before, usually when he was alone in the house (on this occasion there was only Roger Hebb, Paul and me present in the house).

The call did not seem to worry Paul and he took the calls as a piece of nonsense. Berthold Schwarz, a leading American ufologist, has noted how his own and UFO witnesses' telephones have created unexpected electronic trouble and have become a nuisance.

Schwarz notes that Dr Hopkins, a 58-year-old family physician in the resort town of Maine, was visited by a Man in Black (MIB) and had lots of strange things occur to him after having a UFO encounter. Dr Hopkins said that after the MIB encounter: "We... had a lot of trouble... with the telephone being cut off, clicks followed by background sounds indicating that there was an open line to another telephone somewhere, but never any voices. Also, people kept breaking in on phone calls. At the present time, however, the phone has not been disturbed any more. I hope this is the end!"

The very bizarre nature of some of the phone troubles, Schwarz has noted, would suggest that American covert agencies (such as the CIA) are not involved in these activities, who or what is causing these troubles is an open question.

Paul had another unusual telephone call not long after my visit. He related the incident as follows:

"It would seem that quite a lot of people know of my close interests in ufology. I occasionally get people phoning me about certain UFO sightings, even though I don't know the person on the other end. One such happening occurred way back in December of 1977. It involved a film of UFOs taken by the air force.

"Jon Tilleard, Robert Hopkins and myself were in our house, when the telephone rang. On the other end there was a voice of a man who called himself 'Thompson' (with regard to this case, I can say that I am not 100% certain on his name – it could have been Johnson, I'm not sure). The man's voice was very hurried, and he seemed very anxious to tell me something.

"It was as if he didn't have much time to tell me of the event. As far as I can remember this is what the conversation was like:

Mr X 'Hello, Mr Paul Bennett?'

P.B. 'Yes, that's me.'

Mr X 'I'm from Leeds/Bradford Airport. I work there... I don't know whether you're interested, but the air force has just filmed a UFO combat over Bradford tonight.'

P.B. 'What?... who are you?'

Mr X 'Thompson(?). Thompson. It's been recorded tonight by the air force.'

P.B. 'Do I know you?'

Mr X 'I know you. Look, are you interested? There's been a major sighting up here. We've got the films...'

P.B. 'Look how'd you know me, and how'd you know about this?'

Mr X 'Take my word for... (garble)... O.K.? Or I'll hang up.'

P.B. 'Tell me that again, I didn't hear it.'

"Then the phone went dead, seemed like either he had hung up, or someone had cut the phone line at his end.

"I believed that man. His voice seemed to be rushed, and he seemed fairly frightened when he was talking to me. That has been the only phone call of that kind which I have had. True, there had been a UFO seen in the sky that night, but it was only a light-in-the-sky sighting. Nothing elaborate involving a combat was seen."

Ghosts and Invisible Walkers

Wood Lane House just off Kings Road, Bradford, is a favourite haunt of Paul's. The house is inhabited with the exception of three rooms which are claimed to be haunted. Surrounding the house is waste land and a couple of derelict outbuildings. I asked Paul what had attracted him to the house in the first place and he replied: "Well I had a report from somebody, somebody had seen a ghost up here. So I came up for a little look around to see if I could see or hear anything and first of all I heard the invisible walker so I came back the next night to see if I could get anything else, nowt then, came back the night after still nowt. So once or twice a week I kept coming back up looking for things."

Two of Paul's friends, Brian Lawson and Richard Hale have heard the invisible walker, as has an anonymous "witness".

Paul and a friend, Paul Davis, went to the house on 22 February 1977, and as they neared it they noticed a flashing light in one of the windows. After that they both heard footsteps. I asked Paul where he had heard the invisible walker and in reply he said:

"Well, it was just footsteps we heard on the other side of the bushes and trees. We were stood there just stood looking at the house, and (we) walked around (the) corner to see if there were any ghosts, looking for ghosts.

"Then we came back round and we heard somebody walking, just footsteps walking. First of all we saw flashing, a light flashing in the house and it wasn't... like an ordinary bulb light..."

As the footsteps approached them the nearby bushes rustled and then parted. They couldn't see anything that might be causing the footsteps or rustling, and there was no wind that might have been responsible. Paul wrote: "If it was an animal, it must have been very flat, but have massive feet, and would need long but very thin arms."

On 27 March 1977, Paul and Jon Tilleard visited the house which is rumoured to be haunted by a dead woman. They approached the place at 7.45 p.m. when the sun had just set. Wanting to evoke the right atmosphere for their adventure, they had waited until it got dark.

At first they heard a strange kind of loud squeaking noise, which eventually went away. Paul crept up to where the ghosts are supposed to frequent, but he saw nothing. However, as Paul and Jon walked away from the house, they both turned around and saw a head bob quickly behind a wall.

Paul went back to the house for another look – but at a slower and more cautious pace – and he and Jon saw the outline of a middle-aged woman, with dead skin, reflected against a window.

Paul climbed a wall to have a better look into the window. The room of an outbuilding slopes down toward this wall, and this outbuilding is said to be haunted. Anyway, Jon shouted, "Ey Bennett, I've just heard something on the roof, 'ave a look in that 'ole up there."

"I looked up," said Paul and, "up there, looking upwards into the sky was a transparent figure. As I looked upwards at it, it looked down at me. To my horror, the person had no eyes. This must have been the ghost that everyone had seen and heard about. I saw the ghost for about two seconds only, because when I looked up at it, and it showed its face, I had no second thought and I instantly reacted by clambering down an eight-foot (2.4m) wall in a split second; almost breaking my leg in the process."

In a written account Paul noted:

The ghost was of a middle-aged woman with dead skin. I only got a brief look at it and what I saw was horrific. The worst aspect of the ghost was that it had no eyes at all. As I clambered up to look in the hole in the roof, I saw the ghost staring into the sky, but just as my whole head popped up, the transparent figure looked down at me. As well as having no visible eyes, it only had one shoulder, the other half of the body was not there.

The most mysterious thing about the ghost was that it was moving a large stone, one about as large as a shoe box.

Concluding his report he added: "When I got home and told my parents, they burst out with laughter at my story. Later that night I had two nightmares about it."

When we interviewed Paul on 5 September 1977, he said the eyes of the ghost looked like the blackness of the ghost's mouth featured in the BBC programme *The Signalman* which was based on a story by Charles Dickens. (The film was re-run and broadcast for Christmas 1976.) Explaining this Paul said they "was, a bit like a void, you know just stove-in, that's how it's [sic] eyes were like, eyes just like a void. Just absolutely nothing at all".

It is worth adding that the *Folklore of Prehistoric Sites* by Leslie V. Grinsell (David & Charles, 1976) contains legends of stone carrying women who were reputed to have created cairns, and other forms of rock monuments. Interestingly enough, these stories travelled from Ireland, Northern Wales and then to Northern Britain.

Paul told me that sometimes he heard tapping sounds emanating from his bedroom ceiling, and he described the sounds as being "scary". Also, from 31 November 1977, he "heard, literally every night; footsteps! Not, I suppose, very unusual: but when you take into account that whenever I look out of my bedroom window – no one is to be seen. The reason for me looking out of the window was that these specific steps sounded as if they were walking up the road in front of our house; then veering left and up the garden path. The invisible walker immediately came to mind. Yet what reason had he/she/it to come here?"

On 21 December 1977, Jon Tilleard, Harvey Caswell and Paul visited the house in Bradford, only to find the haunted section of it completely demolished. Apparently, three days after Paul's last visit – which was on 26 November 1977 – the destruction had been carried out.

Paul spoke to a male occupant of the house and the man agreed with him that it had been an evil area. Considering the fact that he had had visitations from the invisible walker ever since the demolition of the haunted section of the house, he linked the two events together as can be observed in Paul's following written account:

> Did the invisible walker think he/she/it could take refuge in our house? After all, I had been to the house to seek the invisible walker more than anybody else I know. If the invisible walker had a mind of his/her/its own, then it would, to myself seem very logical, that if it knew somebody who would like to have a ghost, apparition etc., as a good sort of friend (it would go to them – N.W.). Which is what I would like to have – on the condition it was friendly.
>
> Could this invisible walker have been walking outside our house to attempt to create a type of sympathetic contact. By sympathetic this has a specific significance. The invisible walker always walked when it was either raining heavily, freezing weather or high gale force winds. This could bear special resemblances to my subconscious emotions. Because in my own mind, I can have pity for everything (including plants), or in the case of the invisible walker; even dead things!

It seems that the invisible walker has not deserted Paul, because in 1979 he wrote:

> For more than a year now, I have been hearing footsteps parading up and down our garden path. I told nothing of this to my parents or anyone else in my family.

Sometime in May of 1979 it was my parents and one of my brothers who told me of footsteps they heard parading outside the house. In a way, I was a little amazed to hear that my mother had heard these 'footsteps' for many months also. But it didn't stop there.

On one occasion my mother went downstairs to find all the lights in the house on, and the night before, poltergeist-like noises were heard from downstairs (that was on a Wednesday night in May, I don't remember the date), but the most dramatic manifestations were heard by me, and me only.

It was on Sunday morning on July 1st, 1979, between 4.00 and 5.00 a.m. I was awoken by the cat jumping on my bed. Just then I heard all hell let loose downstairs. Doors were slammed, someone was walking up and down in the rooms down there, voices and mumbles were heard, and some strange drone (music) was also heard. After about ten minutes, it all stopped and I went back to sleep.

About 20 minutes later I woke up again, to hear identical noises, and after about ten minutes the noise stopped again. I then went downstairs to see who/what was making the noises, but there was nothing down there.

The next part was the most dramatic. After trying to get to sleep again, I was once again woken up by a very strange, and very loud noise outside my bedroom window. It sounded as if two giant birds were screeching and fighting but there was nothing to be seen. Then there were noises of someone running down the stairs making a hell of a noise, the door at the bottom of the stairs opened and then slammed shut. Loud sounds of someone walking downstairs were heard again and mumbles of people talking could again be heard. By this time I was getting sick of it, so I stormed out of bed, but just as I reached the top of the stairs all the noise from downstairs stopped. I still pelted down, but there was nothing and it was all silent. Just to make sure that nothing else went on, I stayed downstairs, that was at about 7.00 a.m. Nothing else happened. But something was going on down there, and the fact that not only me had heard those footsteps outside the house on other occasions satisfies me that I do not imagine the things.

Sigma the Angel

Paul's "angel" sightings occurred from late 1977 to the early part of 1978. Before telling me about the sightings of this angel, Paul claimed that he had seen something so fantastic he could hardly believe it himself. He only gave me a short verbal account of this series of events, but he wrote about them in detail in a letter to Ian Cresswell, and with their permission I reproduce below Paul's written description.

On 30 December 1977, 8.05 p.m., my younger brother, Phillip, 7, came downstairs claiming he had had a nightmare. Being interested in nightmare phenomenon I asked him what he had dreamt about, but because of his state of mind he was unable to tell me; so I forgot about it. 9.27 p.m. After doing a stunt ghost act on my brother (which we did by flashing a torchlight onto the bedroom window and playing synthesiser music). The light (in the bedroom) was off, and as the flashlight hit the curtain again the most amazing thing occurred. The stunt ghost-scare turned into a reality. By crouching on the edge of the bed and looking at the reflected light on the wall: I saw a faint silvery-white transparent figure, which, at first appeared very faint and got fractionally brighter. The apparition was – an angel! Yes I did say it – a 100% Biblical Angel!! Complete with wings, and an astronauts helmet!!!! Hallucination? Definitely not!

I instantly shocked 7-year-old Phillip and he saw the same thing and became hysterical. Phillip saw the angel's wings but not the astronaut's helmet; although he described the angel as wearing an astronaut suit. No, Phillip was not the only witness, there were two other people, Paul Davis (to whom I instantly screamed out, "There's a ghost, an angel, a bloody angel") and – inevitably – Jon Tilleard. This was no hallucination, figment of the imagination, or any type of mass hysteria – there was definitely an angel. When all of us gathered in the bedroom, I cautiously approached the angel and put my hand straight through it. The angel looked like the following description:

The figure was approximately 2 feet 6 inches (0.76m) in height and not too well built. The wings on the back were folded in, and the whole of its body was silvery-white in colour. The astronaut suit had no special shading; the suit appeared astronautical even though it may not have been one. The helmet I saw disappeared as the sighting continued and the angel simply hovered several inches above the bed at the side of the wall. The angel appeared as in this very simple diagram (unfortunately I have been unable to obtain a copy of this diagram, and Paul was rather reluctant about it being published – N.W.).

The diagram does look a little pathetic but that is what the angel (who will be called "Sigma") looked like. The speculated astronaut suit could not be drawn in, even though it was fairly simple and gave me the impression of the "Great Astronaut God" in the Tassilka Mountains (a reference to the Great Martian God found by French explorer Henri Lhote in Yabbaren, Tassili – N.W.). The helmet which could be seen at first, had two large vertical slits in it and these gave the impression of eyes.

As I said earlier I put my hand through Sigma and when I did this the angel became invisible to me, yet Jon, Paul and Phillip claimed that as my hand passed through Sigma, the angel stayed in the same position, but seemed to rise up a few more inches. The Sigma could only be seen from one specific corner of the room. If you were at any other position then the outside streetlight would block out the dull light which emanated from Sigma. Therefore the figure was not easy to see. After attempting to communicate with Sigma it began to fade away. The Sigma did not reply and made no audible sound and performed no replying gestures; there were no physical effects anywhere in the room. The diagram may not give you the impression of an angel, and probably looks like a crazy monster out of a silly SF comic, but that is what it looked like.

The other three witnesses were scared by Sigma yet I felt very calm and was not frightened in the least by Sigma. What would your reaction be? My attempted contact with Sigma continued for about nine minutes, yet each time I approached it, the angel simply faded away. Yet every time this happened, the "terrified trio" in the corner said that the Sigma stayed there and they could still see it. When Sigma faded away I remembered about Phillip's nightmare... "Er Phil, what was your nightmare about?" I asked. He replied by saying that he had dreamt of an invisible entity in his bedroom against the wall, giving off heavy breathing. Connected? Anything is possible. Well, what do you think of the experiences so far? We are going to try and see if Sigma is there tomorrow.

31.12.1977:- Negative Results.
01.01.1978:- Negative Results.
02.01.1978:- Negative Results.

03.01.1978:- Negative Results.

04.01.1978:- Conclusive results:

This time the body of Sigma was further above the bed, perhaps by several inches or more. This time the body of Sigma had no wings attached to it and as Jon stated, "...it looked like a side view of a human leg, but it was a transparent silvery-white." The angel this time appeared much more like a human on the "first view" as if in a monk's robe. Jon saw no arms but I did. On the second view the angel appeared to have some wings but they simply looked like protrusions; but in this case I will call them wings.

As I went out to shine the light against the window, Jon saw, "These bright lines of light, like neon lights, around the angel's head, and half way down the left side of its body. It looked to me as if he had a trilby-type hat on its head." Phillip did not see this. This occurrence only went on for two minutes or so. I did not see this, even when Jon went outside to shine the light. Paul Davis was not present on this occasion. We will try again tomorrow.

05.01.1978:- Negative Results.

06.01.1978:- Negative Results.

07.01.1978:- Negative Results.

08.01.1978:- Negative Results.

09.01.1978:- Negative Results.

...no more appearances of Sigma have occurred since the reappearance of him on the 4th. It is now the 11th and all activity has ceased. I see no further reason as to why I should continue.

UFO

On Monday, 30 January 1978, Paul was out with Jon Tilleard. Paul noticed a couple of jets in the sky, but Jon also saw a bluish-white object towards Cleckheaton. Paul thought the jets might have been investigating this unknown object. The next day on the school bus about six children asked Paul about the object they had seen in the sky towards Cleckheaton. Including the various children's parents Paul estimated that there had been about 15 witnesses to that UFO, which was sighted between 8.35 and 8.40 p.m.

An Accident

This incident is worth revealing in Paul's own words:

> Sometime around August 1st, 1978, I began feeling very uncertain about my own life, and I felt convinced that before long I was going to die. Also at about the same time, photographs of me began acting strangely and literally flung themselves to the floor. Evidently, something beyond conscious comprehension was at work.
>
> Monday, August 21st, 1978. It was then that a mass formation of UFOs were seen by a camping expedition outside Pateley Bridge, Yorkshire. There were several tens of witnesses to the phenomenon, many of them being teenagers between 14 and 17.
>
> Tuesday, August 22nd, 1978, I was on my bicycle racing my friend Paul Davis down his street. It got to about 9.05 p.m., and I looked into the sky, and saw the most beautiful cloud I had ever seen. It was in the perfect shape of a bird of prey, and the cloud was very dark, almost black. "Hey look, a black bird of prey up there. It's a sign of death." I said jokingly. "Someone's gonna die!" That was the last thing I remembered. The next thing I remembered was looking at my parents in hospital, with me being the patient.
>
> I didn't know where I was, and even when they told me where I was, I didn't know what I was doing there. Apparently, I had been racing Paul Davis, when my chain

slipped off, and stuck into the spokes. The bike stopped dead, whilst I flew in the air coming to rest with my skull stuck on the side of a tree. On reaching hospital it was found that one whole half of my cranium had separated from the other half; my left jawbone was completely smashed into tiny fragments "which were like pieces of a jigsaw puzzle". It took hours to fix it back together again. And just to make it a little worse, I had lost something like 2 pints of blood. Other than that, I was in perfect condition!

When I was taken into hospital Tuesday night, doctors were sceptical about me staying alive. They thought I would die. Wednesday came, and I seemed to be in the same condition, with no improvement or deterioration in health. Thursday came, and it seemed that I had edged on to a slight improvement. On Friday, I regained consciousness (so I have been told – I don't remember). Eight days later I left the hospital: "Much sooner than any of us expected," said one of the nurses.

So my prophecy had not come true, I did not die – or did I? When I was supposedly unconscious, I can remember my body floating through a dark void. It was beautifully desolate and quiet, and mental euthanasia was added to the experience. I remember thinking to myself, "I must be dead", because it was so tranquil. At first, the doctors would not tell me if I had died, but late in April, they gave me a blatant "No!" to my question. So what had gone wrong with my prophecy?

My accident took place on Tuesday, and on either Wednesday or Thursday night, my closest friends were apparently keeping watch on the hospital I was in. This wasn't known to me until I had left the hospital. It was the local newspaper (the *Telegraph & Argus*) which carried the report which encouraged my interest. Apparently, a woman, Miss Elizabeth Dunn, was driving home in her car when she noticed something near the Bradford Royal Infirmary which had never been there before and hasn't been there since, and as far as I can work out, that thing saved my life, of course, you know what that thing was don't you? No, it wasn't the Loch Ness monster, nor was it a Yeti, Miss Dunn reported it as a UFO.

Orange in colour, it was just hovering there, above the hospital. "Bradford Woman Spots UFO" read the headline, and it was just described as being no more than 30 feet (9.1m) across, and looked like a flattened sphere glowing like a phosphorescent light. Did that UFO above the hospital stop my prophecy from coming true, after all it was hovering there when I was in a critical state? If that UFO did save my life – and I am more than certain that it did – then you can mark my case as UN-unique: there are hundreds of reports of people being cured of certain ailments by UFOs, I'm just glad that I have had an unusual experience.

In confirmation of Paul's accident and eminent death prophecy Mrs Susan Stead, a correspondent of mine who has met Paul on several occasions, informed me that:

> He apparently does have "premonitions" of a sort and the day before his accident (when he came to see me) the feeling of something going to happen to him got worse. It had been building up for a while and he said he had told a lot of people about it. He came to collect a UFO folder he had borrowed. He kept going on about how he was sure something was going to happen to him, and he was having dreams about "death" and that he would die before he was 18!

Well of course I tried to re-assure him that it was probably his imagination working overtime. It was sometime later that his mother told me over the phone that Paul was in hospital with a fractured skull.

Paul seems a normal schoolboy in many ways – he was upset that he was forbidden to play football and swim for six months or so after his accident – two things he likes doing very much. He does not seem to me the type of boy to "fantasise" because he is bored with life or needs this sort of stimulus.

Mrs Stead also passed on the information that David Lawson, a Spiritualist friend of Paul's family, "knew Paul was going to have an 'accident' but lied to Paul (when Paul asked about it) and pretended he didn't know anything about it. David told Paul afterwards that he didn't want to upset him but he had 'known' all the time."

Another interesting comment made by Mrs Stead was about the very short period of time Paul spent in hospital, a mere 11 days as opposed to the month-long stay most people with such injuries are detained for. Although Paul had to take it easy for a long period after his accident, when I visited him a few months later he seemed in good health and none the worse for his experience, the only complaint he had at that time was that he was deaf in one ear.

Perhaps Paul's accident was caused by his own wish-fulfilment, he really wanted his prophecy to come true (although I don't suggest that he had a conscious death-wish), and in a bizarre way it did. Since he evaded the jaws of death, due to the intervention of his UFO friends, and since he also believes that his prophecy would have come true had it not been for them, his belief in both the power of prophecy and the existence of friendly UFO occupants was further reinforced.

More Dreams

Throughout this chronicle of Paul's experiences, dreams seem to occur with some frequency, and there appears to be a grey area where Paul and his friends cannot distinguish between objective reality and subjective experience.

Paul notes how his friend Jon Tilleard had a dream on Monday, 29 May 1979,

> just after midnight (12.21 a.m.) Jon was in bed trying to get to sleep, facing the left-hand-side of his bedroom, when he noticed a light shining on the side of the wall. Jon says, "I looked up, and there was a really bright light in the sky, and it got larger and brighter as I was watching it... until it was about the size of a light bulb in the sky."
>
> Originally Jon said it was a bit brighter than a normal star in the sky.
>
> After it had "grown" to such a size it began to shrink again, until it was as large as a bright star. About as bright as Venus. Then it moved over to the left, and just disappeared.
>
> The part of the story which intrigues me the most was the beam of light, and on asking him where was the light shining on his body, he told me that it was on his lower abdomen, down to the bottom of his legs. Strangely enough, when I woke up the following morning, I had a rash (like large heat-spots) on the lower part of my body and legs – Jon didn't. And even stranger, that night, I had dreamt of being abducted by a UFO in a scene similar to one in *Close Encounters of the Third Kind* (which Paul has seen several times – N.W.) setup. Coincidence?
>
> Jon didn't seem too sure when I asked him whether it was the UFO which was glowing, or whether it was just a glow which was enveloping the craft.

After he had seen the object, and after it had gone he went downstairs to telephone me, but at that time I was asleep.

Whether UFO dreams have any relevance to the phenomenon as a whole or not, is worth considering. Jung, however, seems to relate it sufficiently to the phenomena (in his book *Flying Saucers*).

One dream UFO was told to me by Sarah Whiting, an exceptionally beautiful female who I know. Like most dreams on UFOs, this one was very short. She was downstairs in the kitchen when she noticed a bright orange spheroid in her back garden, hovering a few feet above the Earth. She then called her mother, and Sarah just stood transfixed looking at the object. That was it. Sarah has never had any involvement in the UFO phenomenon all her life, whether it be in dreams or in reality, but recently since she has got to know of me, her dreams seem to consist of UFOs and a direct relation to my life.

Although my mother's interest in the subject of ufology is totally negative, she does say she has had the occasional but rare dream on the subject. One such dream involved her being in a large shopping precinct when a massive orange ball of light began flying through the shops. The UFO was seen by hundreds of people in the town. Again, the dream was exceptionally short, as it ended with the object flying above everyone and suddenly disappearing.

Mrs Kathy Nicholson, a ufologist in the Bradford area, also has had many dreams on UFOs (as well as that, she has shown me a very good photograph of a UFO which she took – she also had a visitation once, of three "friendly" men dressed in grey who questioned her on UFOs. She didn't know who they were, where they were from and why they wanted to talk to her). One such dream involved a UFO hovering above her home when she used to live in Australia. Another one was of a humanoid entity emanating from within a dome-shaped, orange object.

Jon and Paul

One feature which is exceptionally prominent in mine and Jon's frame of reality, is a possible telepathic connection between the two of us. Of course, I cannot prove this, but the "coincidences" in how the pair of us think is shown whenever we are together.
You've probably had the experience when your friend says something, and you were thinking of the very same thing at that moment. One such experience involved UFOs.

It was 10.25 p.m. Saturday, 23 June 1979, when Jon and I were crossing Idle Moor. We both sat on a fairly large tumulus on the moor for several minutes, then moved on (passing a standing stone, another tumulus and an earthwork – which I think could be the remnants of a previously unknown hill fort surrounding the hill fort known as Idle Hill Reservoir). As we reached the edge of a track Jon said something about a massive UFO appearing over the nearby reservoir. "Hey, I was thinking that" was my reaction. Jon then told me that he was also thinking of a major UFO flap in the Metro Triangle, and the two of us watching a giant white mothership coming from Idle Hill. That was on the tumulus, and strangely enough that is exactly what I was thinking. Jon also told me what he had been thinking of in the last five minutes; both our thoughts were again identical.

This thought of a massive UFO appearing over the nearby reservoir parallels the scene in *Close Encounters of the Third Kind* when a gigantic UFO suddenly appears from behind Devil's Tower Mountain. Certainly, it is a very memorable part of Spielberg's film. Paul adds: "I don't know whether it could have any direct association with our strange coincidences, but both Jon and I are descendants of Romany Gypsies: a race of people who have unknown origins and also a race of extremely psychic individuals (in many cases...)."

On 27 August 1979, at 3.10 a.m., Paul was on the edge of Idle Hill Reservoir when he noticed a bright light low on the horizon, which moved down towards the horizon and out of view. Within a few seconds he saw a couple more lights which copied the first UFO's motion and method of disappearance. They had an absolute magnitude of about -1.8 with a minimum magnitude of -1. On returning home Paul discovered that his brother Phillip, had seen a light in the sky with a magnitude of -2, late on Thursday night, 26 August. In a speculative mood Paul wrote:

> The UFO dream, the two mid-MIBs, the prophecy, the five minute telepathy contact, the double-headed sperm cell UFO: do each of these nexuate (sic) an occult/UFO connection between Jon and I? I've pieced together all of these facts in my mind over and over again to try and find a suitable theory – and there isn't one!
>
> That UFO I saw in 1972 seemed to be an "enlightenment" in some sense of the word. I believe that I am being worked on, for better or for worse. My life is an experiment. Why should a UFO save my life (as I believe)? Do they need me or Jon for some future purpose? Or am I asking these questions to hope for a boost to my own ego?
>
> The secrets of the mind are many. The forces and powers within are phenomenal. It is the psyche which is

the truth in humanity. Too few people realise the energy which can be exerted by the mind. But minds can be overcome by external forces. The psyche of humans can, and has killed others, but there are other forces beyond the mind, a force of control which can be controlled through UFOs. That force controls us...

Without doubt, ufology is the strongest of all the pseudo sciences. The many theories within the field, the many books, the many witnesses and photographs, all coalesce, to create an oddity.

Is Paul telling the truth about his observations and experiences? There is no clear-cut answer to that, as far as I can see. Certainly, in his accounts we can see the influence of books on his experiences. He compares his very first UFO sighting to an illustration in Brinsley Le Poer Trench's *Flying Saucer Story*. Other experiences he compares to the monster sightings detailed in Ivan Sanderson's *Uninvited Visitors* and to the sightings made in Warminster, which are noted in Arthur Shuttlewood's *Warminster Mystery* book. In fact, parallels to many of the events described earlier are easy to find in the UFO literature. Could it be that Paul Bennett has an over-active imagination which has been put into overdrive due to reading too many UFO books?

Many people, including some ufologists, would say that he is either deluding himself, or is simply seeking attention. However, I would argue that he has created his own "reality". To him his UFO experiences are as valid as any other mode of consensus reality. This is borne out by his statement: "I once had a dream, or semi-dream, I don't know whether it were a dream or not..."

Perhaps he did dream his sightings, but they are dreams which have been shared by his friends. We saw that Paul has a powerful influence over his friends, for example, after viewing the tall green robot, Andrew Hammond said: "I thought I saw something, but I thought 'oh, it must have been you (Paul) trying to make me think so.' He always does that."

Even Paul's mother told me that Paul "believes what he sees, but his sightings have no basis in reality". Paul's thoughts reflect the contents of the literature he reads which is a mixture of fact and wild speculation.

Peter Rogerson commented that this dissonance,

> in itself this is probably not sufficient to explain Paul Bennett's behaviour. Many hundreds of people may have "factional" intellectual systems without projecting them onto their own experiences. Paul must, however, have some powerful motive for creating what his own family (and no doubt many of his school friends) regard as a delusional system. Perhaps it is a mixture of artistic impulse, a desire to brighten up the tedium of everyday existence, a spirit of rebellion or a yearning for attention. In other words a similar constellation of factors which lead other less articulate teenagers to commit various anti-social acts. As for Paul, perhaps in other cultural contexts he would have been the "pious child" who receives a religious vision or is the centre of poltergeist activity, or even the "victim" of witchcraft attack.

At the end of his article Peter Rogerson stated that the record of Paul Bennett's non-consensus experiences could provide "useful information on the early stages of the 'Contactee Syndrome'".

In reply to Peter's statement Paul wrote:

Contactee ...? No, Not Me!
On the 12th of October 1975, at about 4.05 p.m., a very strange encounter with a robot brought my life alight. Ufologists, for some obscure reason, have tagged me a

contactee after the event, the reason of which I am still trying to work out.

A contactee in the ufologists term, is an individual who has a close (contact) encounter with a ufonaut – who ever said the robot was a ufonaut? It came and it vanished, there was no craft. For all I could care, it could have just been a deity of Keel's superspectrum!

Although I do not regard myself as a contactee, I do feel that that "robot" was meant to materialise, in order for me to see it. Some "external" unit caused the robot to manifest (don't ask me what the external unit was/is).

I would also apply a similar explanation as to why the case of the "little black humanoid" does not make me enter the heading of contactee.

Paul also made mention of his prophecy that he was going to die in 1978. It: "would have been fulfilled, but for the UFO above the hospital the night I smashed my skull." And he added: "Ufologists would probably pass that off as an adolescent fantasy. It seems that teenagers are not reliable in the field of ufology, but that it is an investigation which is best carried out by adult researchers – that seems the general philosophy. I'd like to know what differences are made in teenagers seeing a UFO, and adults seeing them. Ufologists may well be sceptical of my sightings (I couldn't care less!) but trying to suggest personal sightings of mine are being enhanced by 'factional' reading seems to be unrealistic."

In defence of Paul, Mrs Stead wrote in a letter to me: "he does seem to have quite a mature attitude towards his critics – a far cry from the mere fantasies of a teenager! The comment I have to make is that the possibility of Paul being psychic does not seem to have arisen as an alternative reason for Paul's experiences. It is a fact that psychics do often see things that the non-psychic does not see – the implication being that these 'things' are really there and 'they' exist outside the 'sense' perceptions of ordinary people."

The reason why I wouldn't call Paul psychic, is because it, to my way of thinking, would be nothing more than a meaningless label. To term something psychic (paranormal or ufological) is nothing better than an attempt at papering over the cracks of our limited concept of consensus reality and explaining one unexplained phenomena with another.

For Paul a UFO sighting is almost a religious experience, the ufonauts with their supernatural powers which govern the universe, and their craft are a symbol of that power and mystery. Whether he believes they dash from dimension to dimension via the superspectrum, or whether they are mundane space visitors, the fascination of visitors from elsewhere has clung to his imagination, and fuelled by his books, his mind hurtles through the, almost, unimaginable depths of time and space.

Whatever we might say or write, Paul sincerely believes in what he has seen, and he is no liar. His youthful enthusiasm sends him in directions of thought and research which seem bizarre, but countering that is his ambition to become a UFO expert, his pursuit of educational qualifications, and his personal integrity which should keep him from losing complete touch with consensus reality.

He regards himself as a pioneer, and as such he has some strong views about the state of humanity and the future of mankind. This is what Paul has to say:

Our planet is in a bad enough state as it is. Bit by bit, over the last hundred years, man has been gradually rupturing the very innards of this globe. Oil, by the year 2000 will not be around. The same applies to natural gas, petrol, and coal could be in small supplies also at the end of the century. Cars, on the road, could well become extinct; man too may be having problems in surviving, and sooner or later man will be discussing his Judgement Day. Such a paradise shall flourish, the day Homo sapien is dead.

What has happened to man recently? He has been destroying himself, yet this doesn't seem to be enough. He is picking on animal wildlife for the sake of it. At the moment, wildlife is the essence of beauty, but idiots don't seem to realise how precious animal wildlife is. Take this into account: "Although wildlife can exist without man, Man cannot exist without wildlife."

Man doesn't find destroying himself good enough, he just picks on other things. There are only two alternatives for man. We are either going to have to change ourselves dramatically, and hope for the Aquarian Age to come, or to just annihilate the whole human race. Which are we going to choose?

If we listen to all the prophets and seers, then we must expect something to happen at the end of the century. Nostradamus: "In 1999 and 7 months. A great king (of terror) shall come from the skies..."

Predictions are continually told of the "end of the world", or even of an amazing UFO sighting. These prophecies never seem to come true. If and/or when a contactee is told a major event will happen to them which will affect his/her life, it very rarely seems to come true if the individual concerned informs hundreds of people. The ufonauts are simple liars who hand out phoney stories and seem to turn some of the predictions into eccentric riddles. Philosophy and riddles of a philosophical nature also come under my great interests.

Ufology, now, is becoming more of a religion than a belief. Not just for people like George King (the leader of the Aetherius Society – N.W.) or contactees, ufology is a religion for believers.

The science fiction of the last century has now become science fact. It shouldn't be too long before today's sf becomes fact. And if man can manage to keep himself on this planet for another thousand years, then science fiction will probably not exist, and it would be almost impossible to write any form of literature on the subject.

But sooner or later someone must hand in the true piece of evidence to show the world that UFOs actually do exist. The ufonauts are much too clever and sensible to land en masse. Maybe they will appear in the skies in massive numbers or do something outrageous like kidnapping the Whitehouse!

The Bible tells of Satan "rising from the pit" after two millennia. Contactees have been told of many things which will happen at the end of the century. Some have been told of horrors like the coming of the "Second Sun" (a prediction made by Dino Kraspedon in *My Contact with UFOs* – N.W.) whilst there are others who tell us that UFO believers and great believers in God will be saved by the ufonauts at the end of the century.

The Pennine Pterodactyl Flap

Just to underline the bizarre way fiction blurs with reality, Paul reported that William Green saw on the afternoon of 12 September 1982, a bird with grey leathery wings emerge from a location called the Devil's Punchbowl, below Shipley Glen, northwest of Shipley. The witness said, "It appeared to be flying in a rather haphazard way, keeping fairly low. The silhouette was quite eerie. Its wings seemed to represent the shape of a bat, or, more realistically, a pterodactyl!"

He estimated that it had a wingspan of at least six feet (1.8m), and it had short legs and a medium-sized beak.

Only three days later, another large bird, estimated as having at least a ten-foot (3m) wingspan, appeared over Yeadon, near Leeds. Witness Jean Schofield said it was being mobbed by a group of rooks, and to escape them it flew up from her garden and headed in the direction of Leeds Bradford airport.

During the third week of September, groups of green and white lights, UFOs rather than flying reptiles, were seen over the moorlands of Baildon, north of Shipley Glen.

In the same month, Richard Pollock of Pudsey was walking his dog when he was dive-bombed by a pterodactyl. As it did so it made a piercing high-pitched shriek that he said he would never forget. His dog whined and whimpered at the sight of this four-foot (1.2m) tall, flying creature with huge leathery wings. It made another shriek as it flew towards Richard, making him leap to the ground to avoid being hit. Looking up, he saw it soaring away.

A zig-zagging white light was seen by teenagers over Yeadon at the end of September, and a light was seen at Woodside. A further sighting was made of a big bird flying from Shipley Glen, at the beginning of October, and on 3 October, a couple saw four revolving, red flashing lights speed over their home in nearby Saltaire, heading for Bradford.

So, there was a mixture of UFO and pterodactyl sightings and the whole matter was compounded by Paul mentioning that before the bird sightings. "[R]esidents from Baildon and Shipley were watching frightening processions of people clad in white robes and hoods, after dark. Nearby woodlands became the centres where these figures were being seen. Burning crucifixes, enchanted moans and ceremonial dances were being reported. Strangely, however, local witch covens and magicians had nothing to do with these bizarre goings-on. Even they were baffled by these antics."

The Buck Woods area of Thackley, Bradford, became the location for white robed and hooded figures carrying out yet more ceremonial dancing on 12 October. The next evening two girls heard a screeching sound followed by the appearance of a reptile-looking creature that flew out of the woods and glided at tree-top height towards Thackley.

By implication, was Paul suggesting these ceremonies were magically bringing these UFOs and pterodactyls into existence? Some even thought they were flying ghosts whilst the more sceptical thought that birds like herons, buzzards, kestrels, crows, ospreys or even a lost American Condor, eagle or vulture were responsible. Radio-controlled models, outright hoaxing or just plain old misperception were also wheeled out as possible explanations.

The local publicity generated more sightings of the pterodactyl over a period of two years. Also, a Mr Morris said he saw a large reptilian bird with a long dog-like head with razor sharp teeth and red eyes, glide over him in November 1977. Much later, on 13 March 1999, a husband and wife filmed a big bird riding on thermals over Mexborough, near Sheffield.

Miracles

Strangely enough science fiction writer Ian Watson wrote a novel titled *Miracle Visitors* that features a teenage boy who uses his mind to conjure up a flying reptile with a 20 feet (6m) wingspan, that soars over the Pennines.

Jenny Randles notes that "this novel did not take a straight 'aliens have landed' perspective. It looked much deeper and explored consciousness, how witnesses and their close encounter experience interact and even the nature of reality itself."

In her book *Mind Monsters*, Jenny notes that the creation of this fiction paralleled what Paul lived out in the real world in the very same geographic locations. Jenny went on to speculate that there is a "symbiotic link between fact and fiction". And, that Ian Watson was as much a "contactee" as Paul Bennett, plus she points out the coincidence of two Watson's exploring the same landscapes of the imagination. Perhaps as she says, Ian and Paul were drawing on the same primitive imagery that lurks in our subconscious.

Jenny adds that: "I had some correspondence with Ian at the time of these events and discovered that he wrote his book over a period when, as he told me, UFO reports seemed to home in on the locality where he lived as he was writing it."

For her, *Miracle Visitors* "was hugely influential in my then nascent research as it gelled so well with where I saw the real evidence leading my thinking.

"To this day I believe that Ian Watson's *Miracle Visitors* – fiction that it is – has to be one of the most significant UFO books by a British writer. Without my reading it I suspect that I would never have seen the nature of the 'Oz Factor.'"

Backstone Circle

The references to dancing hooded figures is probably explained by Paul on his *Northern Antiquarian* website where he describes camping at the prehistoric Backstone Circle in July 1989. Here, he and a friend did a ceremony for a spirit incarnation that brought about the vision of several hooded, humanoid figures walking faster and faster in a circle, which created a vortex followed by the appearance of four horizontal orange-red lights. One of the lines of light seemed to run from Idol Rock to the Swastika Stone, like an illuminated ley line. When the lights vanished, Paul went into the circle and felt an intense coldness.

Numerous bizarre experiences have occurred at this circle, and the locality often terrifies people so much they never want to return here.

Carol Oliver writing in the comments section of Paul's article wrote:

> The sight you saw at Backstone that night sounds very much like an old Wiccan "mill" or round dance where

they circle rapidly while chanting to raise energy to use for various "work" (curing animals, potato blight etc). I really wish I'd been with you, especially for the "light show" afterwards :-) I'm sure it was pretty scary though.

Neil Rushton on his *Dead But Dreaming* blog, makes the point that:

> Stone circles were almost certainly used for a variety of purposes, both metaphysical and practical ... I suggest that they were partly utilised for shamanic dance rituals, designed to alter the state of consciousness of participants. We cannot find a direct archaeological route into prehistoric ritual dance, but the Neolithic and Bronze Age stone circles of Western Europe are highly suggestive of monuments built for a ritual that involved circular movement.

Looking Back

In 2018 I got back in touch with Paul, via email, and got this reply:

> What am I up to? The same old, really. Seeking out new and unrecorded petroglyphs, megaliths and prehistoric sites; contextualizing them in the landscape and striving to give as coherent a mythic relationship (mythic, in that Eliadean sense) to the modern mind as is possible. I put some of this material on my *Northern Antiquarian* website (presently being given a huge upgrade behind the scenes).
>
> I've done a few books on holy wells (some on Kindle); and am, as ever, slowly, getting some others done for the same e-platforms. But I take my time...
>
> On the Fortean scene: I occasionally pop in to have a look at what's going on – but find most of it very superficial and, even the so-called good stuff, is pretty low-graded

psychosocial repetition, without a clue about the nature of transpersonal psychological necessities, nor keeping abreast of the outstanding findings in non-behavioural physical sciences. These elements are fundamental requirements for students if they wanna get a lucid idea on the nature of the subject/s they're exploring – but, as John Keel once said (I'm paraphrasing from reading it as a 14yr old!), "Forteans and ufologists simply lack the IQ to investigate their own subject credibly."

He was right then – and it still seems to apply. Look at the debacle Deveurex, Persinger et al got over their works. I keep telling myself to get back into Forteana for a few years – to give it the kick up the arse it sadly needs. Maybe I will, sometime...

Anyway, hope you are well Nigel. I'm living in the Scottish hills these days. We've just had some stunning blizzards – sadly the rains are washing it all away as I write. The wilderness is still my home – and the olde places and Her waterfalls still my inspiration, as they were as a kid.

About Paul

When reviewing Paul's book *The Old Stones of Elmet*, David Raven observed:

"In places humorous and irreverent, the prose is obviously the musings and ideas of a man with no precious 'reputation' to prevent him from discussing more 'exotic' theories. Or from pondering the relevance of the sacred sites he describes to our modern-day (missing?) spirituality. It's written with a passionate appreciation of the region's megalithic heritage and a love of the northern landscape."

In another review, Gyrus, summed up Paul as:

"A mutant hybrid of a party animal, Taoist mystic and obsessive scholar, Paul's reference points and expressions will no doubt send fussy academics and shamanism-shy pedants running for cover."

Paul, writing on his *Northern Antiquarian* website, lists lots of interests but there is no mention of aliens or UFOs. He notes:

"Over the years I've been described invariably as a lunatic, a fruitbat, a tosser, Barmy Bennett, a genius, a poet, an arrogant bastard, The Gazelle, a hermit, guru – along with 'the Very Irreverent Paul Bennett' (as author and publisher Bob Trubshaw once called me); 'an old Earth shaman if ever I saw one!' by the great Paul Devereux; as well as an 'intrepid megalithic explorer' by the honourable Aubrey Burl. It's a disease I've had over many incarnations I think!"

Notes and References

A condensed version of this chapter appeared in two parts, under the title "Anatomy of a Percipient" in: *MUFOB*, New Series 11, Summer 1978 and *MUFOB*, New Series 12, Autumn 1978. In *MUFOB* New Series 11, Peter Rogerson added some editorial notes about Paul Bennett.

The Paul Bennett case is also featured in:

Mortimer, Nigel and Randles, Jenny, "Protected by Angels?" *Northern UFO Network Case Histories No. 4*, September 1982.

Mortimer, Nigel. "The Paul Bennett Story," *Northern UFO News*, No. 101, March/April 1983, p. 11.

This chapter is also based on the following sources:

At least five meetings and interviews with Paul. The first took place on 5 September 1977, when Roger Hebb and I visited him. I interviewed Paul on 9 October 1977 and 1 February 1978. Shirley McIver and I visited Paul on 27 October 1978 and in early 1979.

Paul's books on his experiences were quoted extensively. They fill an exercise book each, and he spent several weeks working on them:

Bennett, Paul. *UFOs and Psychic Phenomena in the Bradford Area*, 1977.

Bennett, Paul. *Encounters with the Unknown*, 1979.

In 1978 he wrote a book titled *UFOs are Magic,* but I have not seen this.

Postal communications by Paul, all posted in early 1978, to Ian Cresswell, *The Daily Express* and the author.

A press clipping from the *(Bradford) Telegraph and Argus,* Circa 1978.

A letter from Trevor Whitaker to the author dated 11 November 1977.

Letters from Ian Cresswell to the author dated 8 August 1977 and 24 October 1977.

Letters from Mrs Susan Stead to the author dated 6 September 1978, 17 October 1978, 7 March 1979, and 12 June 1979.

Other sources and references are:

Berlitz, Charles, *The Bermuda Triangle*, Panther, London, 1975.

Bord, Janet and Colin. *Mysterious Britain*, Paladin, London, 1974.

Daniken, Erich von. *Chariots of the Gods? Was God an Astronaut?* Corgi, London, 1971.

Doyle, Sir Arthur Conan. *The Coming of the Fairies*, Hodder and Stoughton, London, 1922.

Grinsell, Leslie V. *Folklore of Prehistoric Sites*, David & Charles, Newton Abbot, 1976.

Holiday, F.W. *The Dragon and the Disc*, Sidgwick & Jackson, London, 1973.

Schwarz, Berthold. "The Men-In-Black Syndrome," *Flying Saucer Review*, Vol. 23, No. 4., January 1978, p. 9–14.

Shuttlewood, Arthur, *The Warminster Mystery*, Tandem, London, 1973.

Trench, Brinsley Le Poer. *The Flying Saucer Story*, Neville Spearman, London, 1966.

Watkins, Alfred. *The Old Straight Track*, Methuen, London, 1925.

References to winged beings:

Barclay, David. "Pterodactyls or Condors in the Aire Valley?" *Earth*, No. 14, June 1989, pp. 16–17.

Bennett, Paul. "The Case of the Missing Pterodactyl," *UFO Brigantia*, No. 9, July 1995, pp. 6–7.

"Pennine Pterodactyl," *Obscure Legends Wiki*, at: https://obscurban-legend.fandom.com/wiki/Pennine_Pterodactyl

"Pterodactyl Sightings?" *Ludchurch* blog, at: https://ludchurchmyblog.wordpress.com/places-further-afield/pterodactyl-sightings/

"Paranormal Pterodactyls in the U.K.?" by Nick Redfern, *Mysterious Universe* website, 27 July 2017, at: https://mysteriousuniverse.org/2017/07/paranormal-pterodactyls-in-the-u-k/

Randles, Jenny. *Mind Monsters*, Aquarian Press, Wellingborough, 1990, p. 23–27, p. 151.

Watson, Ian. *Miracle Visitors*, Panther, London, 1980 (orig. Pub. 1978).

"Northern UFO News: The Story," by Jenny Randles, *Oz Factor Books* website, at: http://www.ozfactorbooks.com/northern-ufo-news-january-2019.html

References to Backstone Circle:

Bennett, Paul. "The Backstone Circle. A Brief Record of Recent Paranormal Phenomenon", *Earth*, No. 15, February 1990, pp. 20–21.

"Backstone Circle, Ilkley Moor, West Yorkshire," by Paul Bennett, *Northern Antiquarian*, 22 September 2014 https://megalithix.wordpress.com/2014/09/22/backstone-circle/

"Stone Circles," by Neil Rushton, *Dead But Dreaming* blog, 19 October 2016, at:

https://deadbutdreaming.wordpress.com/tag/stone-circles/

"The Old Stones of Elmet by Paul Bennett" by David Ravn, *The Megalithic Portal*, 27 January 2004, at:

https://www.megalithic.co.uk/article.php?sid=2146411375

"The Old Stones of Elmet by Paul Bennett," by Gyrus, *Dreamflesh* blog, 06 March 2004, at: https://dreamflesh.com/post/2004/the-old-stones-of-elmet-by-paul-bennett/

Bennett, Paul. *The Old Stones of Elmet*, Capall Bann Publishing 2003.

"About me ... Paul Bennett," *The Northern Antiquarian*, at: https://megalithix.wordpress.com/tna/about-me/

Chapter Two

Close Encounters and Children

Children and teenagers have as many UFO encounters as adults. Usually these are ignored because most UFO investigators prefer the testimony of people employed in a profession or career rather than that of children.

The reason for this prejudice is because some UFO investigators do not want to discover anything too bizarre since it might jeopardise scientific recognition of their subject. It is surprising that people investigating an unknown (unknown since we know little about it) phenomenon have such fixed ideas about what is and what is not relevant to their studies.

Typical is a letter I received from a UFO investigator:

"Concerning the reference made by the schoolboy to a 'stick man': I dismissed it partly because there was only one person who saw it, and secondly, that the lads had claimed to have seen so many UFOs in that area. (Woodhall Spa, Lincolnshire).

"Anyway, I'll quote from the letter I received from the lads.

On Sunday afternoon boys are allowed to go to Bardney. In the summer term, 1976, about mid-June, we saw a "stick man" jolting along. It was black with a round head, not making any noise. It was about 150 yards (137m) away from us, and it was quite hard to see.

"In my letter to Ken Phillips (BUFORA National Investigation Co-ordinator – NW) I said that if the 'stick man' had been seen by more reliable people, and also if these young boys had not seen so many 'UFOs' (and many of them sounded like phantoms) I might have felt that the report justified an intensive investigation. However, even if the report was investigated little could be achieved because (a) it took place (allegedly) in summer 1976, (b) its value is very limited as I certainly would not hope to have to resort to reports made by young boys who; (i) could not be bothered to report the incident in 1976, (ii) probably have very strong imagination, (iii) seem to be searching very hard to find a UFO."

It is obvious that we are losing a lot of useful material because of prejudice and the need to be "scientific", even though not many ufologists know what that term means anyway!

Investigators must not be deluded into thinking that they know the answers before they examine the evidence. Children can deal with their environment in a huge variety of ways. They are adaptable to new situations, and their behaviour reflects the conditioning they receive or inherit. If they report UFOs and various other experiences within the UFO context, we should examine why they have such experiences, and compare their experience to those of adults.

UFO books might inspire a child to look for UFOs, but why should they trigger experiences which are nothing more than "pure fantasy"? To ask "what is pure fantasy?" or "What is the mechanism behind this mental phenomenon?" are more relevant responses, than dismissal. Their relevance to adult UFO experiences is clear.

A typical UFO report was sent to me by a nine-year-old boy from Gainsborough, Lincolnshire. He wrote:

"I saw the UFO, it was spinning round across the sky, sometime in summer, it had a red light at the top and a little white light at the bottom. First it just missed our tree, in our back-yard, then it went across Whites Wood Lane. After that I got back into bed, then half past one in the morning I saw something flashing so I rushed to the window and I saw the UFO again but about six seconds later it just vanished in thin air, I could just see stars so I got back into bed. It was a Tuesday I cannot remember the date. It did not make a noise."

This sighting occurred in 1971 and the boy sent a drawing of the UFO which showed a bell-shaped object with a door at the side. He thought that the object was spinning on its vertical axis. The boy told his story in a straightforward, logical manner with no attempt to embellish or speculate.

Compare that with one I received in 1978 from a 27-year-old man, also from Gainsborough:

"The time was 10.20 p.m., Feb 1st. I saw a large silver disc shooting across the night sky, it made a landing behind some trees, I observed 2 figures standing by the spacecraft about 6 feet (1.8m) tall, the saucer made off at more than the speed of light, I estimate in about half an hour. What was it? Could it have been a space craft from the star system of Andromeda or beyond the Milky Way?"

The letter ended with a request for space enthusiast pen pals. That letter was written to seek attention and friends; in comparison the child's letter was a simple attempt to record a memory.

The following account, had it involved an adult, would have been classified as a sighting of a good old intergalactic spaceship.

Stradbroke Landing

On 4 November 1977, 12-year-old Timothy Pearson, his younger brother Nicholas, and their friend Roger Shaw were building a bonfire on waste ground near their home in Stradbroke, Sheffield, Yorkshire. At about 8 p.m. they all saw a strange light in the sky.

"It was like this star what (sic) kept moving in circles," said Nicholas. Timothy also saw it but was unimpressed. He described their sighting: "We saw a light... Like it went across the sky, it vanished. Then about 10 minutes later it came back in (the) same place, went back across and vanished in (the) same place again. I don't know what that was." This light was seen towards the north moving left to right on a horizontal trajectory.

Nicholas went home shortly afterwards and Roger at about 9.15 p.m. Five or ten minutes later Timothy, who had remained, saw a blue/white light that "seemed to appear from nowhere". This "strange glowing object" was seen approximately in the north-east. "It moved across, from the right-hand side, over then hovered for a bit, then it just, like went down," he said.

"It were biggish, about as big as a garage and although it was glowing it did not illuminate the rest of the countryside. About five minutes I saw it in the sky," he commented. "Then I watched it for about five minutes while it were down."

This light landed in a field at the top of the hill in front of the witness. The field was bounded by four or five trees and Timothy said: "I could see like some bits of light behind (the) trees."

He ran home and "I told my mum to have a look outside, but she didn't." Both parents were sceptical of his story. During the sighting he was scared: "I hardly got any sleep that night because I couldn't wait to go and have a look where the strange object landed," he said.

At 8 a.m. he awoke and went to the field. I asked if he was apprehensive about visiting the spot to which he replied that he wanted to see the area, especially since his mother had laughed about his sighting.

The field had a grass crop approximately a foot (0.3m) high. Timothy discovered "a [sic] oval section of the grass flattened down. On one side of the oval was some green sticky stuff. I dipped my finger in it and it was warm. I wiped the scuff off and went home. I didn't tell anyone because I don't like being laughed at."

He said the sticky stuff resembled darkish-green jelly and attached to the side of some of the flattened grass in the middle of the flattened portion was "a brown patch".

Timothy's observation comes from an interview with him and Nicholas and from a letter Timothy wrote to Jenny Randles, in response to an article in *The Sun* tabloid newspaper.

Roger Hebb and I found Timothy and his brother helpful and articulate. Timothy admitted an interest in UFOs and had read books about them. He said that on 0 November 1977, "We had been looking all night for UFOs." He particularly likes stories about UFOs and "little green men" and had read about the famous Kelly, Kentucky, humanoids seen on 21 August 1955. He claimed that he did not believe in UFOs until his sighting.

A transcript of Roger Hebb's and my interview with Timothy and his brother, and the former's letter, reveal two discrepancies. In his letter he wrote: "About ten minutes later (after first seeing the UFO – NW) it took off and disappeared into thin air." When asked if he saw the UFO take off into the sky after it had landed in the field he replied: "No, I just went in."

His letter stated that he had seen similar things since then, but in our interview, he claimed not to have had any other kind of experience with the unknown. I do not think these discrepancies are sufficient to doubt the rest of the testimony. We must bear in mind the time which elapsed between the UFO sighting and the interview.

The relationship between the observed UFO and the alleged landing traces are circumstantial, and several things could have accounted for them such as farm machinery, fungi or the remains of a campfire.

Wawne School Sighting

Two weeks after Timothy's sighting, 20 six- and seven-year-old children saw a UFO from the playground of Wawne Primary School during their afternoon break time. Wawne, North Humberside, is a small, secluded village north of Hull.

At 2.45 p.m. on 18 November 1977, the children saw what they described as a spinning, silvery object resembling an upside-down dish surrounded by a top cupola section with windows. As it moved swiftly from east to south on a horizontal trajectory it made a whistling sound.

Lisa Pattison, aged seven, said: "It was a silver colour and seemed a long way away. It went in a straight line."

Six-year-old Caroline Swift added: "It was quite high and had a hump. I thought it was a helicopter at first. But then it didn't look like one. And it was whistling."

Robert Stevenson, also six years old, said: "It went very fast over our school round to the right and very fast up into the sky. No one could have thrown anything as high."

Headmaster Mr Michael Yates separated these three witnesses and asked them to make plasticine models of what they had seen. They were placed in different corners of the classroom, and they all produced remarkably similar models.

That these children observed something in the sky, disc shaped and spinning on its vertical axis, cannot be denied.

12 miles away to the north-west of Wawne, on the same day, a mother and her seven-year-old son were going to the youth club at Middleton when they saw a brilliant cone of blue light. It was in the north-east and travelling silently at a high speed. It travelled cone-first and as it moved it got larger. They saw it for only a couple of seconds and the boy's description of it as "like a rocket" suggests they saw a meteor or fireball.

UFO Landing

It is noteworthy that earlier that year on 4 February 1977, 14 children at Broad Haven primary school, south Pembrokeshire, Wales, saw a UFO land near their school. At first their headmaster, Ralph Llewellyn, was sceptical of their story but after interviewing them separately he came to believe they saw something unusual.

The boys aged between nine and 11 years old all said they saw a silvery craft with a big dome on it behind trees at the top end of their school playing field, after 1 p.m., and later at 3.35 p.m., when they were leaving school. Some reported seeing a silver-suited figure with long ears near the craft and some heard a humming sound and saw lights on the top of the dome. It was initially dismissed as fantasy, but their teachers eventually took them seriously, and reported the matter to the local police.

Further sightings of UFOs and a humanoid in a silver suit were made in the area during 1977 and it became known as the Broad Haven Triangle or Welsh Triangle. In 1996 a local man confessed that he had gone round the area in a fireproof silver suit as a prank, although the original witnesses remain unconvinced of this explanation.

"You Are from Far Away"

A family in south Wales alleged they had numerous UFO and paranormal encounters in the summer of 1976 onwards and were inspired to tell their story after the release of *Close Encounters of the Third Kind* in March 1978. It could also be that the sightings in the Welsh Triangle were also a big influence.

The prime witnesses in the family were a 11-year-old boy and a 12-year-old girl. The investigators found the boy to be imaginative and clever, who was apt to inject a certain amount of exaggeration and melodrama into his story. He said he was walking down a road when he noticed a shiny object in a nearby field, accompanied by five or six men who walked in a stiff manner and appeared to be very angry. The source of their rage was they were unable to shoot out some light bulbs mounted on poles. Their guns did not seem to work well, and they resorted to hitting the lights out.

Near these "men" was their spaceship that looked like a silver aeroplane. It had a tailplane, and a periscope-like apparatus on top of a dome. Inside the craft, Douglas could see someone who looked like one of his neighbours operating the controls. At this stage a green and red dinosaur emerged from the craft. One of the men growled at it and the creature reluctantly went back inside.

An unusual aspect of the craft was that it had an elevator that made anyone who left the ship look bigger. For example, the men inside the ship seemed three feet (0.9m) tall but when they went outside, they gained one and a half feet (0.45m) in height.

The evening of the same day of his encounter, he went to bed and felt very frightened. His bedroom curtains were open, and so fearing that something might look in on him during the night, he got out of bed and closed his curtains. As he did this he saw, in the southeast, the "same ship" he had seen earlier in the day, climb away into the sky from behind a group of houses.

The girl, perhaps on the same day as her brother's sighting, said she was riding on her bicycle when she saw a silvery craft with a red light on its top in a nearby field. In a letter to UFO investigator Terry Bellis written in 1978, she wrote:

> In about five minutes a person came from around the back of the ship. After he had taken a few steps I knew he wasn't human but I still didn't think it was a spacecraft – but I was scared.
>
> He walked stiffly and seemed to have no knees. He couldn't turn like us but had to swivel. He moved away from the craft with side steps – very stiffly. He was holding a gun (brownish colour with a red half moon button on the top corner). His arms were short and very square elbows and he couldn't bend them properly. He had four long, very thin pointed fingers. His legs were very short and thin and his body seemed long compared to his legs.
>
> He had a helmet on that fitted very closely to his neck. He didn't wear clothes but had on a silver suit that was like a skin all the way down without any break even on

his feet (except they had a thin black shapeless sole). It covered his hands as well. The helmet was silver like the covering on the body except for a clear front. It was a pretty tight fit on his head. His face was the palest I have ever seen. It was long and his chin didn't stick out as far as ours. He had very small very white teeth but he looked as if he had more than us. He had no lips, just a thin, thin line, round his mouth. His (nose?) was broader and flatter without nostrils. His eyes were bigger and round. The pupils were about as big as the bottom of a match. The eyes were white with tiny pale, pink pupils with no other colours. There were no eyelids but a small rim all round. No eyebrows, and I didn't see ears because the helmet fitted so tightly. I couldn't see hair, except some sandy wisps. The forehead was very high.

He made about four holes and felt the ground. All the time he knew about me but ignored me. He moved back to the craft and I saw the silver arm again in the flap and they were murmuring again, very high pitched, very fast. I feel that they were talking about me. The flap closed and then he went around the back of the craft.

The next thing was someone else came from the back. She walked and looked like the man except smaller. I think she was a woman because she had a bit of shape, but not very much. She had a long thing with a wavy edge stuck to her side. She went to the holes the man had made and stuck this thing in. I could hear the noise of the earth scraping, but the stick thing was absolutely clean when she pulled it out.

In all, her sighting lasted for about 31 minutes, and she described the craft as being cigar-shaped with a rim, this was 27 feet (8.2m) long and she saw it from a distance of between 17 and 18 yards (15.5m and 16.4m).

Following her encounter, she found that whenever she became frightened, a mental image of the two beings would appear and it had a calming influence on her. Also, she dreamt of the entities returning and whisking her away in a craft filled with electronic buttons and moulded seats. She, in her dreams, goes with them voluntarily, but after take-off she tries to get out, whilst the entities just murmur in a peculiar manner.

On 25 June 1979, her dreams that the aliens would return, came "true". She went to bed at 8.30 p.m. and was reading until about 11.00 p.m. Suddenly whilst looking at the ceiling, she became dizzy, and she felt she was travelling along a dark tunnel. The next instant she met the two aliens she had seen earlier in a brightly lit field.

The male alien appeared to be wearing trunks beneath a green top, and he had "wings" on his shoulder. The female alien wore a pink dress which reached down to her knees. Wearing a similar outfit to the man was a two- to three-year-old boy who stood between the aliens.

A short conversation took place during which the female alien informed Gloria that she was called ARNA, and her male companion was named PARZ. "You have come far away," the lady told her.

On touching Arna's hand, she found herself and her friends flying over a fascinating city which nestled beneath a very large and dark red-coloured sun. After this flight they returned to the field. Here another conversation took place. The aliens told her that they would help her obtain a gift, they encouraged her to live in peace, and they said that they would return, adding that "we come to you in your darkness".

Once more the black tunnel returned, and she awoke to find herself in bed, the time was now about 11.45 p.m. After this experience, she easily returned to sleep. It is significant that at 11.20 p.m. during the time of her experience, her mother had gone into the bedroom and found her in an unusually deep sleep almost "as if in a trance".

In August 1979, she was warned that a being was preventing Arna and Parz from entering our dimension. To banish this being she recruited members of her family and in a field at midnight, and as they held hands in a circle, she mentally admonished the being to "go back". A vortex of wind blasted the field and a flash of light illuminated them like a bolt of lightning from the heavens. After this, the being was no longer blocking entry to our dimension.

This exorcism episode is reminiscent of a science fiction story serialised on British Independent TV at about the same time in July and August 1979. The series, called *Sapphire and Steel*, starred David McCallum and Joanna Lumley who played time detectives who possessed psychic abilities. Sapphire and Steel were sent to Earth to stop nasty, evil creatures and forces from punching holes in the fabric of the Universe; an activity that would create general havoc amongst us innocent and puzzled Earth people and would ultimately cause the Universe to be flooded with inter-dimensional, spatial and time absurdities. The very first story, in this six-part series, features a house where the evil forces of the Universe have broken into our dimension, and Sapphire and Steel had one hell of a job plugging the gap. In the house lived two children whose parents had been sucked into the other dimensions, and the area of the dimensional holes were in clearly defined areas of the house.

In about the same period the family became involved in psychic questing, and they lost contact with aliens. Their story was so fantastic that it did strain belief as objective, real events, and it has been a source of controversy ever since.

Paul Whetnall and Jenny Randles investigated the case but Jenny notes: "I suspect nobody in that family really believed it but just went along for the ride. And might even have ended up believing parts of it. It does have important lessons about the subject, and I can never prove whether the family believed it or not. But it was part of that era so not something I ever write about today but I am not sorry it is on record as we should not self-censure events."

Alien on the Roof

This first came to my attention when I participated in a Radio Humberside phone-in programme on UFOs in February 1978. A woman identified only as Barbara described a UFO sighting made by her seven-year-old son, whom I shall call for the sake of privacy "Peter".

This was alleged to have occurred on Wednesday, 18 January 1978, at Anlaby Primary school. Anlaby, North Humberside, exactly two months after the Wawne sighting which is only six miles away.

Peter was in the playground at lunch time when he heard a sharp whistling noise "similar to the sound of someone blowing into a pen top". He looked up to see a round object with small windows in it which looked "how you would imagine a flying saucer". It was changing colours as it came to land on the flat school roof.

Three humanoid beings got out of the craft and walked onto the school roof. Peter said that they appeared armless and wore gold suits. From their backs hung wires or tubes which connected them to the craft.

Peter ran to tell a friend who was a few yards away, but when they looked back the three beings had turned around and gone back to their craft. The craft took off slowly, and because the base of the vehicle was transparent, he saw the three occupants returning to their seats. Once clear of the buildings it went away "just like a boomerang".

That evening Peter was rather nervous about going to bed but otherwise he did not suffer any after-effects.

His mother supplied this information in a clear, precise manner without trying to sensationalise and she sounded genuinely puzzled about the whole affair.

The story contains a wealth of bizarre detail, including the changing colours and sound of the UFO; the transparent underneath of the craft; the small windows; its motion on take-off; the occupants in their gold suits; their lack of arms and the wires or tubes connecting them to their craft. This all parallels the equipment used by human astronauts in carrying out extravehicular activities.

I was unable to contact Barbara or to obtain further information about this intriguing case. Little can be added which offers any explanation. One ufologist in a position to investigate this case in more detail stated that it was a "classic" encounter and left it at that. He knew Peter had seen a visiting spaceship and that was sufficient for him.

Mike Covell, a UFO investigator in Hull, did look further into this case. He was able to find a fellow pupil of Peter's and said, "I remember it well; the boy was actually called Peter, which was his real name. We didn't see anything or hear anything, and we were on the same play time too, but I do remember him coming in really excited and telling everyone his story. The class wound him up until he left school!"

The informant said he would put Mike in touch with Peter but so far this has not happened.

The Jelly Man

Are such high strangeness UFO encounters caused by visiting aliens? Many ufologists seem inclined to believe this. An example of investigators' belief in the physical existence of UFOs is illustrated in a report investigated by Andrew Collins, Barry King and Graham Phillips. This involved a young boy who is referred to as "Trevor P" and lives with his parents at Hutton, Essex.

On Tuesday, 22 July 1975, whilst in the vicinity of Dovey Vale, near Machynlleth, Powys, Wales. Trevor decided to walk up a nearby 250-feet (76m) hill, whilst his parents inspected a cottage. On reaching the top he saw in front of him, at less than 50 feet (15.2m) away, a strange craft. Because of his exposed position he leapt behind a boulder and watched from there.

The craft had a round hemisphere mounted on top of a "paddling pool-like" circular base. The latter had large bright round lights and the top of the hemisphere had one mounted light. The base lights gave off a colour Trevor could not identify. Inside the dome, the boy saw two translucent, white jelly-like entities. Their outer surface moved constantly and inside them he could see hundreds of doughnut-like discs. The entities appeared to be attending to a large metal control unit in the centre of the craft.

Trevor took in details of his sighting in a frightened state of mind for 20–25 seconds, then a ramp was lowered from the right-hand side of the craft. It took about eight seconds to descend and one of the entities began to float towards the exit.

It was at this stage that the boy ran as fast as he could down the hill. He cannot remember what he said but his father testified that he cried out, "You won't believe me – come on!"

The father watched his son run back, lay down on the hill for a few seconds and then run down again in a petrified state. The boy shouted, "A jelly man got out of it."

Apparently on his return trip he saw the object with the two jelly entities in their former positions and with the ramp raised. This time he heard a constant noise like "a car revving up but quieter". The craft's lights flashed simultaneously and took on the colours of the surrounding countryside so that they blended with the environment and, consequently, disappeared.

Trevor and his father visited the spot but found no traces or other physical evidence. His father did notice that the wind blowing through the grass created a peculiar sound – an explanation for the strange revving sound.

The next day Trevor could not speak, and his brother suffered from a sore throat, a doctor diagnosed tonsillitis. A few weeks later Trevor complained of a thumping noise in his head and became blind in his left eye. For six weeks he could not sleep normally. The blindness travelled from the boy's left eye to his right. A psychiatrist said that the condition was probably psychosomatic. From being a quiet, introverted child Trevor became aggressive and argumentative. Three years later (1978) he still had the same eye disorder and consulted a psychiatrist on a regular basis.

We do not know Trevor's age or anything about his family; from the few facts we possess it seems that he suffered an hallucinatory experience. The UFO had no objective reality, but it might have been a projection of his unconscious mind attempting to externalise his own thoughts and feelings.

The UFO had strange lights and a metal control unit, presumably the product of a superior technology. Yet the technology derived from the intelligence of grotesque jelly-like creatures. When one creature was about to emerge from the UFO, Trevor ran away (he cannot remember much about this part of his experience) and then returned to watch the UFO and crew merge into the environment. The UFO could be anywhere due to its ability to blend into the environment and the occupants could visit and frighten him once more with ease.

Investigators described Trevor as a loner, perhaps like the UFO he wished to merge into the anonymity of the environment. This hallucinatory experience was probably the first initial onslaught of a psychotic condition which might have a root cause in neurosis or organic lesion. Aggressive behaviour and a psychosomatic condition are further evidence for such a hypothesis. We can say with some confidence that this experience was psychological in origin with the witness suffering from a rare childhood psychosis.

Andrew Collins in *Flying Saucer Review*, Vol. 24 No. 4. stated: "Everything points to the fact that Trevor P. did have an objective encounter with a strange craft and entities that were very real to him. Whether it would have been possible for others to have seen the object would have depended on how physical the object really was."

The reasoning behind such a conclusion is that the experience created the psychosomatic after-effects a view often held by UFO investigators when they find that a close encounter witness starts suffering from psychological problems. A great number of UFO investigators cannot accept that a UFO experience could be but a part of an individual's emotional or organic disposition, and not caused by something "out there".

Nottingham Noddy Cars

Sixty or more Noddy-like gnomes were seen riding cars at Wollaton Park, Nottingham, 23 September 1979 at 8.30 p.m. in the evening. Several eight- to ten-year-old schoolchildren said that the gnomes had green wrinkled faces, white beards, brightly coloured clothes who laughed in a strange fashion. Two gnomes rode in each car that soundlessly chased the children. When two boys thought that some gnomes were jumping down on them from some trees, they plunged into a swamp in their panic to escape them.

The day after this sighting, the children circulated their story round their school. The headmaster interviewed the children who all confirmed that the event was true. Not long afterwards, I telephoned the headmaster who dismissed it as a rumour and did not want to talk about it anymore.

Marjorie Johnson, a local investigator, said that other people had seen little people in that area. In contrast, a spokesperson for the Nottingham UFO Investigation Society (NUFOIS) informed me: "We do not investigate figments of people's imaginations, only UFO reports."

NUFOIS would have been pleased to learn that in the Wollaton area, a white light with a haze around it was seen in March 2010, and several orange lights were seen moving upwards into the sky on 12 June 2010.

Pure Fantasy

One reason why UFO investigators are reluctant to examine the pure fantasy of children's UFO reports is because they do not want to deal with the psychology of such experiences. The implication of the word psychology is that the UFO witness is mentally deranged. This bias results in UFO literature being filled with material that could easily be explained in psychological ways, rather than being offered as evidence for extraterrestrial visitors.

Trevor P's encounter is an extreme example of the kind of psychological explanation that can be offered to diminish the majority of close encounter evidence. The psychological interpretation of UFO cases casts light rather than darkness upon UFO evidence.

I would recommend all UFO investigators examine every close encounter case however bizarre, and on completion of the investigation the case should be analysed as critically as possible. In this survey of English sightings by children, their observations supply valid material equal to reports by adults.

Playing with Our Minds

Since at least 2008, several schools throughout Britain have staged fake UFO crashes in their grounds. These are inspired by the Everybody Writes project, run in partnership with the Booktrust and The National Literacy Trust and is funded by the Department for Education (DfE). Their purpose is to stimulate the imagination and critical faculties of children.

In their attempts to make the UFO crash seem real teachers have gone to such lengths as having local police cordon off the site and organising press conferences with real journalists in attendance. In their rush for authenticity, many children have been frightened rather than stimulated by these events.

These exercises ignore the playground panics of the past, and the harmful aspects of using authority figures to trick children. Some internet bloggers believe this is all part of a long-term disclosure project, which just shows that even in adulthood we never really know what the authorities are up to or what is caused by our own imaginations, rumours or something beyond our ken.

Notes and References

Parts of this chapter was originally published as "Close Encounter Incidents and Children" in *BUFORA Bulletin*, No. 7/8, 1982/1983, pp. 12–18.

Also see: Watson, Nigel. "Enigma Variations," *Fortean Times*, No. 33, Autumn 1980, pp. 42–43.

Remarks about the stick man were contained in a letter to the author dated 25 July 1977.

Details of the Gainsborough UFO were contained in a letter from the witness dated 2 January 1977, and from a questionnaire completed a week later.

The information on the close encounter and entities made in Gainsborough, Lincolnshire, were contained in a letter from the witness dated 24 February 1978.

An interview with Timothy and Nicholas Pearson was conducted by Roger Hebb and the author on 22 March 1978. A letter written by Timothy dated 23 February 1978 was also used as a source.

Information on the Wawne UFO was obtained from *(Hull) Daily Mail*, 21 November 1977.

Interview with the witnesses 1 and 7 December 1977.

Paget, Peter. *The Welsh Triangle,* Panther, London, 1979.

Mike Covell in his book *The East Yorkshire UFO Files,* Next Chapter publishing, 2020, notes that the headmaster is now deceased., and that further research indicated that the records show a Robert Stephenson not Robert Stevenson. Some accounts give Lisa's surname as Patterson not Pattison, and Caroline Swift is sometimes called Claire Swift in some reports.

Middleton sighting; Mike Covell in his book *The East Yorkshire UFO Files* citing *Northern UFO News.*

Randles, Jenny and Whetnall, Paul. *Alien Contact,* Coronet, London, 1983.

Randles, Jenny. *Star Children: The True Story of Alien Offspring Among Us,* Sterling Publishing Co., Inc., New York, 1995.

Details of the Anlaby encounter are taken from the transcript of a *Radio Humberside* programme "Countrywide" broadcast on 7 February 1978 and Mike Covell in his book *The East Yorkshire UFO Files,* Anlaby section.

The Machynlleth encounter is reported in:

Collins, Andrew, "Jelly-like Entities at Machynlleth," *Flying Saucer Review,* Vol. 24, No. 4, January 1979. p. 14. Andrew Collins clearly states that he believes the witness happened to chance upon a physical object.

"The Bubble Car Gnomes of Wollaton Park," *Fortean Times,* No. 200, Special Edition 2005, p. 34.

Young, Simon (ed.). *The Wollaton Gnomes: A Nottingham Fairy Mystery,* Pwca Press, Nottingham, 2022.

Wollaton UFO sightings, see the *UK UFO Sightings* website, at: www.uk-ufo.co.uk/2010/03/nottingham-wollaton-2nd-march-2010/ and www.uk-ufo.co.uk/?s=wollaton

Did Wollaton Park Fae come out to play?" by Dan Green, *World Mysteries* blog, at: https://blog.world-mysteries.com/guest_authors/did-wollaton-park-fae-come-out-to-play-arousing-with-dowsing/

Chapter Three

The Liverpool Leprechauns

Exceptional things were happening in Liverpool during 1964. When the Beatles returned to the city on 10 July for the premier of their first film *A Hard Day's Night*, 150,000 people lined the streets to greet them. A less well-known fact is that a few days earlier thousands of children, and curious adults, went hunting for leprechauns in a Liverpool park.

This incident is of interest because of the rapid spread of the rumour and because it appears that the rumour was especially strong among pupils of Roman Catholic schools in the area. According to the *Liverpool Daily Post*, 2 July 1964, the leprechauns were first seen on the night of Tuesday, 30 June. Nobody knew how the rumour started, but one nine-year-old boy told the Post reporter, Don McKinley, that "last night I saw little men in white hats throwing stones and mud at each other on the bowling green. Honest mister, I did".

The centre of this leprechaun activity was the bowling green in Jubilee Park, which is to the east of the city centre in the Edge Lane district. On the second night of the scare, on 1 July, the bowling green was so crowded that the police had to clear the park and guard it from the marauding leprechaun hunters who were prone to tear up plants and turf in their search for the little creatures.

A rather bewildered Irish park constable, James Nolan, who had to wear a crash helmet to protect himself from the children's stone throwing, told the reporter that:

> This all started on Tuesday. How I just don't know, but the sooner it ends the better. Stones have been thrown

on the bowling green and for the second night running no one has been able to play. The kids just won't go away. Some swear they have seen leprechauns. The story has gone round and now we are being besieged with leprechaun hunters.

Such was the violence of their search that the police had to set up a temporary first-aid shelter to treat at least a dozen children who suffered from cuts and bruises.

The Liverpool Echo and Evening Express, 2 July 1964, described the strange visitors as: "little green men in white hats throwing stones and tiny clods of earth at one another."

The newspaper article indicates the little green men part of the story was possibly inspired by the testimony of a Crosby (north of Liverpool) woman who said that on 1 July, she had seen "strange objects glistening in the sky whizzing over the river (Mersey) to the city from the Irish Sea".

This, apparently, explained how the leprechauns managed to emigrate from "auld Ireland", though it was more likely a tongue-in-cheek addition by the editorial staff to create a neat story appropriate for the flying saucer era. This supposition is supported by the fact that no exact date or any information about the witness was given, and the local paper for the Crosby district did not report anything of this nature to its readers. It is also worth noting that the leprechaun hunt had already been going on for two days before this report was published, so the newspapers cannot be regarded as the originators of this scare.

However, the newspaper reports could well have inspired or fuelled a second leprechaun panic in the Liverpool area a few days later. Details of this will be given later, but for the time being this local panic shows leprechauns were linked with UFOs six years before the British publication of Jacques Vallée's book *Passport to Magonia*.

Brian Jones Confesses

The Liverpool leprechauns could have remained in our files as another datum of the damned if it had not been for certain revelations published in the 26 January 1982, edition of the *Liverpool Echo*. In this report a man called Brian Jones claimed he was responsible for the scare when he started to tidy his grandfather's garden in Edge Lane, which backed onto the park. He wore some clothes suitable for gardening, which comprised a red waistcoat, a pair of navy blue trousers, Wellington boots, a denim shirt and a woollen hat with a red bobble on it. As he sucked on his pipe, no doubt reflecting upon his sartorial elegance, he saw some children sitting on the ten-foot (3m) high wall which separated the garden from the park. He heard one of the children say "It's a leprechaun".

Realising that his short stature, emphasised by the height of his grandfather's weeds, and his extraordinary clothing gave the children this impression, he decided to capitalise on their deluded perception. So, he claims that: "I bounded into view, babbling made-up words, I jumped up and down, picked up turfs and threw them at the children." Not surprisingly the children ran away in a "blind panic".

The next evening, he was again in his grandfather's garden when he heard the noise of a crowd in the adjacent park. Looking over the wall he saw 300 children on top of a covered reservoir which gave them a good view of the bowling green. On seeing him they shouted: "There he is. There's the leprechaun!" However, the children remained where they were, so for the next hour Brian entertained them by angrily shaking his fist at them and by tossing turfs into the air.

Afterwards he changed his clothes and visited the park to find out the reaction to his leprechaun impersonation. Here he found children boasting that they had seen two leprechauns, although some had to top this by saying they had seen six, or more!

The next day, a Saturday (according to Brian), crowds of children and adults went to the house in Edge Lane in search of the little people. Despite the efforts of the police, the crowds did not disperse until after 11 p.m. In the next two weeks children raided the garden in their search for the little people, causing damage to a shed and the garden itself.

Things came to a head when Brian overheard two boys saying that they planned to shoot the leprechauns with an air rifle and deposit the bodies in jam jars to prove to their teachers that the story was not a figment of their imaginations.

At this juncture Brian decided that something had to be done, so for three evenings he put on his leprechaun act in the garden of an empty house six doors from his grandfather's home. This did the trick so effectively that within a couple of months the city council had to demolish the house because of the devastation caused by leprechaun hunters.

Is Brian's confession the solution to the great Liverpool leprechaun panic? More than a brief glance at his statements will show that he simply makes matters more complicated, rather than clearing them up. His story is full of contradictions and errors when compared with the contemporary press reports. For a start, Brian claims that the leprechauns were first seen on Thursday and Friday, and that on the Saturday crowds gathered near his grandfather's home; yet the press tells us that the creatures were first seen on Tuesday, 30 June. Perhaps with the passage of time he just forgot the correct days and dates of the sightings, and just remembered the dates of the newspaper reports?

It seems odd that the newspaper descriptions of the leprechauns do not tally with Mr Jones's description of his elegant outfit. None of the children noticed his red waistcoat, the red bobble on his hat, his navy trousers or his denim shirt. The ten-foot (3m) high wall is of interest too. It could not have been the simplest thing in the world to climb, either for the children, or particularly for Mr Jones considering his short height and Wellington boots.

It is also difficult to understand why the children on the second day did not approach the wall in large numbers and scale it to catch the "leprechaun". The children of Liverpool are not normally that shy! Furthermore, all the children's reports speak specifically of leprechauns in Jubilee Park and bowling green; there was no mention of any sightings in private gardens – and many of the children said they saw more than one creature. A search through the two Liverpool daily newspapers for the period covering July, August and September did not reveal any more reports of leprechauns seen in the neighbourhood of Jubilee Park, and no mention of the rather newsworthy event of a house being demolished through the depredations of their hunters.

Another factor is that leprechauns were also seen in other parks in Liverpool, namely in Stanley Park, in Newsham Park, Abercromby Park, and in Sefton Park a 13-year-old girl said she grabbed one of them, but he escaped her grip and ran away laughing.

For these reasons we suspect that Brian Jones might be mistaken in his belief that he was responsible for starting this panic; perhaps after twenty years two separate events have become confused?

Whatever the explanation for the start of the rumour, it is noteworthy that it spread very quickly, and generated sufficient interest for substantial crowds, including many adults, to gather in the park. It is also intriguing to see the injection of the UFO sighting into this context, even if it was a humorous attempt at an explanation for the presence of the leprechauns. In addition, the children who wished to insert the entities into a jam jar remind us of those ufologists who believe (or hope) that the USAF has succeeded in preserving little green men in bottles.

Little Folk in Kirkby

No sooner had the Liverpool rumours subsided than a similar scare erupted several miles to the north-east of the city in the overspill town of Kirkby. *The Kirkby Reporter*, 17 July 1964, under the headline "Little Folk and Flying Saucers" noted:

> Flying saucers and leprechauns came to Kirkby last week – at least according to local children. What the connection was the children were not quite sure, but scores of excited youngsters invaded the *Reporter* offices on Friday, eager to tell they had seen both these things.
>
> A "strange object in the sky", which changed the colour of its lights from red to silver, and was moving slowly at first, then very fast, was their description of the flying saucer.
>
> The "flying saucer" faction vied with the "leprechaun" group for colourful descriptions. About eight inches (20cm) high, with red and green tunics, and knee-breeches, thus the little people were described. And, of course, they spoke with a strong Irish brogue.
>
> Origin of the wee folk remains a mystery, but so convinced were the children that hundreds of them plagued the vicar of Kirkby (Rev. J. Lawton) by invading St. Chad's churchyard in search of the little people. At times the numbers were such that the police had to chase the children away.

The Liverpool Echo, 13 July 1964, carried the first account of scores of children searching the churchyard at St Chad's for leprechauns. After what was described as two days of hectic activity, which probably began on Friday, 10 July, a relieved Rev. Canon John Lawton told the *Echo's* reporter on the night of Sunday, 12 July, that: "The children seem to have been convinced at last that there are no leprechauns." During the same period, children had also searched the grounds of St Marie's Roman Catholic School and Mother of God Church, Northwood, Kirkby.

In many ways this panic seems to have been a continuation of the primary rumours originating in Liverpool. We should note that they could have been influenced by many reports from the general Liverpool area of UFO activity that July, which by their very quantity might have linked leprechauns with UFOs more firmly in the minds of the Kirkby children.

Newcastle Inspiration

We might even speculate that the original Liverpool rumours were inspired by a report in the *Newcastle-upon-Tyne Journal*, 9 June 1964, which may have reached some of the national or regional press. *Flying Saucer Review*, Vol. 10, No. 5., p. 18, reproduced the following from that paper:

> Flashes of light ... loud buzzes in the night ... little green men chasing each other round haystacks ... egg-shaped flying saucers ... the leprechauns aren't loose and it's no Irishman who is telling this tale – just the good people of Felling. For stories are going around Leam Lane Estate (Gateshead, Durham) that flying spacemen in egg-shaped flying saucers are using the area for manoeuvres. So persistent are the stories that a full-scale investigation has been launched by one organisation.
>
> And the little green men? They were seen by 14-year-old David Wilson. He said: "I saw several small green creatures about two feet (0.6m) high running around a haystack on a farm near the estate."

David saw this on the afternoon of 2 June 1964, along with several other children. Joining the group who were a few yards from a haystack, at about 5.30 p.m., 14-year-old Mike Smith said he saw "around six or eight tiny human beings on top of the stack: they were about two and a half feet (0.76m) tall and dressed in bright green suits. They appeared to be digging into the haystack, as if searching for something. Their hands seemed like lighted electric light bulbs".

The newspaper added: "But not everyone believes the stories. Last night Mr M. Coates, headmaster of Roman Road junior school, denied that he had called a special assembly of pupils to discuss the little green man, or that he had told the children to stay away from the farm. He said: 'There is no truth at all in these silly rumours.'"

An anonymous witness came forward years later, to say that she was five years old in 1964 and recounted that the little people in green suits and a silver disc were seen in her school field several minutes before they were seen at the farm. They went through a gap in the hedge and crossed Leam Road heading for the farm. It was also claimed that lots of "military" turned up at the scene.

A Prelude to Their Arrival

Going further back in time, Tom Slemen reports in his article "The Summer of the Leprechauns" that a mother and daughter saw little green men sitting on the windowsill of their living room window in 1957. Their home in Wimple Street, Kensington, Liverpool, was not far away from where the leprechauns would appear several years later. The mother, thinking they might be dolls, went outside where she saw two domed craft hovering five feet (1.5m) above the ground. Her daughter, Joan, stayed indoors but was able to see these mini craft through the window. As her mother called to a neighbour and pointed at the craft, it fired a bolt of light at her. The neighbour didn't see the small UFOs, only the flash of light. Seconds after the flash, Joan heard her mother groaning, and she rushed outside to find her on the doorstep with her eyes closed. By now the craft and the little green men had disappeared, and later her father told her mother not to say anything about it because "they'll think she is crazy". Tom wonders: "Is there some connection between the miniature UFOs (which may have been probes of some sort) and the enigmatic 'leprechauns'?"

Glasgow's Gorbals Vampire

Ten years earlier young children besieged Glasgow's Southern Necropolis cemetery looking for vampires rather than leprechauns. Edward Cusick, headmaster of St Bonaventures primary school helped police disperse the crowd by telling them it was all a silly rumour.

The story that a seven-foot-tall vampire with iron teeth, had kidnapped and eaten two local children had spread round school playgrounds and prompted them to search it out en masse after school hours.

For several nights at the end of September 1954, the school kids scaled the walls of the cemetery, armed with sticks, stones and penknives. The nearby ironworks added to the drama by casting smoke and an eerie red glow over the scene, where any shadow was the vampire.

The Iron Man, as he became known, hit the headlines in the local and national press. On investigation, not surprisingly, no children had gone missing or been eaten. No firm reason was found for the cause of the rumour, but blame was put on horror films and imported American horror comics.

The moral panic found solace by introducing the Children and Young Persons (Harmful Publications) Act of 1955 that effectively banned comics that might show contents of a repulsive nature to minors.

Those who claim that something strange was seen or that the real source of the rumour was never discovered, note that many of the children had never seen the likes of *Tales from the Crypt* or *The Vault of Horror*. In addition, it is claimed no Gorbals Vampire with iron teeth is to be found in the pages of such comics. The latter is certainly untrue as a story titled "The Vampire with the Iron Teeth" by Hy Fleishman appeared in *Dark Mysteries*, No. 5, December 1953.

More Explanations

Obviously, Brian Jones could not have been responsible for all the Liverpool scares. So, if he was not the cause of them, who or what was? In the case of the Liverpool happenings, it could be argued that a tall story got circulated at a local school and rapidly spread by word of mouth. The stimulus could have been the factors already discussed or might have been an invented story that came to be regarded as relating to a real event.

Sigmund Freud in his essay "Creative Writers and Day Dreaming" claimed that fantasies are mental constructs of the imagination, liberated from the constraints of reality, and that "the motive forces of fantasies are unsatisfied wishes, and every single fantasy is the fulfilment of a wish, a correction of unsatisfying reality".

In support of this, most of the children attended Roman Catholic schools and (in the Liverpool and Kirkby areas at least) were most likely of Irish descent. Their Irish cultural background might well have had a strong influence on the way such wishes were expressed. Leprechauns play an important role in Irish folklore, and Katharine Briggs in her *An Encyclopaedia of Fairies*, reminds us that the leprechaun was a fairy cobbler who lived underground beneath a fairy hill. Attempts at capturing him always failed. Another version of the leprechaun legend asserts that a boy with fairy blood in his veins can recover treasure from a cave guarded by a leprechaun.

Can this legend, or some remnant of it, have been the reason why the children so vigorously sought to discover the leprechaun? Or was the rumour just an excuse for vandalism and some excitement? As with most aspects of folklore, and ufology, such rumours can be generated and sustained by a multitude of purposes and reasons. These rumours were short-lived in the media of the period, but memories of the events are still recounted on social media and by local historians.

As a postscript to this report, when it was first published in *Magonia* magazine, Granville Oldroyd and Ian S. Cresswell noted:

> We feel that there is a very real danger of making the mechanisms at work behind Liverpool leprechauns more complicated than need by be the over-use of complex sociological theories when more simple and easy to understand explanations are near at hand. We would rather suggest that the more likely cause behind this series of events was rumour which very quickly spread within the restricted confines of school, playground and neighbourhood, which got out of hand and spread to other groups of children within the Liverpool area, before finally becoming just another silly season story and dying out.

John Rimmer, the editor of *Magonia* magazine, who at one time lived only a couple of miles away from these events was not convinced about the religious and Irish influences on these stories, instead he thinks, "the point raised about the Merseybeat phenomenon is valid. This had a tremendous social effect in Liverpool, not just restricted to teenagers. In many ways this was a period of massive social change in the city, which has yet to be adequately charted by social historians."

In contrast, Simon Young in his article "Fairies across the Mersey" makes a strong case for Irish immigrants passing on their fairy beliefs to third and fourth generations in Merseyside and helped form the basis for this scare.

Besides, Brian Jones's belated confession about causing these sightings, Liverpudlian comedian Ken Dodd told the *Liverpool Daily Post*, Monday, 25 January, 1965:

> Just before all these rumours started, I did an item on television. We used a special technique by which the cameras were able to "diddify" people. It was rather like looking through the wrong end of a telescope. We arranged everything so that television commentator Bill Grundy... was reduced to about four inches (10cm) on the screen and I described him as a diddy man from Ireland – a leprechaun. Immediately afterwards, there were all sorts of stories about leprechauns being sighted...

Ken Dodd is associated with making the mythical Diddy Men, who work in the jam butty mines of Knotty Ash (an area of Liverpool), famous. He regularly used Diddy puppets, children or short adults to perform "diddy" related songs! Although, as Steven Tucker notes in his book *Paranormal Merseyside*: "This programme... could have fed into the scare, certainly, but not have caused it alone. Liverpool's schoolchildren do know the difference between television and reality..."

Yet another explanation is given by John Hutchinson who worked with Jim Nolan in the Liverpool Parks Police department. Jim told him that he made it up as a bit of fun and the kids did the rest. John noted: "His antics came to the notice of Police Superintendent John Buchanan, who was head Constable of the Liverpool Parks Police — Constable Nolan was warned off and to keep his mouth shut. The exercise had resulted in many officers having to work overtime — and as Nolan said: 'The money came in handy with Christmas coming up'."

This seems a bit odd, as Christmas was a good six months away, and includes a neat bit of conspiracy theory.

Leprechaun Memories

Whatever the real answer, several people do recall "seeing" the leprechauns. After this story was put on the *Magonia* website it prompted a few people to send in their memories, Mike S wrote

> As a child, living in Fairfield, I remember the "sightings" in the park in Kensington. I remember what seemed like thousands of kids congregating at the park and eventually getting chased off by the police. I was six at the time so the exact details are not totally clear in my memory banks but I do recall going to the park with my brother and sister along with the rest of the kids in the area. Everyone was excited about the prospect of seeing a leprechaun.

Many years later he read that the sightings were caused by circus folk who were staying at a house near the park and were mistaken for leprechauns.

Linda Tahmasebi recalls attending "Brae Street school (located near Jubilee Park) and we all saw them popping in and out of a window overlooking the school yard, there were about 4 of them all tiny dressed like a school book idea of a typical gnome and they sat swinging their legs on the window ledge getting in and out."

Bri remembers "the siege of St Marys (sic) church when the police and Father Rose (or Father Spain) appealed for calm. I was one of the huge crowd of children shouting out 'there they are.'

"Someone said they had crossed the road into St Marys infants school and were now hiding in the lockers (small cube-like cupboards then) I never slept for days, and have had a fear of these type of cupboards to this day, which is still tested as my grandchildren's nursery school use something similar. Ah memories."

Chris Jones said that when he was nine years old, "I was one of the swarm of children who invaded St Chads in Kirkby. I was also a pupil at St Marie's school. I too had come to think that this event was a figment of my imagination. I was not aware that the mass psychology of the events involved Catholic children predominantly, though it does not surprise me. Religious education in school was full of stories about children being favoured by visitations: Lourdes and Fatima being two of the better known examples. However, why leprechauns were involved and not something more pious is a mystery to me now."

Eddie McArdle was also a pupil at the same school and gained a permanent reminder of this incident:

> I remember the story well as I have a scar as a constant reminder of the event. We, the kids from St Marie's, Kirkby, went en masse into the church and as we hunted the little people, some bright spark shouted that they were coming out after us. Panic ensued and as we all fled quicker than we entered a boy who is sadly no longer with us swung the church gate in his haste to escape, and I was hit on the forehead by the metal cross on it. The lad, Danny Callahan, didn't even know he had injured me as he was well up the street and along Elric Walk where I lived. I had to have my head stitched by Dr Cole. As far as I know I am the only person injured by the little visitors. Unless you know different.

Notes and References

A substantial part of this chapter was originally published as "The Case of the Liverpool Leprechauns," in *Magonia*, No. 18, January, 1985, pp. 12–16.

"Leprechauns in Liverpool," *John Knifton* blog, dated 12 August 2016, at: johnknifton.com/tag/brae-street-school/

"The 'Little People,'" by Tom Slemen at: www.wirralglobe. co.uk/news/23610075.tom-slemens-haunted-wirral-column-little-people
He notes some 11-year-old boys saw a small two-foot (0.6m) tall man near the Farmer's Arms pub in Frankby, in July 1963. The man said "hello" and then disappeared. He also carries the story of two 13-year-old girls who saw tiny people inside a one-foot (0.3m) tall, beautiful crystal when walking through Birkenhead Park, in July 1971.

Vallée, Jacques. *Passport to Magonia: From Folklore to Flying Saucers*, Tandem, London, 1975.

"The Leprechauns of Liverpool and the Bowling Green from Hell," *Beach Combing* blog, dated 14 May 2012, at: www.strangehistory.net/2012/05/14/the-leprechauns-of-liverpool-and-the-bowling-green-from-hell/

"Fairies across the Mersey," by Simon Young at: www.academia.edu/44392039/Young_Fairies_across_the_Mersey

Rimmer, John. *The Liverpool Leprechauns*, UneXplained Rapid Reads, Windmill Books, London, 2015.

Tucker, S. D. "Invasion of the Diddymen – Liverpool's 1964 Leprechaun Invasion," *Fortean Times*, No. 299, April 2013.

"The Gateshead Gnomes. and more Little People," *John Knifton* blog, dated 2 September 2016, at: johnknifton.com/2016/09/02/the-gateshead-gnomes-and-more-little-people/

"The Summer of the Leprechauns," by Tom Slemen, September 2011, at: web.archive.org/web/20221106231529/http://www.slemen.com:80/leprechaunreality.html

"Child vampire hunters sparked comic crackdown," by Stuart Nicolson, *BBC Scotland News*, at: http://news.bbc.co.uk/1/hi/scotland/8574484.stm

"Iron Man of Gorbals (Scotland)," *American Monsters* website at: http://americanmonsters.com/site/2010/03/iron-man-of-gorbals-scotland/

"The Gorbals Vampire" at: http://potrzebie.blogspot.com/2010/03/ec-comics-gorbals-vampire.html

"The Re-Post with Iron Teeth," *THOIA* blog at: http://thehorrorsofitall.blogspot.com/search?q=Vampire+with+iron+teeth

Freud, Sigmund. "Creative Writers and Day Dreaming" in *Creativity*, edited by P. E. Vernon, Penguin, London, 1970.

Briggs, Katherine, *A Dictionary of Fairies,* Allen Lane, London, 1976.

Tucker, S.D. *Paranormal Merseyside,* Amberley Publishing, Stroud, Gloucestershire, 2013.

Chapter Four

Shadowlands of Ufology

The Mrs Trench Case

The prime witnesses to these series of events were Mrs Trench and her son Edward (both names are pseudonyms). Most of the details of the incidents are based on and quoted from the correspondence that Mrs Trench sent to UFO investigator Carol Tonnessen. Initially, her UFO sightings were not particularly exceptional.

Her first sighting was in the spring of 1957. On a clear bright morning she was taking her son (then aged six months) to a day nursery before she went to work. The time was about 8.15 a.m. and she was walking towards Queens Park, London, NW6, when she saw a silver, Saturn-shaped object, motionless in the sky. After a few seconds it glided behind a cloud and disappeared. She wrote: "I was scornful of UFOs and I remained scornful until 1959 when a colleague assured me that the object I saw could not possibly have been man-made as our technology was not so far advanced ... Even then I was doubtful."

Her second observation was at 1.30 a.m. in November 1959. Whilst in her home in London, she saw a blue-green flame which was very brilliant, and in shape resembled a horse-shoe magnet. She saw this, she said, "when I was in bed, my husband was asleep and I was just admiring the bright stars, when the object came into view and quickly out of view. I thought it must be a sputnik crashing to Earth. I expected to hear a crash by the time it passed from view, but there was no sound at all. I wondered how the middle section of the object remained without flame, and years later I had to concede it was a UFO."

In 1967 Mrs Trench became a UFO believer, and consequently she bought and read a few books on the subject. At about the same time the family moved to Thetford, Norfolk. Here Edward, who was by now about 12 years old, had a couple of UFO sightings himself.

"On one particular day a friend and I were standing on top of a garage, plane spotting," wrote Edward, who explained it had been a light evening, as they watched some jet fighter aircraft. These aircraft followed the same flight path, so the two boys knew exactly where to look. Also, they could hear some booms (not sonic booms) just before a jet would pass over. The planes were flying over at regular intervals and the booms were regular too.

> After several booms and jets we heard the next set of booms and waited for the next jet to fly over. We waited longer than usual for the jet and by this time we were scanning the whole sky ... I saw something coming, which I quickly pointed out to my friend. It took exactly the same route as the jets but was utterly silent except for a kind of swishy noise. It was disc shaped (and at about the same height as the jets) and had coloured lights going around the lower circumference ... another set of booms was heard and a normal jet passed by. By this time my friend was scared witless and was struggling to get off the garage to tell his father. I knew there was no danger, since the object had passed. I think this sighting is very important because of the way in which the disc fitted in with the jet manoeuvres, almost as if with the co-operation and/or control of the air force base.
>
> My second sighting was shortly after that. It was about 10.30–11.00 p.m. I was lying in bed looking out at the sky (my curtains were open) and it was still lightish. A disc-shaped object went past at a fair distance, but it was not the same as my first sighting. This had a large circular white light in its underside, flashing on and off at regular

intervals. (It was tilted as though changing direction.) Its shape was rather taller than the first.

On several other occasions Edward saw zig-zagging lights in the sky. In fact, he claims to have had so many sightings of various kinds of lights in the sky that he has now forgotten many of them. During this period Edward maintained an interest in astronomy, and with his two telescopes he would study the constellations and simultaneously keep an eye open for any visiting UFOs.

Mrs Trench became aware of many of the UFO sightings in the district. She spoke to many UFO witnesses and discovered that one night a young man had been walking home alone, from a school dance, when he saw a UFO. He told Mrs Trench how he had felt compelled to look upwards, and on doing so had seen something (he did not use the term UFO) which had coloured lights about it and was descending towards him. Alarmed, he ran home as fast as he could.

In the same locality there had been incidents of travelling lights following cars, and one night Mrs Trench, with some friends, "saw UFOs like fireflies darting about the eastern sky. On another occasion Edward and I watched a small light trying to catch a large bright light."

It is noticeable that Mrs Trench's early sightings took place at a time when there was a great deal of public interest in space exploration, due primarily to the launch of Sputnik 1 in the early hours of 4 October 1957. More than ten years later Mrs Trench and her son saw UFOs when there was another period of intense public interest in space exploration due to the Apollo moon missions.

Edward thought his first UFO sighting was important, because "the disc fitted in with the jet manoeuvres, almost as if with cooperation and/or control of the airforce bases". This, he claimed in the same letter, lead him to believe that some but not all UFOs have their origin on Earth and wonder if there is a secret government cover-up.

Returning to the experiences of Mrs Trench, she said that in the early 1970s when glancing through her kitchen window, an unusual light appeared. The window faced south and directly opposite there was a block of flats and shops, and to the southwest of these, and close to them, was the full moon, which was at the centre of an enormous crucifix-shaped light. Vertically, it covered from 10 to 15 degrees, and the crossbar was in proportion. Each shaft of white light was the width of the full moon. She wrote:

> I was so astonished I called my son (his dad took no notice at all) and together we stared at it for a moment, then with one thought in mind (that it might be caused by the glass of the window) we made for the garden door. From the door it was clearer than ever. Recently I found an article in Edward's *Scientific American* on the subject of crosses of light in the sky, which explained the effect of light from sun or moon through ice crystals which, it was said, sometimes form crosses as parts of arcs which cross. However, what we saw were definitely NOT parts of arcs. The shafts were dead straight, almost as bright as the moon itself.
>
> I, myself, have always held the firm conviction that "Truth is one and indivisible" but I see no reason to doubt that spiritual truth (if we can ever find the wisdom to understand it) will teach us how causes beyond the reach of material science produce effects which can be evaluated by material science. That is no reason, however, to ignore the latter. The Biblical prophecy "The Sign of the Son of Man in the Heavens" could well be as scientific a prophecy as our weather forecasting!

It could well be that technological civilisation which we know has produced environmental changes which affect the upper atmosphere, has thus produced the conditions in which such a cross of light may occur in certain local conditions. And it could be that observation of that cross and the search for "the how" of it could draw attention to more profound changes in our environment than science has to date monitored ... perhaps it (the cross of light) has always appeared before cataclysms as a natural result of environmental change – as natural as clouds appearing before a thunderstorm...

This sighting is reminiscent of the star or cross seen by two police officers in the early hours of 24 October 1967. Their observations received a great deal of publicity in the media, at a time when the population of England was confronted by many hundreds of UFO reports from across the country. This has been explained as being a sighting of Venus, but the two officers several decades later still felt that they had not been given an adequate explanation.

Mrs Trench regarded her cross sighting as "the sign of the Son of Man in the Heavens..." and then expressed the feeling that our technology has provoked the conditions for the appearance of the cross. To her, the cross is a warning that unless we respect and understand the earth our greedy vandalism of the planet will result in a cataclysm.

The cross is indicative of a sign that by coming to terms with our environment, both physical and mental, all will not be lost for humanity. It is noteworthy that she remarks that Edward's dad took no notice at all (of the cross), aware that her husband, and rational science, are blind to the fate of humanity. She can only try to come to terms with the impending cataclysm with her son.

The fact that other UFO witnesses have reported similar sights, and given importance to them, adds relevance to the interpretation of such visions. Such a report was made by the Shade family who live in Louisiana, USA. During a partial eclipse of the moon on the evening of 26 July 1972, they saw a perfect gold cross on the moon. Mrs Shade said that the road was lit up bright as day from the cross. Not only had the Shade family been witness to UFO activity but they also interpreted their cross observation as an omen from heaven.

Hilary Evans cites the case of Mr and Mrs Frank Harley who regularly saw a glowing cross flood the bathroom of their mobile home in Pontiac, South Carolina, with light. Sometimes an angel or a burning bush could be seen next to the cross of light. There was even a "Great Cross Flap" of similar sightings throughout the USA in 1971.

On another occasion Mrs Trench was talking to a friend, late at night, and as they were walking to a bridge which lay between their two homes her friend Teresa suddenly gasped "Good Lord, what's that!" Mrs Trench wrote:

> I looked and ran to the middle of the bridge to get a better view, Teresa following. It changed course then and came towards us. It may have been a coincidence, but when it reached the half-way stage towards us I felt uneasy and thought at it "Please don't come any closer" and it blinked out immediately. I then regretted my cowardice, and it blinked on again, now in the woodland, boughs dashing across it as it moved. Again it changed course and came at us, and again at the half-way mark I felt uneasy and thought "That's far enough" and immediately it blinked out again. Teresa was now willing to go home; all the way home I felt something behind me and, indeed, just after leaving the bridge I instinctively spun round but there was nothing to be seen. I never felt uneasy before on that route, or since.

With this sighting Mrs Trench was no longer a passive observer. She had the power, or at least thought she had the power, to interact with UFOs. Similar instances have been recorded in the UFO literature – and although they might support Jung's hypothesis that some UFOs are projections of the collective unconscious, we cannot give much validity to this idea without better investigation of such alleged events, or through controlled experiments.

A few months after the above experience, Mrs Trench was lying awake in her Thetford bedroom at 1.30 a.m. when she saw inside her room a 12-to-14-inch (30cm to 35cm) diameter sphere like a million-faceted ruby, with sharp red gleams from all over the surface. The sighting lasted a few minutes, and describing the encounter she wrote that:

> I was trying to get to sleep, my thoughts on tramlines, I decided to get up for a drink to break the pattern of thoughts, opened my eyes and saw the object described ... I felt no alarm whatsoever ... It did not move or do anything at all to keep my interest, and with the train of thought which had been keeping me awake broken, my eyelids just wanted to close. So I turned my back wearily and went to sleep. Next morning I found it incredible, but I wasn't dreaming or even thinking about anything to do with UFOs.

Mrs Trench's bedroom encounter was probably a hypnagogic hallucination, which is a common feature in the UFO literature. Mrs Trench's attitude to this experience was one of disinterest, yet during the previous encounter she felt distinctly uneasy and afraid.

Most UFO contactees seem to have an intuitive nature, and Mrs Trench seems no exception. She claims that since childhood she has been prone to precognitive insights. One of her premonitions was of a group of schoolboys falling from a funfair structure; a year later this apparently came true.

She wrote that,

> this upset me so much I have taken a long time to get over it and "tune in" once again. And in that connection I have to say that in 1964 I began to get the words "As in the days of Noah", until after some years I looked them up in the Bible, and found that other impressions I had been having were confirmed by Biblical prophecy, by Jesus. Which leads me to think that Jesus was a Master of Science (i.e., of that truth which is one and indistinguishable), and that the churches, all of them, missed the point in creating their dogmas, and repressed the very faculties Jesus was trying to awaken. The UFOs are certainly "signs and wonders in the heavens", Jerusalem certainly is "encompassed by armies", etc., etc.

Since childhood Mrs Trench has experienced strange insights and seen wonders in the sky (whether illusory or not is another matter). However, she is able to seek answers within the Christian Bible.

Contrary to Mrs Trench, who found solace and vindication in the words of the Bible, the clergy, as represented by the Christian UFO Research Association (CUFORA), looked on this kind of interpretation of the Bible with considerable trepidation. Their leader, the Reverend Eric Inglesby, concluded using a fundamentalist interpretation of the Bible that UFOs are demons that have arrived here to draw mankind into perdition. In his book *UFOs and the Christian* (Regency Press, 1978), Inglesby quotes from Mark chapter 16 verse 16, "he that believeth and is baptised shall be saved but he that believeth not shall be condemned".

The meaning of UFO experiences has caused as much debate among divines as others, though all sides have a decidedly apocalyptic tone. The Reverend Prebendary Victor Pear has claimed, much like Inglesby, that "These (UFO) sightings could be the gathering of spiritual or angelic forces preparing for Armageddon; the final event".

A Roman Catholic priest who made his opinion known about UFOs is Padre Domenico Grasso, a Jesuit who taught theology in Rome. His opinions are contrary to those of the Christian UFO Research Association because he claimed that:

> The existence of extraterrestrial creatures does not go against the scriptures. I believe they do exist ... it seems logical to me that there are other worlds with living, thinking beings all created by God. Naturally they are not part of our human family descended from Adam, but they are God's creations. They exist for the glorification of His immortal being. And they have not sacrificed Christ as we have, so I'm sure they would be much better people than we are.

Dr Larrakas, a Chicago research psychologist, carried out a survey of 378 people regarding their beliefs and found that of the four variables of age, sex, education and religion, religion was the strongest correlation to belief in life in outer space. He noted that people who have religious beliefs also hold the highest belief in extraterrestrial life.

A decade later, the Rev. Millican erected a stall in the foyer of the Bristol Odeon cinema to persuade viewers of *Close Encounters of the Third Kind* that the UFOs were coming here "to seduce us into the forbidden world of the occult".

Opposing this viewpoint are such people as Barry H. Downing, who regard the Bible as a record of UFO sightings and believe that Jesus himself was an extraterrestrial visitor. As with the majority of Jesus "was an astronaut pundits", Downing interprets most of the visions of the Bible in terms of present or imagined future technology. It cannot be denied that the Bible contains many accounts of UFO-type phenomena in its pages, the interpretation of which is the main topic of debate.

The reason for this theological confusion boils down to the fact that they fail to have a sufficient grasp of the psychological and sociological factors involved in both the interpretation of the Bible and the interpretation of present-day UFO sightings.

The experiences of Mrs Trench and her son highlight the confusion, bewilderment and paradoxes inherent in both the individual and society when confronted by the vexed questions which surface due to the multi-faceted nature of what is loosely described as the UFO phenomenon.

Notes and References

Mrs Trench and Edward's real name and address are on file.

Originally published as "The Shadowland of Ufology," in *Magonia*, No. 2, Winter 1979/80, pp. 13–16 and *Magonia*, No.4, Summer 1980, pp. 9–10, p. 17.

"Devon 'Flying Cross' of 1967 Revisited," *Ian Ridpath's UFO skeptic pages,* March 2021, at: http://www.ianridpath.com/ufo/flyingcross.html

Evans, Hilary. *Visions. Apparitions. Alien Visitors,* Book Club Associates, London, 1984, pp. 113–114.

Inglesby, Eric. *UFOs and the Christian,* Regency Press, London, 1978.

"Suffer Little Green Men," *Reveille,* 19 June 1979.

Newman, Jeffrey. "Religious people are more likely to believe in outer space life," *National Enquirer,* 6 June 1978.

Davies, Shan. "UFOs are the Devil's Messengers, says Vicar," *Sunday People,* 23 April 1978.

Downing, Barry. *The Bible & Flying Saucers,* Sphere Books, Great Britain, 1977.

Chapter Five

"We Are Here"

Josephine Elissah's Sightings in Hull

The percipient involved in the following account is Mrs Josephine Elissah who lives in Willerby, a satellite village of the City of Hull, North Humberside.

Jane Humber in the *Hull Daily Mail*, 6 September 1977, described Mrs Elissah as a "young, very attractive, dark-haired housewife, wearing mod gear, living in an up-to-date home and working part-time as a chemist's assistant, she is the last person one would associate with weird phenomena".

In 1974 Mrs Josephine Elissah started to write about UFOs, extraterrestrials, and their influence on humanity. These writings were to constitute a 27-page-book which she titled *Through the Minds of Others*.

The essence of this book is contained in the following text, but before dealing with this it is worth quoting from her introduction which tells how she first became aware of the UFO phenomenon.

> One might say that the wheel started turning for me in 1964, I had just gone to live in France at a place called Descine, which is just outside of Lyon, what I saw there I can only describe as an "Alien Craft" an oval metallic disc which moved rapidly through a break in the clouds. The experience left me rather stunned, but, as the years went by I forgot about my "Flying Saucer" and so it came as quite a surprise when some ten years later I put pen to paper, and started to write upon a subject of which I had no knowledge whatsoever, as far as I was concerned, what I had experienced those previous years

had been completely wiped from my mind. But had it? or is there a store of hidden knowledge built within us all that at a given time in our lives, permitted, will come out, a breakthrough in subconscious, the realms of the unknown....

I pondered upon this for quite sometime and eventually, as far as I was concerned, come up with a solution.

I recollected an incident that had taken place that year in 1974, the year I had put pen to paper, something could well have attributed to the fact, for it happened again in France only this time I no longer lived there but just visiting.

It seemed that I was drawn back to Lyon, for while in a shop down the main street I was aware of a man at the side of me, a little nervously I moved along, but the man was still there. He looked rather strange and his clothes took the appearance of someone not from the present day, his height was a little over six foot (1.8m), he had fair hair and blue eyes and towered way above the heads of those around him, he spoke in a way that seemed to suggest he knew me, but the tongue he spoke was not French, but one which I would have said was very much akin to German, however not being familiar with it I was not quite certain. For a moment he stood, half smiled, turned, then walked away.

I noticed he took long strides and on his feet he wore boots, certainly not the custom on a hot summer day France.

The incident left me quite puzzled and when reflecting on this sometime later I wondered if perhaps this "Man" could have been a "Humanoid" an "Extraterrestrial Being".

From this bizarre beginning, she began to write her book, which starts off from her own (inspired) viewpoint on the implications of the UFO phenomenon.

The Initiation of the Mind

Perhaps there lies a strong possibility that each sighting, made, of a UFO could carry... a being who is able to build up his body into solid matter, and control his craft through the mind.

One who is able to do such things must indeed be advanced, for their means of communication is 'Telepathy,' and to any who have read of contacts with Space Beings they will find this method frequently used.

It would seem to them that words mean little, but the Mind being a very powerful asset enables them to communicate from one Craft to another. A Mother Ship carries these smaller craft in concentrated energy form, thereby making these, Projections.

The saucers leave the Mother Ship, but now they must build up their power to create energy forms through 'Thought Transference,' the Mind must Radiate this power, it is only then the craft is able to enter Earth's Atmosphere as Solid Matter.

But so it continues, for one susceptible Earthling Mind will pick up those waves, thereby, sighting the craft, maybe even two or three at the same time might see it, this is then transmitted to yet another, one who is not necessarily situated in the vicinity at that time, but on the same wavelength, perhaps even in another part of the world.

So the message is put out all over the globe, the message that states, 'We Are Here.'

Millions of years ahead of Earth time exists a race, their intelligence so superior that no man could question, their infinity makes them, 'the power of the Universe,' their knowledge, as far advanced as any could see.

To be a part of their world is not difficult, for 'They' possess a craft known as the 'Flying Saucer,' but people know little of these beings for who or what they are remains unknown.

'The Mind,' to work through this for them is of great value, an asset, they do not 'manipulate' but 'attune' themselves, it is here there lies a 'Telepathic Power,' through this one either sees a craft, or a being, and his craft, who has attuned himself at that time to one suitable to accept.

The human brain is little advanced in this way, but through the media of yoga meditation it is possible to 'contact' even at will, a being from another world, but the human must be found wholly suitable on the part of a ufonaut for 'contact' to be upheld, if he were to ridicule and not stick to his firm beliefs in Interplanetary Life, if he were to sensationalise, in order to create a disturbance then 'contact' would be withdrawn.

A suitable contact must at times learn to be silent, for there are those with whom such topics cannot be and therefore to them it is necessary to say little.

When their craft enter your Earth's atmosphere they do not travel as you would expect, they come from their time into ours, 'they' travel back in time.

The thing to understand is that 'they' have lived as perhaps you have also, but in a different context have existed for billions of years before even Earth was created. Many earthlings of today are the 'incarnations' of Space Beings in a sense one might say, 'I have been Born, I feel a different person,' and in many cases true.

If you have seen a UFO the effect afterwards may be unusual, by this I mean you may feel ill, perhaps not yourself, a strange sensation, a head bursting with 'ideas' things that were not there before, you suddenly see the World in a different light and begin to criticise your fellow man for what he is.

But you have lived in this world for many years. Why then is it now you begin to see the faults of the Human Race?

It is because you have acquired an awareness of a different source, you are not seeing the world through your own eyes, but through one who has lived many an Era before.

This is the Re-Birth of a Planetary Being, being brought Earthwise, with him come his ideals and intentions, his purpose to put over a True Existence.

You are ready to be initiated into the realms of the Superiority you have seen what so many before have ignored as just pure imagination, and are now ready to walk the road of true posterity. As a candidate you must now disregard the materialistic side of life as child's play, and must take upon yourself to be dedicated to your 'Master',[sic] for there are many tasks at hand and you must prove yourself to be trustworthy out of all degree, for there is far more to a 'Flying Saucer Story',[sic] than meets the 'Eye.'

There is background work to be done, by this I mean, not only putting ones [sic] words over, but finding for yourself the way to stabilising a relationship between the 'Two Minds' in question, the earthling possessing the weaker of the two.

He must learn therefore to 'Control' the mind so that a stable and sincere relationship between himself, and his 'Contact,' can proceed on the required basis.

To have 'Mastery' over your mind takes an Era, many a 'Life' gone by, for it is not an easy task and above all you must strive to achieve your Highest Goal, the objective being complete 'Oneness' that is a perfect understanding between 'Mind' and 'Soul.'

The following extracts from her book are from a more alien viewpoint than the one above which tends to read like Mrs Elissah's own conscious (or sub-conscious) viewpoint on the UFO subject. This gravitation towards a more alien viewpoint of the subject matter occurs approximately half-way through the book.

The Ascent of Man

'I' am a cog, in the wheel of a Vast Universe.

I 'have seen' the Ascent of Man, his achievements and failures in the Scientific World, followed your Moon Landings, Space Probes to other Planets, and your use of Satellites.

It is but a game you play, for your knowledge will never be far enough advanced ever to conquer space.

'We' have achieved such things, but then our knowledge is by far greater.

You think you have your means of power in Atomic Weapons, this never conquered a Universe, only 'DESTROYED.'

What is it that makes you as you are? A somewhat weak-willed race, lost in your own little world, going around in ever increasing circles, always being led by the hands of others. While your governments rule they make all the moves, they use your countries as chess boards, your people are but the pawns in their silly game. They have no real power and could never be fully justified in judging.

For 'We' have no governments, we are each his own.

The Time Benders

'Time' is always against you.

In my world this is not so, there is no time as such, our existence goes on 'we' re-establish ourselves and can therefore continue with what has been placed before.

A strange concept? perhaps, but to us we know no other, you see 'we' are 'THE TIME BENDERS,' the Prophets of years to come, and of long since past. Once 'Masters' of the World, now the inhabitants of a planet as different from yours as could be imagined.

The years pass, yet I am as I had once been, to come and go as I choose, the 'uninvited guest.'

But I will make my mark, I will be heard by the willing listener, for few heed their own thoughts when there is much to be achieved.

What is my purpose in this world of yours? for no one has heralded my arrival, an unidentified object streaking across the night sky. Yet, I am here, to express the feelings of those around me, who speak not for their rights but for the rights of others, words such as were spoken in your past, but were not heeded.

Atlantis

For it is no myth that once this hidden continent existed, and will do yet again. Get your facts right, read between the lines, for the long lost will reign once more.

It is not an impossibility that there is life still beneath those deep waters, if only to prepare the way.

Perhaps now you will see our reasons for frequent visits beneath your oceans, for of resources we need none.

Our intention is to bring forth 'ATLANTIS,' reiterate, the work of another Era.

The raising of a continent? Yes, for us a great achievement, for you, the thought only of impossibility.

But do not scoff, for 'we' carry on the work first started 'AN AGE PAST.'

I recall 'AN AGE PAST,' the dawning of a day, 'THE BIRTH OF A CIVILISATION.'

To be Re-Born in another world. Could you survive?

You must determine a way in life for you know little of what really goes on in the Universe around you, there is much you must learn, and you have but a short time.

You discover new stars in your galaxy, 'WE' know of every star and the gases contained therein, 'WE' have discovered all.

Do not shake yourselves by the hand for your achievements, they are negligible, you have attained nothing, but 'WE' have the wealth of a knowledge that is by far greater, 'WE' have conquered all.

It is a lack of power, a confidence you could possess by knowing and believing that life has more to offer than materialistic values, oh, so important to many.

You choose to ignore our existence now but you cannot put behind you what has always been there, our work still goes on in many walks of life.

As yet I remain unimpressed by the whole system on which your people choose to run their lives.

Far be it from my intentions to put to rights your wrong doings, I can only 'PLANT' an 'IMPRESSION' in 'THE MIND.'

Tuning In

In a letter to me, Mrs Elissah explained how she wrote her book:

> The pieces came on average every four to six weeks. I have written (things) since, but nothing that would form into anything.
>
> The chapters were written separately, not in one session, and the time taken to write each would vary from say thirty minutes. Some bits of it would come at different times in the day, even early morning when I've had to rush out of bed to find a pen and paper. They were all written in longhand, but didn't come in the order presented in the book.

In the same letter she told me of some of the other experiences she has had along with some comments on where, she feels that mankind is going.

> I have never been hypnotised, or put in a trance. Meditation yes, but I have never been trained to do so.
>
> I've had no other (UFO) sightings. Premonitions, the odd one, telepathy (I have experienced) frequently... Very early one morning I was awakened by a clear voice in my ear, to be truthful I nearly jumped out of my skin, I felt a cold wave of electricity in my head and down my spine and the voice said, "Me, its [sic] me again" but didn't say who. I have also had vivid dreams, one where I was floating through the clouds eventually to find myself looking down on the planet, and another where I was walking with a man in long white robes. I believed the place to be India. The next thing I was being pushed into a river up flowing water. Where once again I experienced a flow of electricity down my spine.

I put both of these experiences down to the astral body, out on one of its jaunts.

I feel that where the future of mankind is concerned we have a long way to go, but as people go on having "Contacts," so they will be enlightened and guided along the Road, until they will finally reach the state of higher evolution. This may take more than one "Lifetime" to achieve, but eventually, we will attain our highest goal, the objective being complete "Oneness."

We will no longer need the habitation of this planet, but will be free to come and go as we choose, pure in Spirit and Mind. This will be the future of mankind, when all will exist peaceably.

Notes on the Alien Drawings

"The Aliens" were in a sense communicated, I can't be sure how that came about except that I felt I wanted to draw, and I'm usually not a drawer.

The colour I'm not sure about, but the little marks outlining the body are to give a glowing effect or aura.

The feet are not shown on the page but they do wear boots, there are no faces or hands.

One point I would like to add, is that, while doing some automatic writing one day, I got a name for the head and shoulders portrait, it was "MOVOS" who emanates from the planet "URANUS."

A curious feature of Mrs Elissah's "alien" drawings are the lack of both facial features and hands, a characteristic which is prevalent in Paul Bennett's encounter with the faceless "robot" and the faceless and handless black "entity".

Many humanoid encounters reported by other people contain similar accounts. These might be unconscious expressions of faceless science, or it might be an emphasis of the anonymous and superhuman qualities of the space people.

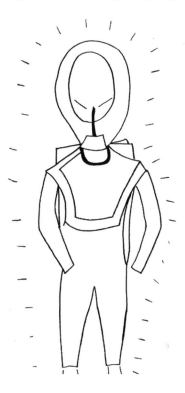

Flying Saucer Dreams

Josephine Elissah's experiences and dreams are far from unique. In the early 1980s Mrs Ann Adams, for example, created inspired oil paintings which she only understood when she "began having Space Dreams. These dreams are where I see space craft and the beings sometimes watch or take part."

The paintings of the space beings show that they wear unusual headdresses and richly coloured garments. The beings have different coloured eyes and faces, and the male beings often appear to wear earrings and beards.

Some strange lettering appeared on the garments of the beings and later she began producing a lot of "alien writing" which filled more than 52 pages of her notebooks. Unfortunately, even Mrs Adams does not understand what this writing means but she hopes that someone in the future might be able to translate it.

As she says in a letter to me, these paintings and writings emanate from "real people as I see them in my dreams and at other times".

Mrs Adams described one of her dreams:

> I dreamed that I saw a flying saucer. Everyone on the Earth saw it. We saw it change shape, then land. The space people were much more advanced than us and set about to set us right. And some people did not like that – at all – never-the-less they were caught. They could not get away from them. They all seemed to be dressed alike in sort of suits. They had some device over their shoulder, could be a weapon of some kind. Perhaps it is a good omen. I think they will surprise us.

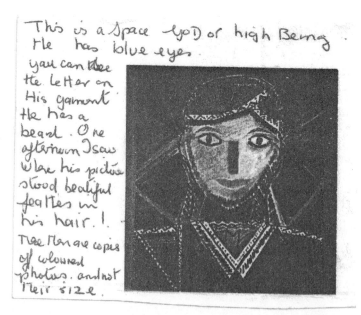

Summary

It is obvious that Mrs Elissah has a great feeling for the destiny of mankind, and I do feel that her book is a genuine work of inspiration and not a conscious vehicle for her own views. Her writing flowed from her on an unconscious level, and it expresses her deep-rooted fears and desires through the acceptable UFO paradigm. Along with Norman Harrison profiled in the next chapter, Josephine expresses a dislike for governments or politics of any kind, as she wrote "we are each his own". We have to achieve this level of being, and become our own judge and jury, unlike in our present state where we are mere pawns in a gigantic and incomprehensible chess game.

The intervention of the aliens in our normal routine on an individual level offers us a way of escaping the terrors of our impersonal society. The human psyche uses metaphorical, symbolic and analogical terminology.

In her writings much is made of the concept of time i.e., "there is no time as such, our existence goes on..." and "'I' am a cog in the wheel of a vast universe". The wheel of time is eternal, and free from the mundane limitations of modern civilization, one can through the psyche see the enormity of existence. These emanations of the psyche break down the prejudice of cultural and social thinking and reveal the power and glory of the Universe. Although our human bodies have a finite life on Earth, our mind can soar beyond such restrictions and limitations, the liberation of the psyche allows us to accept the petty injustices and downfalls which we encounter in our everyday reality.

We become numbered and dehumanised robots when we really want to be treated as individuals. As Josephine wrote, "the objective... (is) ..complete 'oneness' that is a perfect understanding between 'Mind' and 'Soul'". This concept is a yearning for the integration of her conscious mind with her psyche which is trying to tell her in symbolic language what her real feelings are. She looks forward to when we "will be free to come and go as we choose, pure in Spirit and Mind. This will be the future of mankind, when all will exist peaceably".

Her references to Atlantis contain much of interest: "for the long lost will reign once more. Perhaps now you will see our reasons for frequent visits beneath your oceans, for of resources we need none". This strongly suggests a subtle analogy to the mirrored images of the psyche raising up into consciousness.

As Josephine points out, our minds are limited and are not very advanced, it needs effort and awareness to perceive the projections of the aliens. A susceptible human mind that picks up these projected waves will see a UFO and the message "We Are Here" is delivered. To be one of the chosen few adds a tremendous boost to the individual who can look beyond their own cloudy and dark environment into the brilliance, splendour and mystery of the Universe. It is a paradox that the military impetus that created the inter-continental ballistic missile and the worldwide threat of annihilation also made it possible for us to advance into space. This expansion of both our fears and our dreams is dramatically contained in Josephine's writings and thoughts.

Notes and References

The bulk of this chapter is based on:

Elissah, Josephine. *Through the Minds of Others*, an unpublished manuscript, circa 1974.

Further information was supplied by Mrs Elissah in letters to the author, dated: 20 February 1978, 04 October 1978 and 10 December 1978.

Other information was from:

Humber, Jane. "Clue to the Mystery of the Universe?" *(Hull) Daily Mail*, 6 September 1977.

An interview with Mrs Elissah by the author in late 1977.

The Ann Adams case is cited in:

"Paintings from Afar?" *Northern UFO News*, No. 103, Jul/Aug 1983, p. 10.

Chapter Six

Alien Messages and Impressions

Norman Harrison

When I was interviewing people in northern England about their encounters with aliens, during the late 1970s, John Rimmer, the editor of *Magonia*, suggested I should contact Norman Harrison. In a letter to John, dated 6 January 1978, Norman revealed: "THIS EARTH is now under close surveillance and profound scrutiny by alien intelligences from distant star systems. I am not being silly, I know what I am saying and doing as well as you."

Norman, who lived in Sheffield, Yorkshire, at that time went on to outline the different races of beings which inhabit this galaxy. The first race populate the fourth and fifth planets of Epsilon Eridani (a star that was targeted by the SETI Project Ozma in 1960), and are "four feet (1.2m) tall on average, spindly and yellowish skinned and totally devoid of any hair. Their heads are disproportionately large due to further evolved brain capacity."

A second race inhabits three planets orbiting Canopus; a third race derives from Proxima Centauri III and IV. A fourth inhabits the two planets of Capella. Describing these latter races, Norman wrote that they are quite similar to each other and that they are "over 7 feet (2.1m) tall on average, powerfully built and extremely agile, [have] fine blonde hair and [are] musically and artistically gifted. These three are of one Root Race type, corresponding to Earth Nordic."

The stars of Betelgeuse IV, V and VI in Orion are the location of the fifth race of aliens, and a sixth populates the constellations of Ursa Major and Cassiopeia. This race occupies the solar systems of Merak, Alcor, and Dubhe in the Ursa Major constellation. The whole race is linked in a confederation and their colonies are densely populated. Other than being humanoid, Norman does not describe the appearance of these two races.

All these aliens have spacecraft capable of exceeding light velocity several times over and have the facility to set up impenetrable force fields as well as invisibility shields. They make use of unimaginably advanced energy propulsion technology and have extremely powerful electromagnetic – gravitic (sic) devices at their disposal, all capable of effecting vital changes in this world. Force fields and rays are extensively utilised at enormous distances: in spite of the long distance these are resolved to fine focus and can be intensified as required to influence the course of events on Earth.

Many of their Earth contingents are military task-force or scientific field operatives. The remainder engaged in collating or compiling vital information, making regular operational shuttle trips and submitting data reports to their base planets.

Norman received this information about our galactic neighbours by way of telepathic communication from aliens. These communications began in 1975 and occurred with increasing frequency over the next three years. In a letter to me dated 17 March 1978, he wrote that "these 'contacts' can occur virtually at any time ... I still hardly know what to think about the whole business – if these are hallucinations, I don't see how they could contain information about the Universe which I never had before".

Apparently, he does not hear or see things when having a "telepathic" communication: "The information comes through direct without any sensory impressions, vision or delusions whatever."

He said that much of the information he received came when he felt rather tired and hungry when he wrote it down: "my mind wasn't preoccupied with anything, I just felt more or less 'neutral' or indifferent. The words just flowed without any conscious direction on my part. This is always the case with either writings or drawings set straight down 'automatically.' Very often the physically weaker or hungrier I feel, the more clearly the contacts are received."

He notes that there are a group of aliens that he calls the Observers, who have similar views to Norman:

> Human Western society is rapidly falling into catastrophic decline and Mankind is now falling into chaos and absolute folly. They believe there is virtually zero survival probability as a result of mental degeneration and moral decay combined with political corruption, greed and militarism. These and other factors, they feel sure now will destroy all human civilization within another half-century.
>
> This isn't just pessimism or gloom-and-doom alarmism – these people are infinitely more intelligent, more truly civilized and more mature than any race on Earth, and have reached their conclusions via strict mathematical extrapolative calculus based in historical, social, psychological and economic FACTS. Most of these races have had an intimate exhaustive knowledge of Man for tens of thousands of years and the wisdom of their logic is undeniable.
>
> I have little to add, except that I am notified that a final terrible war will definitely take place (whether atomic or not) between East and West within three decades, and pollution poisoning will soon endanger all vegetation and animal species of the globe. All the most recent incidents positively indicate to me personally that the aliens are

correct. We ignore and gloss over such dire warnings at our peril, and we have no-one but ourselves to blame for the destruction of our own world-home by our madness, ignorance and blind folly.

These communications, transmissions, impressions, whatever we might label them, were preceded by a UFO sighting, sometime in 1974. Norman was then staying with a friend of his in the Beeston area of Leeds for a few days when he saw his first and only UFO. His friend had just gone outside for a few minutes, the time was between 8 p.m. and 9 p.m. when Norman had a "distinct urge to get up and look out of the door".

Opening the door, he saw between the doorframe and the rooftops of the houses across the road, a box-like shape silhouetted against the night sky. Upon it were banks of multi-coloured lights. The object was slanted at an angle towards the ground and was moving from right to left in the direction of its central axis at slow speed. He heard no sound from this phenomenon, which he estimated to be gliding at a height of 1,000 feet (304m). After twenty seconds, it drifted out of view, although: "Why I did not step out into the street for a better look I don't know."

Norman's reaction to the sighting was interesting, as he wrote that: "I wasn't in the least bit frightened of it, but it did disturb me in an eerie way, as if hypnotic." He went on to speculate as to what it might have been.

> It must have been a huge carrier vessel of tremendous motive power, capable of containing a number of smaller saucer type craft or several hundred passengers. By proportion and distance, I feel sure it was anything up to 300 feet (91m) long. A massive vessel like that must be able to traverse the whole galactic radius at speeds far in excess of light velocity who would logically build that big

for merely planet to planet journeys. Who would employ that much propulsion and that scale of motive energy?

My belief is that this "ship" was from a giant planet in the hub of the Milky Way (Bigger than Texas!!!).

Early Psi Experiences

Having read Norman's correspondence with John Rimmer and having arranged to meet him, what could I expect on visiting his household? Norman had anticipated this question by explaining his circumstances in one of his letters.

> I must point out that I live in a working-class area and my house is not too beautiful, being a Victorian terrace council house and rather decrepit now. (I was away when my parents died and the old place was left empty for a year and bad weather and neglect have taken their toll. I'd do a lot but I've been unemployed for a long time and live only on State benefit.)
>
> So my surroundings are not ideal for social contacts as you can imagine, I'm embarrassed about this! I'll probably sell the house before long and then I'd like to travel around – the Continent perhaps, who knows.

When I first met Norman on 26 February 1978, he told me about how he had experienced distinct impressions from 1968 through to 1969. He felt he had been picking up thoughts that were being powerfully projected towards him. However, he could not pick up any words or language, but it was a "kind of thought expression that doesn't rely on language. And not a true voice that you could hear ... but the sensation of words virtually spontaneously," he said.

Usually he had these experiences when in a state of meditation, when sitting down or before going to sleep. Norman described his condition as in a "diminished state" when he had these experiences, but not a condition like a trance or under the influence of drink or drugs. On most occasions he was on his own when this phenomenon happened, but once he was walking along a city street when he felt that he could tell what people were thinking.

On another occasion during this period, he and a friend visited a Spiritualist Church in Sheffield, when he was "awakened to Christian faith". The Church was quite full when they entered, and the minister was delivering a sermon. As the minister spoke, Norman felt a knot of tension build up in himself. They stood to sing a hymn and halfway through it, he felt a distinct physical sensation of a twisting knot of tension in the solar plexus.

"I felt this oppressive, almost hostile, presence in the church, I felt a strong hostility, a threat," he explained. At this juncture, a nearby usher approached Norman and his companion, and said in a quiet voice to them: "Would you mind leaving please, I'd like you to go."

"Just before he approached me this thing was building up to a real climax... as if something was tearing me inside out, literally," and he added that: "This man sensed that there was something amiss." Norman's friend experienced nothing untoward in the church, and was no doubt puzzled as to why they were asked to leave.

In 1966 Norman knew a girl called Angela who lived in London. He took her out for about four months, and was very serious about her, and "cared an awful lot for her". However, in due course they went their separate ways. Later in a period when he was feeling emotionally low, very depressed, anxious, physically depleted and under-nourished, he saw Angela's face distinctly in front of him as he was lying down one evening. She seemed to be speaking to him, but he cannot now remember what she was saying, except that she might have been asking him what he was doing, where he was, had he been thinking about her, had he missed her, etc.

Alien Intervention

Norman explained how he received extraterrestrial communications:

> I've had occasions, not just recently but I should say over the last two or three years, when I've been walking outside in the open, in a sort of park or recreation area something like that. The more open air the better. If I was in a large crowd of people... nothing. But on occasion I thought "Oh, that's a daft idea, where did I get it from?" and then I'd suddenly realise that it's not an idea, but it's information. I'd have a sort of powerful influence to get a pen and notepad and jot it down. On some occasions I did this; I didn't keep the notes, but there have been times... when I've drawn pictures, and I've had these images which were very clear when I draw them, what I myself perceived was not very clear at all, but in the act of drawing it came through with clarity. And it seemed to me that I'd sort of acted as an unwitting unconscious intermediary and I've had this distinct sensation that someone is using me in order to transmit knowledge.

In particular, he has frequently had recurring impressions of three figures.

> None of them sort of stand on the ground, they all seem to be just suspended in space, and there are no buildings or anything recognisable around them at all. As though they were suspended in vacuum. They all have a powerful projection and I've not been personally intimidated, it

doesn't seem to me that they are threatening me or in any way warning me, but they have an air of warning or admonition, if you like. Sort of "take care" or "watch it" pay attention.

The three figures are Aroniel, Mik-Ael and Uriel, whom Norman described in more detail.

Aroniel

This personage is a "tall figure very straight, dressed in a long yellow robe, a flowing yellow robe with a high collar and he looks oriental. He wears a medallion in the centre of his forehead, and his own colour, his skin colour, is yellowish or shall we say golden and he's like a sort of gold appearance generally... He carries a book in one hand and the other is raised as if in greeting. The book looks like some sort of old book."

Mik-Ael

According to Norman,

This is an image of what you might call something like a Crusader or armoured knight figure; chain mail with a tabard or tunic. It's a white tunic with a broad belt which looks metallic and has buttons on, and the tunic has a... red cross on it. He's like a crusader, but the helmet is rather strange... it completely conceals the features, you can't make out the face. It's not like an ordinary visor but it's a solid, transparent sort of plate with a division in the middle. At the bottom (of it) there is a little round disc thing with a wire. He has... full sleeves and gauntlets, heavy gauntlets and he's carrying a sword in one hand.

He sort of stands very powerfully with his legs apart. He presents either a challenging or shall we say an extremely aggressive, intimidating strength or just an image of strength. It's an intimidating sort of an aggressive image. His sword has a sort of red radiance... and he himself is surrounded with red, a deep scarlet or crimson. I should say it is crimson actually. It's like an aura or radiance all around him.

Uriel

The third figure

has long, flowing robes, blue and green, and has like a blue or greenish-blue sort of radiance around him... this third one has white hair and apparently normal skin colour or slightly blue tinge and a white beard and white hair, and he also looks big, powerful but not in a military or a Crusader knight-in-armour fashion, but he looks as though he's sort of... tremendously ancient, tremendously, you know, tremendous power at his disposal. He doesn't seem to carry anything, he's got like a sash around the waist and he wears something like... one of the old fashioned robes of the middle east.

Later during the interview, he explained that the colours of the figures were directly linked with the type of energy they were emitting. He also claimed that he saw these figures in a kind of sequence, sometimes he would "see" them fleetingly for only two or three seconds, other times they would appear for two or three minutes.

Usually, the first figure to appear is the one who has supremacy over the other two. Then maybe a few letters or geometrical symbols will appear.

"They seem to be attempting to express relationships, but as I say, some of it isn't in any sort of expressed language, but there seems to be a logical sequence or progression. It's not logical to me, I don't know it, but it's logical to them."

Many of the letters he has seen are from Greek and Hebrew sources: "I've seen the triangle over and over again," he said about the recurring image he has seen over the past four or five months, and has included in many of his drawings; "I've seen a triangle with an eye in the centre, and I've seen this as a visual image, quite literally as though it was suspended in front of my eyes, in broad daylight when I was fully wide awake and stone cold sober, I hardly ever drink."

This triangle is seen as red coloured with an eye in the centre, which is not like a real eye, but looks effectively like a bright red line drawing of an eye.

He then went on to describe the population of the galaxy, how at the hub there are regions of incalculable amounts of radiance and electromagnetic energy, where discarnate, disembodied "beings" of ultimate intelligence reside. Radiating outwards from the hub, the state of evolution, culture, civilization and society diminish until we reach the very fringes of the galaxy where Neanderthal type beings populate the planets. These lesser planets, including Earth (as our Solar System is much closer to the fringe than the hub) are watched closely by the more superior races who take a parental interest in their evolution. Apparently, at the present time there has been a resurgence of interest in our planet.

This renewed interest might be because, "Man is a very disobedient wretch and keeps veering off, and getting side-tracked one way or another. The guiding hand keeps bringing him back to dead centre. There's this guidance all the way. There is one definite path of evolution of the spirit and mind."

According to him, humanity is being constantly helped by outside, alien forces. It was their influence, which partly established some of the most ancient of all the Oriental religions. He claims that many early religious figures such as Buddha and Moses were inspired by the influence of the extraterrestrials. Even today, a small number of adepts, who have a profound understanding of metaphysical philosophy, and live in very remote regions of the world, are in direct telepathic communication with alien people.

Through alien intervention, and there are hundreds of alien races, some of which are almost immortal, the human mind has been triggered to experience ESP, telepathy, clairvoyance, prophecy, predictions, etc. However, we have misused the forces and energy sources available, claims Norman, and distort things for our own greedy ends. We have probably, in the past, been punished for it afterwards. He quoted the examples, among others, of Atlantis and Babylon, and stated that global disasters are initiated from the outside and convey the alien moral standpoint. These purges occur because the behaviour of humanity can become offensive and noisily wrong.

> Man has destroyed himself as a living specimen at least six times in a row, cataclysm after cataclysm. There have been several cycles of biological life, gradually slowly, painstakingly developing, then flourishing, reaching an apex then declining.
>
> The Golden Age has long passed, none absolutely none of the 20th Century is anything like the Golden Age. It is a period now of the pinnacle of machinery, it's a pinnacle of mechanical contrivance, ingenuity is totally materialistic, physical things. It's a period of total stagnation and decadence in what you might call things of the spirit. There is a complete decline in the ability to understand higher matters... in religious doctrine or philosophical things. Where are the people like Plato, Socrates, Aristotle? Where is the architecture, sculpture and art of Leonardo or Michelangelo?

He answers himself by explaining that the difference between them and modern contemporaries is "self-evident".

Premonitions

In the February of 1974, Norman had his first premonition. This was of a plane exploding in mid-air with people from the city of Leeds on board; an event, which occurred three weeks later over France.

During August 1974, he was living in London when he had a premonition of the Moorgate tube disaster, which happened in April 1975. He also "knew" that the IRA would be posting letter-bombs to people in London in 1975. "All these premonitions seemed to me personally that they are being transmitted to me from an outside source," said Norman, who related that he felt no conscious control over these premonitions.

He also felt certain that humanity would have some crucial contact with extraterrestrials in the near future. It will be with somebody like the Archbishop of Canterbury, or other such celebrity, and their reaction to the encounter will have far-reaching consequences.

After my visit and interview with Norman, he wrote to me on 17 March, stating, "I feel quite sure now that these telepathic communications are only the beginning – there must be something more to follow in the future; I have a 'hunch' about it."

In the same letter:

> Although there have been no new telepathic transmissions or impressions since you came over, I have received a warning in the form of one pen sketch which showed a big explosion. It involves highly inflammable chemicals and will happen in Britain within another month. I have no more exact location than that, but I do know this much – it will involve loss of life and will be caused by criminal negligence and carelessness. This foreboding is very strong and I know it comes from an outside source. The accident must be connected with a big chemical company like ICI or one of the fuel firms like Esso, or North Sea oil.

I hope it doesn't happen because it will be a horrible tragedy, it could be averted if only there were proper precautions taken.

With this situation, it is not surprising to learn that he had suffered four nervous breakdowns and is obsessed by the fate of humanity. Having met him on three occasions, I can vouch for the fact that he is very verbose, and passionately intense about what he believes to be the gloomy and cataclysmic future of humanity. This fear is not generated by any love he might have for humanity; on the contrary, his fear is for himself.

Living as someone who regards himself as being isolated and different from the rest of humanity, it is not surprising that he has transposed his ideas and imagination into an "extraterrestrial" framework.

His concept of the galaxy – pure energy and ultimate intelligence at the hub, Neanderthal beings on the edge – corresponds to concepts of heaven and hell, Jekyll and Hyde or unconscious and conscious, with the mortal Human pivoted between the two.

Even worse, we do not have full control over our destiny; the aliens have intervened throughout human history in order that we follow the "one definite path of evolution of the spirit and mind".

Yet humanity cannot come up to these "parental expectations", so we are punished for our morally offensive behaviour.

After my meetings with Norman at his home in Sheffield during 1978, I had a final meeting with him on 18 November 1979, at his new home in Leeds. This bedsit was even worse than his previous address, but Norman seemed slightly more optimistic about the intentions of the aliens but still felt that humanity was doomed.

He was still receiving extraterrestrial communications, that, "have the power to project their own intelligence, identity and personality, out into interstellar space, and they can communicate this way. They have no need for spaceships, because they use like, astral travel, or out-of-the-body projection. This is the result of advanced mental powers."

My view was that Norman's communications were metaphorical and symbolic expressions of his feelings of guilt, isolation, alienation and emotional stagnation, which emanated from his own psyche. In addition, that it was no wonder that he feared the impending cataclysm.

Norman responded by stating that I was guilty of, "a glib, dogmatic, 'psychological' brand of easy rationalizing. (Nigel's) assumption is that I am a psychoneurotic down-and-out underdog, misfit, trying to compensate for my inferiority by erecting fantasies, and so on."

His opinion is valid, but from a UFO point of view, Norman offers no positive proof for the existence of extraterrestrial space vehicles or aliens. Nonetheless, he reflects the view of many UFO contactees and abductees that the aliens are here to warn us of an apocalyptic end to humanity.

Notes and References

Norman Harrison's real name and address are on file.

Watson, Nigel. "A Stranger in the City," *MUFOB*, New Series, No. 14, Spring 1979, pp. 3–8, 13–15.

"Alien Messages and Impressions," by Nigel Watson, in: Taylor, Greg (ed.). *Darklore*, Vol. 6, Daily Grail Publishing, Brisbane, Australia, 2011, pp. 148 –165.

The information contained in this chapter was obtained from interviews with Norman Harrison at his home in Sheffield:

26 February 1978, with the author.

2 April 1978, with Roger Hebb and the author.

30 April 1978, with Shirley McIver and the author.

Information was from the following letters by Norman Harrison: Dated 6 January 1978, and 4 February 1978, sent to John Rimmer. Dated 17 March 1978, and 18 April 1978, sent to the author.

Chapter Seven

Contemplating Cosmic Questions

Martin Bolton

I first met Martin Bolton (a pseudonym is used to protect his identity) on Sunday, 31 January 1982, and I was accompanied by ufologist Robert Addinall. The interview was carried out in a friendly environment, and Martin was willing to answer all our questions, although he did say that he felt that some things he knew could not be revealed at the present moment. He keeps a record of his experiences, and when we spoke to him, he used a notebook, containing accounts of his experiences, as a reference and launching point for further discussion. For the sake of clarity this material has been re-arranged slightly and checked with Martin for accuracy.

Fifty-year-old Martin is the eldest of four children, and he became interested in UFOs when he was a teenager. The rest of the family have a rather negative attitude towards the subject of UFOs and display no interest in this or other esoteric subjects. He had a secondary modern school education and left school when he was 14 years old. In 1966 he and a partner started a small chemical business which employed nine people until it went into liquidation in 1979. Since then Martin, who is single and lives in Hull, has been unemployed. He is a member of a local meditation group, but the other members of the group do not believe in his contacts and express no interest in them.

For most of his life Martin has been interested in UFOs, psychic phenomena, meditation and ecology. It was not until he realised that other beings could be controlling the authors of science fiction that he became interested in that genre. As a result, he has read and collected many books relating to these interests, they range from the works of Erich von Daniken to

Lobsang Rampa. From his reading and his own experiences, he believes that in the past (approximately 5,000 years ago) Atlantis was populated by evil beings. Consequently, the good forces caused the fall of Atlantis. Some of the inhabitants of Atlantis escaped to the "Americas where they mixed and times became happier, but through the thought process the link with the evil planet (called Oron – N.W.) was still there even though the memory of the previous link had disappeared". So, they have remained an evil influence on that continent.

"The Aryan tribe populated Europe, Greece and down to Egypt," he said. They were originally from the descendants of the escaped Atlanteans. For instance, Martin claims that the Egyptians transplanted animal heads onto human bodies, and impregnated their mummies with germs, and carried out other activities derived from their Atlantean inheritance.

Martin is not keen about organised religion, although he regards himself as being classed as a Protestant, he is more in favour of Buddhism. He thinks that the Christian Bible was supplied by the aliens, and that fairy tales have some truth in them. He commented: "Normal people don't know what the Universe is about. Thousands of aliens have visited us throughout the ages. They are adventurers in space, just as we are attempting to be. But some planets are in an equal state of ignorance as ourselves."

Not long after our interview I sent Martin a preliminary draft of this report, and in response he sent me a letter dated 10 February 1982, and some notes which corrected some of the text. In his letter he wrote, "after our discussion on the Sunday Jan. 31st I started to think of fear of ridicule and I made my mind up to help the world in any way I can.

"The fear I had in the beginning has gone forever so you can print my name if you wish (as a matter of policy I think it is better to keep his anonymity – N.W.). People have to become aware of the dangers of the dominating thought processes going on in their minds without them realising it. Then they can become much stronger individuals able to dissolve any unnecessary thoughts without these forces spreading outwards and effecting the atmosphere."

To see how this psychological cancer can influence one individual, we present Martin's experiences as he described them to Robert Addinall and me.

Description of Experiences

Not long after the liquidation of his business, Martin went on a meditation course in Buckinghamshire. It was during a meditation session when he saw a flash of light occur above him and sixty other meditators. The others did not appear to see this phenomenon. This seemed to be a catalyst, or predecessor, of the incidents that have followed since then. During the course in Buckinghamshire, he also experienced, whilst meditating, a feeling of energy flow up through his fingertips and up his arms and spine. This, he thought, seemed like the kundalini force described by adepts of Yoga. Since then, he has often seen "psychic visions" which he describes as being "a gift of seeing into the invisible world whereas ordinary vision pictures of happenings and events are either put there by unknown forces or... can become a gift of seeing into the future".

A sign of an alien presence are bright flashes of light which can be seen anywhere at any time by Martin. Bright white flashes are a sign of goodwill from the "good forces", black flashes emanate from the "evil forces" and long bars of light are transmitted by flying saucers. However, he explained that:

Black flashes can emanate from good forces as well. In the spirit world high beings of light have to alter the brilliance of light to suit the surroundings of the lower levels so they can alter to black if they desire. Flying saucers can also use black not necessarily evil forces. Long bars of coloured light could be either from a planet or a very large flying saucer's highly evolved beings.

It was at this time in 1979 that he believes that a "microphone", although a better name for it would be telepathic receiver, was inserted into his brain. The good forces were probably responsible for this, although the evil forces also seem to be able to utilise it for their own ends. Coincidently, he had a vision of Earth with one huge radio mast radiating radio signals from its top.

Apparently, we are all capable of becoming receivers of these alien messages by meditating and making one's mind blank. It is then that thoughts that are not your own can filter through to consciousness, so presumably the device placed inside his skull was nothing more than an amplifier for his own natural abilities.

The messages that come to him seem to concern humanity in general. They seem to come from many different levels of existence (e.g., UFOs, the spirit world, etc.) and not from any particular individual or group. The telepathic voices emanate from beings who do not seem to label themselves with names, but they are either working on behalf of good or evil.

When he first began receiving messages the voices that came were faint, despite this, many beings, good and evil, wanted to be involved in communicating with him. In connection with the evil forces is the name "Oron", which often comes to Martin's mind. Oron is an evil alien planet although Martin is not quite certain on this point, as he explained that, "I am not quite sure if it is the evil planet but according to past experiences the name has often arisen from that direction."

The inhabitants of this evil planet seek to obtain psychological domination over human beings. Essentially, they wish to keep our mental processes on a reduced and negative level of activity. This is a preliminary to their ultimate goal of physical domination of Earth and the Universe.

Martin told us that an evil group can focus their concentration upon one person, until that person believes their thoughts are his own. This can cause a prolonged obsession on certain thoughts, and a person can be forced to participate in evil vices such as smoking, drinking, glue sniffing, drug taking, etc. He notes that the assassins of famous people in the past (e.g., the case of Mark David Chapman who shot John Lennon in 1980) had reported hearing voices in their head, and he felt that they had been dominated by more than one evil entity.

As a result of his contacts Martin has constantly had reprisals from the evil forces. Sometimes they have teased him. For instance, he has heard roars of laughter coming through to him. When he "heard" his house plants telepathically "speaking" to him, he thought he was receiving communications from nature spirits, and spoke back to his plants for several days until he discovered that the aliens were "pulling his leg".

Other incidents have been of a more sinister and personal nature. In attempts to make him give up, they have poured chemicals on his head. For periods of up to two hours, he has been subjected to this treatment. Though this has caused great pain, no physical chemical substance was used on him. Other times they have used ray guns on him. He has not been able to do certain Yoga exercises because the aliens have put outside pressure upon his knee joints. His intestines have been doctored, and his head has been subjected to heat. They can manipulate and subject pain to humans by directing rays at certain areas of the right hemisphere of the brain. The most unusual aspect of this torture is the alleged stretching of his penis every night for the past three years. To counteract this, he breathes in and out deeply and this solves the problem.

On two or three occasions they have toyed with him by giving him phantom pregnancies. Often the word "bastard" is broadcast to him. They can also inflict germs upon people (e.g., they can place influenza germs on the end of your nose). As recently as November 1981, he had a week of vomiting which he believes was caused by the aliens.

In his battle against these evil influences, he is just winning. He said, "I'm stronger now than ever before. I'm a fighter and I'll fight on." He can fight them by concentrating on the evil forces and trying to control them, just as they try to control him. He added that, "My personality is now dominating the situation, they can't win. They are out of control."

The good forces are here to fight the evil forces and to protect humanity. Messages from space have informed him that stupid people, including world leaders, are acting in accord with the evil aliens. This is creating a serious situation because some stupid being is likely to destroy Earth by pressing the nuclear button, although he notes that it might "not necessarily be the nuclear button, maybe some other type of button".

Although the evil aliens are a real threat by themselves, they do work through such groups as the IRA and the Mafia, and all kinds of "terrorist troublemakers". To counteract this, we must meditate and make our minds blank, and then we can evaluate any negative thoughts that might appear. "My friends, this is a message of love from the aliens," they told Martin; they wish us to evolve and receive greater technology in the future.

In another message the good forces said that they are great beings of love. They work within a congress of Space and want us to form a link of true friendship. Also, they would like humanity to be aware of certain knowledge, including a better understanding of our history. Throughout time they have been fighting evil.

Martin claims to have had some rather unusual UFO-type contacts with the good forces. On one occasion he was asked if he would like a trip in a UFO. He said, yes, and so they sent an invisible car to collect him. The invisible car parked on a wide path, and he was guided to step inside it. He remained visible inside the vehicle. However, there was something wrong with the car, so he was directed to walk to a nearby clearing. Here he heard the grass snapping as if a being was walking about the place, but either due to the misty conditions prevailing or some other factor, he was unable to see anything to account for the sound. Unfortunately, no UFO came to collect him on that evening.

On another evening he was contacted again, and asked if he would like a ride in a UFO. Again, he agreed to go along with them. This time the rendezvous was at a playing field. In a thorn hedge, he saw flashing lights which resembled eyes. He began trembling; he thought they might use transference technology (a form of teleportation) on him. After a few minutes, he was instructed to go to a wood half a mile away. There he waited and saw more coloured lights. The lights seemed to be looking at him, and he began trembling again. Eventually, he was instructed to go home, after yet another disappointing wait for an elusive UFO ride. On the same night he alleged that a UFO sighting was made by a person in some nearby flats, and this was reported in the local press.

When near Goole, North Humberside, one night, he was told by a female telepathic voice which emanated from a UFO (at this time he could not see a UFO) to go to a nearby field. Here he was collected by an invisible car; when he stepped inside it, he saw nothing but he had a sensation of travelling at speed. He noted that, "when I was travelling at speed I had to keep all thoughts out of my mind but before entry into the flying saucer another thought came to mind."

He had a vision of three females wearing silver suits positioned inside the UFO. It was then he found himself back in the field where he had been collected by the car, and in the distance, he was able to see a line of UFOs. One of the females said in his mind that she would give him heat, and his cold legs were heated up from the outside due to her influence.

He felt that they worked on behalf of the good forces. He said, "The sighting seemed real even if it might have been a vision." Apparently, the three females had initially contacted him when he was on his meditation course in Buckinghamshire.

On one evening, after the Goole encounter, he met the celestial ladies again. This time he was located at his home. At 11 p.m. he went into a room where he keeps his collection of books. Wearing only his underpants, he laid upon a foam-rubber mat to meditate. He heard voices in his head, and lights flashed around him. Then an invisible hand clamped his legs, and he was unable to move. It seemed to him that beings from a UFO were examining his body scientifically. He heard the hum of a motor of some kind, and he had a vision of the three girls, who appeared to be about 21 years old, polishing his fingernails. Then they worked upon cleaning his teeth. The hum of the motor suggested these activities. During this experience the humming sound and the lights attracted the attention of Martin's neighbour. Martin said that he saw his neighbour look through the window and saw him smile. From this he concluded that he had seen one of the girls and thought that he was with a girlfriend. The experience ended when a male telepathic voice said that there was trouble (perhaps something to do with their UFO?) and the girls were told to return to the UFO. The incident lasted approximately two hours, and he felt very tired when they went. This encounter was experienced as real, but no physical traces of their activities were present afterwards.

The aliens use special technology, their use of high speeds and invisibility are reasons why UFOs are not seen so often in our skies. Despite their technology they wish to gain knowledge of our thoughts and actions through people like Martin. Martin has been (and presumably still is) acting as an agent for them, and on their behalf he has read books for them. Often, he has found a book and read a portion of it which has been applicable to his situation or needs (or the perceived needs of the aliens).

Besides book reading, he has attended lectures, museums, cinemas and shops for them to get a better picture of our physical and mental environment. On behalf of the three female UFO beings, he has had to look at female attire displayed in shop windows, because they are particularly intrigued by our fashions. On other occasions he has seen pornographic films on behalf of the aliens. One evening at his home, he played records for the aliens. The telepathic voices had been indicating that they were enjoying themselves, and there was a lively atmosphere. Perhaps as a reward he was told to flicker his eyes. Whilst doing this, with his gaze directed towards the light bulb at the centre of the room a mini grey-coloured UFO manifested below the light for a few seconds before disappearing.

At another time he was enveloped in vibration and light, and it seemed as if the aliens were attempting to transfer him to a UFO, but the operation was not completed for some unknown reason.

Martin even received from the telepathic voices of the aliens an account of his own birth. They said that as his body emerged from the womb a blinding flash of light appeared, and an alien "spirit" body and his own "spirit" body both entered his physical body.

Discussion

Our interview with Martin Bolton lasted about two hours, and we have no plans at the moment to see him again, so any analysis we might make from such a short meeting is bound to be limited. We have decided not to conduct any more interviews for several reasons. Time and money are obvious restrictions on all amateur investigations, but the most basic reason was our feeling that we were not qualified to cope with such a case.

As UFO investigators we are in a rather ambiguous position when confronted by such people. The very fact that we take a serious interest in their accounts, by arranging an interview in the first place, lends a certain amount of credence and value to the experiences which the person has probably told to no other person (or has received only scepticism when they have done so).

In this instance we felt that the experiences were an indication of more fundamental and disturbing aspects of the person's mental state. By reinforcing the validity of the experiences, however mildly, without being able to offer support or guidance, we feel is irresponsible and potentially dangerous.

This is where the ambiguity of our role as UFO investigators arises. Although we might regard the person's experiences as being psychological as opposed to being caused by something of an extra mundane nature, how do we communicate our thoughts to that person? Indeed, the person in question, like most other people, expect UFO investigators to "believe" in the extra mundane origin of UFOs! Sometimes a person who contacts us is probably seeking confirmation of their experiences, perhaps because they are worried that there is something more fundamental bothering them and/or because of ridicule from friends, relatives, media, etc. The question is, can the UFO investigator remain a neutral observer?

In the case of "Gary" noted in *UFOs: A British Viewpoint* by Jenny Randles and Peter Warrington it can be seen that a person can affect the investigator(s) in many diverse ways to the detriment of everyone involved.

However, in the case of some encounters which involve messages from the Space Brothers who wish us to live in harmony, peace, love, etc., the life of the recipient can improve, even if the cynical UFO investigator is rather perturbed by such utterances! Certainly, when one seeks to investigate high-strangeness cases one should be prepared to adapt to the situations which arise, and one should be wary about over-estimating the importance of a case or taking it too literally.

Sometimes UFO witnesses continue to have sightings due to the interest shown by investigators, and they use the knowledge they obtain about UFOs from the investigators as a model for their experiences, particularly when hypnotic regression is used. A classic example of this is revealed by the investigation made by Frank Johnson recorded in his book *The Janos People*. He investigated the story of a family who were taken inside a flying saucer by the Janos people in June 1978. The aliens said they were waiting for the right time to come to Earth and populate it with their people. Johnson believed their story as literal fact and noted: "they wish to come openly and by general agreement. They want to have 'a place which is our own, where we can all be together, and be independent.' Ideally, they would very much like to have an island of their own; it would need to be quite a big island."

The Janos people are likely to have been productions of the imagination enhanced by the use of hypnotic regression, or they are just biding their time. Sceptics think it might have been a hoax influenced by the Betty and Barney abduction case and/or by the recent release of *Close Encounters of the Third Kind*.

During our interview with Martin Bolton, we did not discuss our own thoughts about UFOs, except in very general terms at the end of the session, and we did not discuss our interpretation of his experiences with him.

At the cost of projecting our own prejudices we feel that the following discussion about the Martin Bolton case might prove useful to other UFO investigators and researchers.

We are both struck by the fact that Martin's strange experiences began very shortly after the liquidation of his chemical business. Presumably, the fact that he did not want to, or could not, find another source of employment meant that he had more time on his hands and greater chance to brood upon the unknown as a means of escape from boredom and any worries and problems he might have. It is also intriguing to note that "chemicals" were used by the evil beings to torture Martin. Perhaps they were mocking him because of his failure in the chemical business?

He told us that: "Normal people don't know what the Universe is about." This seems to suggest that he regards himself as someone special or abnormal and this is reinforced by the account of his birth which claims that a spirit body entered his physical body.

The most striking part of his narrative concerns the torture and phantom pregnancies he suffered which are very similar to experiences Dr Daniel Paul Schreber, an Appeal Court judge in Dresden, suffered in the latter part of the nineteenth century. At the age of 51 years old he had a mental illness which forced him to reside in the custody of various German asylums from 1893 until 1902.

A report by Dr Weber noted that at first, he had occasional visual and auditory illusions, but these progressed until, "He believed that he was dead and decomposing, that he was suffering from the plague; he asserted that his body was being handled in all kinds of revolting ways." The report also stated that:

> During the first years of his illness certain of his bodily organs suffered such destructive injuries as would inevitably have led to the death of any other man: he lived for a long time without a stomach, without intestines, almost without lungs, with a torn oesophagus, without a bladder and with shattered ribs, he used sometimes to swallow part of his own larynx with his food, etc. But divine miracles ("rays") always restored what had been destroyed, and therefore, as long as he remains a man he is altogether immortal.

He then got the idea that he attracted God. As a consequence, he was to be transformed into a woman over a period of decades or centuries. Then he would give birth to a new race of men who would achieve a state of bliss and leave Dr Schreber to die a natural death.

Signs that he was becoming a woman were seen by Dr Schreber, and in his own book, *Memorabilia of a Nerve Patient*, he admitted that:

> Something occurred in my own body similar to the conception of Jesus Christ in an immaculate virgin, that is, in a woman who had never had intercourse with a man. On two separate occasions (and while I was still in Professor Flechsig's institution) I have possessed female genitals, though somewhat imperfectly developed ones, and have felt a stirring in my body, such as would arise from the quickening of a human embryo. Nerves of God corresponding to male semen had, by a divine miracle, been projected into my body, and impregnation had thus taken place.

Although he did not investigate it directly, this case did interest Sigmund Freud, who in his *Case Histories II* believed Dr Schreber had these delusions due to repressed, unconscious, homosexual desires.

It is worth adding that Dr Weber found Dr Schreber to have an interest in a wide variety of subjects and was highly intelligent. Unfortunately, "In spite of all this, however, the patient is full of ideas of pathological origin, which have formed themselves into a complete system; they are more or less fixed, and seem to be inaccessible to correction by means of any objective appreciation and judgement of the external facts."

Whereas Dr Schreber based his delusions upon a system which revolved round God, Martin Bolton used the UFO myth as the foundation for his delusions. One conscious or unconscious source for his experiences could have been Stuart Holroyd's book *Briefing for the Landing on Planet Earth*. This mentions the use of brain implants by the space people as a way of improving mental contact with them. Also, their prime contact, "Tom", tells of how Atlanteans used very advanced surgical techniques, which links with Martin's idea that the Egyptians carried out horrifying transplants because of their Atlantean ancestry. Although Martin says that Atlantis was finished by 3000 BC, Tom says it was finished in 11000 BC. Even if he did not get his ideas from this book, he had read and found out enough about ufology and similar subjects for his unconscious mind to plunder them when necessary.

In essence we can see that he uses the space people as an excuse and justification for behaviour and thoughts that he does not wish to accept as his own. Instead of admitting that he wants to see pornographic films and look at female clothing in shops, he claims that the space people cause him to look at such things. He wants young females to admire his body, but rather than admit this, his mind conjures up the three space women who obligingly clean his fingernails, teeth, etc. Because of carrying out these thoughts and actions, even when he does them at the bidding of the good space people, he is tortured and punished by the evil space people. Indeed, the good space people allow him to gratify his id instincts, whilst the evil space people assuage his feelings of guilt by their punishments upon his body for letting such impulses get the upper hand.

As in the Norman Harrison case, Martin fears that some disaster will strike humanity; he says that "the Earth is on a knife edge". Again, we have some confidence in saying that his fears for humanity and the fight between good and evil space people are really metaphors for his own mental struggle. He is frightened of being dominated and controlled by the evil part of his own mind.

Only by expressing it in the terms of a battle over the Universe is he able to cope with this situation. If he loses the battle, it really is the end of the world – for him. In a letter, dated 28 April 1982, Carl Grove claims that this case

> is the clearest instance of paranoid schizophrenia I have come across outside of a textbook. The symptoms are all classical – ideas of reference, social isolation, obvious signs of sexual frustration, and an interest in weird topics. The age of onset is typical, although in this case the collapse of his business was the major trigger. I don't believe there is the least need to invoke an extramundane explanation of any sort in this case.... Interest in UFOs, spiritualism, gurus, etc., seems especially prevalent in such cases, may be because they offer an alternative framework to the socially-constructed reality which the schizoid feels excluded from. (This does not, of course, imply that such subjects are necessarily crazy or worthless in themselves.)
>
> Apart from the danger of becoming further estranged through absorbing himself in such weird stuff, the schizoid is unlikely to be able to contribute anything of value to his area of interest since he totally lacks objectivity, and since the real reason for his interest is covert.

Carl, who is a psychologist, concludes his letter by saying that he does not think that this and similar cases have anything to do with UFOs. Unfortunately, the very presence of the UFO investigator, especially on a regular basis, can induce people to elaborate and multiply their reports of strange events.

When the UFO investigator is confronted by somebody who is "obviously" mentally disturbed, it is possible for the investigator to ignore this if what the person says reinforces their own ideas about the UFO subject. The Martin Bolton case has something to do with ufology because in a gross way it shows how a delusional world-picture can be built from the foundations of the UFO myth and used as a way of masking underlying psychological problems.

With the establishment of what was called the New Ufology in the 1970s, teenage UFO investigators are now involved in cases that could be potentially dangerous. An example of such a case was given to me by David Clarke (then 16 years old) who told me in a letter dated 12 September 1982, that:

> During the winter (of 1981) I began to get several phone calls from a man late at night, who claimed to have had several experiences with UFOs and "knew what they were." He would not give his name but arranged to meet me in town on a certain date. I met him at the given time and he seemed to be quite normal at first until he began talking about his experiences and theories and then it became quite obvious to me that he was "round the bend." He began to make quite a spectacle of himself while talking and eventually I managed to get him into a taxi and home. The following week I met him walking along the same part of town but he just walked past and ignored me.
>
> Following this I began to receive long telephone calls which were linked through from the operator with someone claiming to be a UFO entity. These calls came through invariably twice a week for four weeks at around 4 o'clock in the morning (and by this time my family thought I was going quite mad). The person on the other end of the line seemed to know everything about me: my date of birth, height, etc. – on one occasion he actually told me everything I had got on my school timetable the following morning!
>
> The calls were largely nonsensical and towards the end the person began giving me highly detailed prophecies

about world events which were alleged to happen within the next few years. Already three of these have passed, and all were false.

At first I actually thought I was going "round the bend," but after studying the general mannerisms of the person on the other end of the phone I concluded that this was the same man I had been talking to in town several weeks previously.

Not only do we have the problem of dealing with such cases on an individual level that is satisfactory for both the investigator and the recipient of UFO-type experiences, but we must consider the theoretical problems. If we accept that some accounts of UFO encounters are of a psychological origin, how do we differentiate them from "real" UFO encounters?

It could be that the contactee could be psychologically disturbed or might have had the encounter due to other psychological reasons (e.g., the person might be hypnotically regressed causing a person to "remember" an encounter). If we are not sensitive to such factors the introduction of such cases as a way of reinforcing a belief in objective, physical UFOs, is undermined considerably. However, to get round this problem ufologists in the past have suggested that the UFOs are physical craft which are controlled by an intelligence or intelligences which can manipulate human minds into believing that they have had the more bizarre form of close encounter.

Today, other people suggest that some form of energy emitted in specific geographical areas is responsible for triggering UFO experiences in people who are in the right place at the right time. This type of speculation is certainly more amenable to scientific study than most UFO hypotheses, but it is still a psychological explanation for most UFO experiences. With increasing attention to better investigation techniques and a greater ability to find explanations for UFO encounter experiences, we are left to ask if there are any real objective UFOs for us to discover?

Notes and References

Acknowledgements to Robert Addinall who attended the interview with Martin Bolton; Carl Grove and David Clarke for letting me quote from their letters; Shirley McIver for giving me references to the Dr Schreber case; and last but not least to Martin Bolton for his time and trouble.

Randles, Jenny and Warrington, Peter. *UFOs: A British Viewpoint*, Robert Hale, London, 1979.

Johnson, Frank. *The Janos People*, Neville Spearman, Sudbury, 1980.

"Dr. G. Weber's Report to the Court on the Case of Daniel Paul Schreber," dated 9 December 1899, at: http://schizophreniathebeardedladydisease.com/images/Weber-final.pdf

Schreber, Dr Daniel Paul. (Translated by Dr Ida Macalpine and Dr Richard A. Hunter). *Memorabilia of a Nerve Patient*, William Dawson, London, 1955.

Freud, Sigmund. (Compiled and edited by Angela Richards) *Case Histories II*, Pelican Books, Harmondsworth, 1979.

Holroyd, Stuart. *Briefing for the Landing on Planet Earth*, Corgi Books, London, 1979.

Chapter Eight

Aliens in the Family ... and the Pink Panther Abduction

Stefan Lobuczek

Stefan Lobuczek has had a lifetime of strange experiences and alien encounters, which seem to run in his family. Unlike many abductees who are spiritually uplifted by their alien contacts, Stefan's experiences are deeply troubling to him.

He told me in no uncertain terms, that, "I do not like them. I hate them. What gives them the right to take me and others? I hate them for that. My feelings haven't changed over the years. I'd be very happy to forget about it, but I can't."

Back in 1964, when he was only five years old, he remembers going into his parents' bedroom to shout at them to get rid of the strange people in his room. This early memory only came to him after a series of nightmares in 1973, which prevented him from sleeping at night and made him frightened of the dark. He realised that, "I was conditioned not to remember by those who had taken me. They had implanted a false memory in the form of a nightmare. This prevented me from seeing the truth beyond its barriers."

Meeting the Panther

Stefan was 11 years old when he had a major alien experience. At the time he only experienced feeling a strange presence in his bedroom.

As an adult, he recalls that on the first night he felt a strange presence. Then, a beam of intense light lifted him through his bedroom window and deposited him inside a nearby UFO. Here Stefan found himself naked on a metal examination table. Looking down on him were several aliens. He said, "There were the tall thin ones, which I always think of as the Pink Panthers, but without the tail, they had big black eyes and they floated about a lot. The other being's [sic] of which there seemed to be more were short grey and wrinkly and had a pungent odour I can't begin to describe."

A silver object was put in his arm and he felt a terrible pressure inside his head. And an alien, who looked like a Pink Panther cartoon character, reassured him via telepathy that he would be returned home soon.

Another memory of this, or a similar abduction two nights later, involved him being taken down a long corridor. He said,

> the lighting was blue and was concealed in the recess either side of the walkway. The walls narrowed to the ceiling. I remember running my fingers along the wall. It felt metallic, silky smooth and was cold to the touch. The corridor led to a dark holding area where I was left and the door closed. I was in the room with other children. None of us spoke. I felt sick and very cold.

A striking part of his alien memories is of seeing several clear cases holding human body parts and a cylindrical case containing a severed Neanderthal head.

After writing about these encounters on his website, a person contacted him to say that he had seen a UFO hovering over Stefan's home during the period when he had his encounters. This indicates to Stefan that there is more to his early experiences than just imagination or fantasy.

The same group of Pink Panther-type aliens seem to have kept a regular watch on his life and have made contact on many occasions since he was five. Often his childhood memories come at unexpected moments. One memory was triggered a few years ago when he was looking at an old family photograph taken in the garden of their home in Birmingham in June 1965. As he looked at it, he realised this was the exact spot where he had dragged his older brother in the middle of the night sometime in 1964. Stefan said:

> Then I remembered us both being surrounded by the brightest of light nothing could be seen through it to the outside of it. I have no further recollection of the events that followed.
>
> My granddad, my two sisters and I share these strange encounter experiences but it wasn't until I saw that photograph that I knew that my brother was also implicated in this bizarre nightmare of events.

Driving Lessons

One night in 1986, he saw a bright light in the sky as he was driving down a country lane. He suddenly forgot about driving down this lane and was startled to see a rabbit in his car headlights. Shocked out of his trance, he got out of his car and realised he was lost. He got back in his car, and as he reversed into a field he saw a grey-type alien standing by the gate. Knowing they are not very pleasant characters, he drove off as fast as possible.

In the middle of 2009, he was warned indirectly not to openly talk about his experiences, but he was not intimidated. In defiance of these warnings, he gave a speech into his research into Electronic Voice Phenomenon (EVP) at the Unitarian Society for Psychical Studies Annual Conference on 4 September 2010.

As an indication that he should have heeded the warnings, he said that after the conference:

> On the way back just a little after midnight Sunday, 05 September 2010 between Great Hucklow and Buxton, the car suddenly started to change modes from CD, to radio and Aux input and also in volume, the Sat Nav was also

going crazy in a way not consistent with loss of satellite data. I remember vaguely stopping the car and getting out of the vehicle it was very dark and there were woods either side of the road. The car stereo going crazy had made it hard to concentrate on driving safely and it wouldn't power off.

So by pulling over and turning off the ignition I thought this might somehow reset the sound system. The next thing I remember I'm outside the car for no apparent reason the car door is open yet the courtesy light isn't illuminating the interior.

I then felt very sick for no apparent reason and vomited. Then as if no time had passed I'm standing outside my car miles away in a lay by somewhere on the A38 (my route home) feeling sick. It then seemed to take ages to navigate back home and when I got home at about 2.45 a.m. I continued to be sick. This journey should have taken me no more than an hour and fifteen minutes. I cannot account for an hour plus added to my journey time.

It is Stefan's view that the aliens come from outer space and can use different dimensions to visit us as they will. What most upsets him is the recurring childhood memory of the limbs and severed head he saw onboard the UFO. These alien experiences and nightmares attack him at random, literally out the blue, and he sees them as a lifelong plague. Why are they here and why are they are doing this is a constant mystery to him as well as to the rest of us.

Family Encounters

Stefan's youngest sister remembers that when he was 11 years old and she was five years old, she woke up one night because a bright light was shining through the curtains. It seemed as bright as day in her room, and she could hear people moving about in the house. The same happened again two nights later. This seems to confirm Stefan's alien encounter at that time. She also said that their older sister at that time had a dream of being on an operating table in a spacecraft. When Stefan asked her about this, she became upset and refused to talk about it.

A Strange Wind

In recent years, Stefan's youngest sister was woken in the middle of the night because the bedroom curtains were blowing about. Assuming the window was open, she got up to close it, but found it was closed. Looking outside she saw a funnel of wind that came towards her and entered her mouth.

The next instant she found herself downstairs with her arms outstretched like Jesus on the cross. On her right she saw an angel and on the left a jester. She felt impelled to say the Lord's Prayer, after stumbling over the words she finally got it right. At that moment, the jester turned into an angel, and she was levitated backwards up the stairs. The funnel of wind left her mouth as she banged against the landing wall, and then she woke up in her bed.

Missing Time

When Stefan's Granddad was courting a girl in Poland before World War II, he saw a bright light in the forest after leaving her home. He walked towards the light to see what it was, and then he suddenly found himself walking in the opposite direction. Looking at his watch he found it was two hours later than he expected.

Remote Viewing

When Stefan was 22 years old, he worked nights at a car parts warehouse in Nuneaton, which was built over an old coal mine.

Here the staff reported several strange events, but the most outstanding occurred one Friday night at 10 p.m.

At the time he regarded it as an out-of-the-body experience (OOBE) but now thinks it an example of remote viewing. He was operating a computer ordering system, and when he was satisfied that it was running properly, he placed three chairs together and went to sleep. Then, he says:

> The next thing I remembered was walking out of data control into the open plan office area. I could see Alex the security guard fast asleep. I went into the computer room but don't remember opening the door. I proceeded to the paper console and as it was at waist level, I leant over it to view how many orders were left to process. I would normally place my hands either side of the console for support but don't remember seeing my hands. This didn't seem abnormal at the time I took visual note of the orders left to process and proceeded back through the door into the open plan office. Again, don't remember actually opening the door.
>
> I could see Alex still fast asleep but now he was snoring quite loudly. I proceeded to data control to go back to sleep. However when I got there I could see someone else fast asleep. After a moments viewing and the subsequent shock I realised that I was the person a sleep [sic]. Now just like people claim when they die my whole life seem to flash before me and I just freaked thinking I had died.
>
> Then as if I was on the end of a very powerful elastic band under tension I shot back into my body. I sort of filled up from boots to head with such a force I sat bolt upright and banged my head on the desk that my head was asleep under.

Notes and References

Telephone conversation with Stefan Lobuczek in February 2009. Emails with Stefan, February and May 2009, October, November 2010.

Chapter Nine

Taken Elsewhere

Paula Green

The *Daily Star*, Sunday, 9 May 2021, splashed Paula Green's story on their front page with the headline "'I've been abducted by aliens 52 times...'says Paula from Yorkshire...You've had some bad luck, missus!" she was amazed at how one newspaper clipping had defined her. In reality, she insists she has "a bog standard" life and she doesn't "live, breathe and s*** paranormal." As can be seen she is a very direct and down-to-earth person. She was understandably annoyed that the headline is wrong, as she has only knowingly had six or seven actual abductions. In the past she would have got very angry about it, but now she is slightly more mellow about what people think.

For years Paula has been silent about her encounters, and it was only after being contacted on Facebook that her story leaked out to the *Star*. She thought it was just someone interviewing her and when she found it was going to be in the *Star*, she knew her story would be twisted. She commented; "It quickly went viral. I don't read the news and I haven't owned a TV set for 14 years. It does not matter; people think you are a believer or a nutter. People tend to take things at face value." Another factor was:

"I changed my mind about keeping quiet simply because I know there are others out there going through what I am going through. The more who speak up, it will help those who cannot come forward. Why should we hide in the shadows for fear of ridicule? It is happening and it is real."

Not surprisingly her story caused a storm of interest. Some said she is a fake or just plain loopy, others believed she has really had alien encounters. An article on the *Mysterious Universe* website, not known for being very critical, was quick to rubbish her story and asked:

"Why can't extraterrestrials choose more believable messengers and equip them with more believable evidence? Why didn't Smith (the *Star* gave her the pseudonym Paula Smith – N.W.) ask them for it. Is Smith's story a hallucination or a hoax?"

Paula contacted them and a few days later, *Mysterious Universe* published her side of the story. Regarding her other critics:

> Well. I've been called some right shit these past few days. That goes straight over my head... Zero f**** given. But at least I've got more balls than most to speak out.
>
> Yep, the papers twisted my account, cut loads out and made me out to be a loon. The irony is that those who called me out actually read the newspapers that my account was in and took it as "face value"... you know, because the media tells the truth... (sarc) Delusional... not?... Oh the irony.

As a child she did not have a concept or wording for these experiences, she was not even that aware of the alien subject. And

> the word alien as it equals E.T. I can't answer or speculate about what causes these experiences. It could be otherworldly... Is it random or intelligent? Why do they come here, I've never been happy about it. They traumatise me by the way they look and act. But humanity does far worse things and that is how I cope with it. I don't know what they want of me or other people, not sure if they have a plan. I think they are trying to learn about us, sometimes they try a bit too hard to copy us and

they make mistakes. I cannot answer if they are good or bad.

The experiences do pass through my family, my grandmother had them, but I never really listened to her when she spoke about them. My mother saw a spirit or two, but she kept such things to herself. I didn't tell a soul until 2012. I never read much about aliens, just seeing a picture of one made me physically sick.

Once she woke to see a five-feet (1.5m) tall "grey" at the end of her bed and two similar "greys" at her bedside. She just woke up and it was like they had turned a switch. I asked her if this was probably due to sleep paralysis?

"Sleep paralysis is not the same. They don't shut your brain down. You are subdued and you cannot move. It takes all your energy to open your eyes, but you are fully aware. I've had sleep paralysis and it's nothing like this."

Paula's first brush with the unknown came when she was only four years old in 1974. It came in the form of a small black bird with an orange beak. Over a period of weeks stretching into 1975, it came to her and spoke to her through telepathic communication. It asked her questions like "Do you like school?" and "Do you like your family?" She remembers that it would sit beside her when she was outside her home, and that when her mother appeared, it would fly to the rooftop of the house on the opposite side of the street. Finally, it came to her and told her that, "I won't be coming back. But I will return later in your life." At this she burst out crying.

This experience can be compared to the regular reports of owls and other creatures seen by abductees that the abduction researcher Budd Hopkins regarded as "screen memories" and, of course, many children have imaginary friends. For Paula, unlike most children, these types of experiences have haunted her for the rest of her life. She told me:

"This was the start of it all. I thought it was imagination but only a few years ago my late Mum said 'remember that bird? you called it Inca.' I had forgotten all about that. In my teens I never related it to my other alien-type experiences; it was a separate issue. Now I think it was an introduction."

The Pig

At six years old, one dark evening in October 1977, she was playing in her front room with Candy, the family's Golden Labrador dog. The curtains were wide open because her mother always felt claustrophobic if they were closed, and this is something Paula also feels. Paula for no reason was teasing the dog and kept telling her, "There is a pig at the window." After bounding at the window a few times, Candy suddenly spun round and ran off into the kitchen. Cupping her hands to look out the window to see what had spooked the dog, she came face-to-face with two large almond eyes. She said:

> I screamed and jumped backwards. I looked back again. It was clearly a small person, about my height. Was it a kid? It had a big bald, bulbous grey head. It had long arms and spindly fingers. It wore a black or dark blue skin-tight outfit that finished at the knees and wrists, it was like the Lycra outfits people wear today, but not then. I was so terrified; I had a flood of emotions.
>
> There was a two to three foot (0.6 to 0.9 metre) tall wall outside the window, and it moved backwards over the wall in slow motion. Its body turned and bent forwards to run up the street, but its head stayed straight upwards staring at me. All its proportions looked wrong. It almost glided in slow motion up the street and quickly went out of view. At that age I didn't know what to make of it. Then everything came back to normal, I could hear my Mum and Candy in the kitchen, before everything

had gone silent. I quickly shut the curtains. The whole incident lasted three minutes or 30 minutes I had no way of knowing. I have never forgotten it, and it was strange I had tormented Candy to "look at the pig" as I had never done that before.

Missing Time

Her first UFO encounter occurred in October 1983, when she was 12 years old as she was walking through Judy Woods, Bradford, with a friend. It was after school, and she regarded her 14-year-old friend as a big sister. It was her idea to go to Judy Woods as an adventure. They broke the rules a bit and her mother would never have allowed her to go on the two-mile walk to the woods in the dark.

It was about 6.45 p.m. when they entered a fenced pathway that gave way to a narrower muddy path lined by trees. As they entered a clearing at the end of the path, they could only see their way by moonlight. Then there came a complete silence, and she could only hear her own breathing and heartbeat. She said:

> I heard the lapping of water. We were on the edge of a lake or reservoir, about one foot (0.3m) from it. Then suddenly I saw five to ten feet (1.5m to 3m) in front of me, what I can only describe as a boomerang with an extra arm. This is more accurate than saying it looked like a giant propeller as the ends of the arms were more rounded. It was about 30 feet (9m) high and wide in an upright position, moving slowly clockwise at about one to five mph. The arms were nearly touching the water. As it was in front of me it looked huge and never ending. There was a light at the end of each arm, one was blue, one green and the other I'm not sure about.

At the centre of the object was an extremely black circle or hollow. From underneath a fan of white light appeared. It seemed to be coming from something stationary behind the moving arms. Water underneath the light began to simmer and gave off a vapour or steam. Me and my friend were bathed in a pale blue light. Everything went in slow motion; it was like a horror movie. I remember turning to my friend and saying "F****** run!" I had to drag her as she was so terrified and awed. I knew we had to run. Blackness seemed to close in, and it seemed like running in quicksand. Next minute I was at the bottom of my street.

She was surprised to see children milling about and PC Milner outside her grandmother's door. When questioned she could not tell them where she had been because it would get her into big trouble, plus she genuinely did not know what happened. What really shocked her was that it was 11.55 p.m., there were at least four hours she could not account for. To avoid any further questions, she went straight to bed. The next morning nothing was said by the family and her friend was angry because she said Paula ran away and left her to go home on her own. The friend got home about 9.15 p.m. long before Paula. She said:

I don't remember going home. I can't get my head round it. Where the hell did I go? There was missing time, but I really don't want to go through regression. I don't want to go back there and find out anything more terrible.

It was 20 years before I set foot in Judy Woods again, just the thought of going past it would make me shake.

Legends of the Wood

Judy Woods is very close to the crossroads of the A641 and A58, at Wyke, near Bradford, which due to its high-level of supernatural activity locals have dubbed Hell Fire Corner. It was here in the 1940s a motorist lost control and crashed his car into a wall. Afterwards, he claimed a bright light climbing into the sky from the nearby woods had distracted him.

A silvery hat-shaped object, with windows around its middle, hovering one foot (0.3m) above the ground was seen by Mrs Fowler when she was walking in the area in 1977. It had a red cone of light descending from its base, and after floating near a rocky outcrop it slowly rose, rotated slowly and then with a flash shot into the sky.

In October and November 1981, UFOs were frequently seen between the nearby Wyke Woods and Lightcliffe. Kai Roberts noted that this became known as the Wyke Woods UFO Flap and that, "These accounts tended to involve several balls of light which often split into a greater number and often seemed to repel each other, causing them to dance around the sky accompanied by a faint humming noise, before either disappearing in a single blinding flash or sinking to the ground."

History repeated itself with a bus crash at Hire Fire Corner on 1 November 1981, with the driver claiming that he was distracted by seeing a smoky white light over the woods.

Judy Woods is a popular recreational area established in the nineteenth century and is the closest woods to Hell Fire Corner. When ufologists were investigating the Wyke Woods Flap, the local children told them they avoided going into Judy Woods for fear of the ghostly, white glowing shapes that floated between the trees.

Kai seemed to think the lights that plague the area might be caused by little understood electrical "earthlight" phenomenon, and this is misperceived as ghosts or flying saucers.

The area of Judy and Wyke Woods was also a place of interest to Paul Bennett and fellow UFO researchers Nigel Mortimer and Robert Stammers in early 1982. Robert had spent his school holidays in the late 1960s playing in Wyke Woods and he felt all three of them had a special psychic connection with the place.

Creepy Hands

Since childhood she has had numerous encounters and paranormal experiences mainly at, or near her home, in Great Horton, to the west of the City of Bradford, West Yorkshire. One such unusual experience happened one morning in 1982. Paula woke up and felt a shooting pain in her back, and she got the impression of blood trickling down her skin. Going in the bathroom she tried looking at her back in the mirror, she had three scratches and on touching the area, it felt wet and tacky, and she found a small hole. The scratches looked as if they had already healed up. On touching the hole, she had a flashback to what happened that night in her bed. This is best told in her own words:

> I felt something moving inside my lower back. That feeling you get when you're pregnant and your unborn child moves slightly and gently, rather like a fluttery butterfly feeling. I was in pain, whatever was happening to me hurt me so much on the outside of my skin compared to the feeling I had on the inside of my back.
>
> I didn't have the strength to cry, to move or cry out. Yet, I was determined that I was going to get this thing away from my back, I wanted it out. I tried in vain to lift my right hand, the movement was restricted to a slight twitch of my thumb.
>
> I could now feel the presence of someone standing behind me. That was it I was so mad yet dreamy confused... it's so hard to explain the feeling I had.
>
> I at last found the strength to lift my hand, not only my hand but my entire arm. Although the struggle to keep it up was hard and slowly I managed to move my arm

around to my lower back. There was a struggle with some hand that kept pushing my hand away, I felt the fingers, long and thin, bony, immediately recognizing the shape to the touch. I was in panic mode, I had to fight with what little strength I had in me... I persisted, continued to get this thing out, I fought with myself to find more strength to keep going.

The final fight paid off. I had a hold of a tube-like implement, and I was not going to let go! I estimated that this tube-like implement was about as thin as a pencil, it felt tacky, sticky and wet, I could feel fingers crawling over my hand, very lightly, but strong enough to get my entire hand and place it gently on my knee. I could see the hand clearly. But this hand was different, it was the colour of a dolphin, and had the appearance of rubber yet a bone structure could be seen under the rubber-like skin, its fingernails were charcoal coloured. The wrist was extremely thin with no wide palm or top of hand. The fingers seemed to come from within the wrist, which only slightly widened before the fingers began. The strength of this hand was immense but not rough. I was gone, this time no warning, no seeping darkness from the corners of my eyes coming in. I was out cold, just blackness, then nothing.

Ball of Light

In 1999, when Paula was chatting with a friend at her home, at about 9.20 a.m. they heard a strange mechanical beeping sound coming from the sofa. At first, they thought it was a mobile phone, but after searching the sofa nothing was found and then the sound was heard on the other side of the room. It moved and stopped about three or four times. On resuming their chat, sitting either side of the fireplace, Paula saw at the top corner of the window behind her friend a big ball of light. Looking at the expression on Paula's face her friend asked, "what's happening?" Paula couldn't answer, and her friend had to turn around to see the light.

A tube of light projected down from it coming within a few inches of Paula's head. From the tube came a ball of light with a swirling movement inside it as if it was alive. Looking into the swirling core she was struck by its beauty, and she felt slow motion pulses of pleasure run through her. As the light hovered over her head, little white sparks came out of it that made a "pop pop pop" sound before dispersing. Then the light reduced to the size of a tennis ball and disappeared back up the tube of light.

Her friend regarded the light as repulsive and vowed never to come back here again. In contrast, Paula felt enlightened and that feeling lasted for several weeks and she's never felt anything like that ever since.

They then went to the local Co-op shop. Paula was laughing at everything, but her friend still had the opposite negative reaction. In the shop every time Paula reached into the freezer, a very loud crackling sound erupted. She reached in two or three times and the crackling was so loud it drew the attention of the customers. Not liking the attention, she went to join the long queue at the checkout. Just as she was looking at some tins of Ros's chocolates stacked in a pyramid fashion, and thinking of buying one, the whole stack fell apart as if it had been kicked. The tins rolled everywhere, and it seemed so bizarre and weird to her.

For the next few weeks whenever she was about to touch anything electrical, a blue light would appear, and on touching the object she'd feel a sensation of static.

Phantom Pregnancy

After a period of about ten years without any unusual experiences that she could remember, at the age of 23 years old, she carried a phantom pregnancy for at least six months. At first a friend said Paula was pregnant, but she did not believe her as she was single, and the times did not add up. Then she did experience the symptoms of pregnancy. She said:

> I'm fully aware that this does exist, but I'm unsure of exactly how common or uncommon this is. I had all the symptoms related to pregnancy, the morning sickness, the belly area growing at a rapid size.
>
> All I know was that every time I went to the doctors, I was now convinced the doctors were lying when they said I was not pregnant, my body told me differently. At about six months gone overnight my body was back to normal, it was as though it had all been a dream that had just gone, vanished. I was gutted...

To abduction researchers like Budd Hopkins and John Mack this would have indicated to them that she had been abducted and impregnated by aliens, who then secretly returned and harvested the unborn hybrid child.

Abductions

Paula has indeed gone on to remember abduction experiences, she says:

> On some occasions I'm not really abducted, it implies being taken without consent. I don't like the word "abducted." I black out and find myself somewhere else. How can I say if I've been abducted if at times, I'm not aware? Maybe I've gone somewhere. Where I go I do not know, because I've not been fully conscious of going from home to craft.
>
> About ten years ago I found myself in a moulded, round room. Was I inside a UFO or a front room with

props? Could it have been set-up by the military? A UFO craft is an easier thing to understand. I was sat in a chair, eyes focussed on a screen. People were sitting near me. The totally glass screen was a bit bigger than an iPad. It showed scenery with a 3-D effect. It showed landscapes with rivers, birds and flowers in glowing vivid colours. It was a flow of pictures but no people were in them. They made me feel very happy and elated. Then there was devastation, everything went to a normal colour and the river was now murky and the sky black and red, there were nuclear bombs going off, fires, devastation and buildings collapsing. Now I was crying at the hideous and evil devastation rather than crying with joy at the previous images. I was heartbroken. Everything in these pictures was exaggerated, they were like over-the-top images of paradise and hell.

Just beyond the screen was a black colour thing that had no shape, it was not a person or alien. It did not fit in, and I got the feeling I was not allowed to look at it. Then I woke up, it was not a dream, definitely reality.

Bruises

Paula wrote:

The only time I woke with IRREGULAR shaped bruises was after having encounters with the greys. They do NOT prove I have been abducted, despite what the papers say. Nothing I have or where I have been, whether at work or not, can make those shapes of the bruises. The triangle mark on my face was not a bruise, it was a dark mark, looked rather grey coloured, in contrast to my skin colour – and no matter how much I tried to wash it off, it would not come off. It faded after a week or so.

Seeing Greys

The types of aliens Paula sees are variable:

> The alien is a typical grey alien with the big eyes and grey body, but some of us see them in a slightly different appearance. I'm assuming that is because they (abductees) are focusing on different parts of the body at any one time, so people can describe parts of the aliens better than other people can.
>
> I have also seen grey tans, they have the proportions of the typical grey, except they are tan with more of a mottled brown colour, with deep wrinkles which make them look very old. Their "skin" has more of a leathery appearance. I've only seen the small ones, but some people see them at different heights, or maybe that is all a matter of perspective at the time.
>
> I did a painting that was based on an event where I got the chance to see it without that feeling of fuzziness, like being on heavy medication. The alien is NOT silver ... it is grey. I cannot tell you if it was skin, a coverall or what it was. The reason I painted it silver was because I had no grey paint left.

The Blond

"I have seen a tall blond, dressed in what looked like a pin-striped suit and he was really tall. Later, during this one encounter, he changed into a grey. I have never seen a spirit with a grey – they're both separate entities, but both very real."

She explained that this encounter was like a mash-up of dream and reality. It began when she had a dream of her friend coming round to her house to invite her to a beach party on her nearby street. She went along with her friend to find lorries of sand and water containers to create the beach, and there were already strings of lights there, beach balls, picnic tables, children making sand castles and loads of people. Yet, she was like a ghost, no one seemed able to see her, not even her friend when she stood within inches of her.

As she was wondering what was going on, a tall man who looked like a cardboard cut-out appeared on the main street. He had blond hair, and he looked timeless, he had no lines or wrinkles on his face. He gave the impression of being a time traveller. His suit looked ridiculous as it had pointed edges that tapered outwards to his shoulders. The colours of it changed and shimmered from grey, blue and silver it was hard to tell. Paula estimates he was about seven feet (2.1m) tall, he appeared very broad, and his arms and legs seemed unable to bend so when walking, he looked like a robot.

She had the feeling of knowing him. When he came up to her, he asked if she liked flying? She replied that she was scared of flying and that she had never been in a plane. Through their telepathic communication, he said he did not mean a plane. He said, "Come with me." They went to a snicket (a narrow passageway between houses) and he told her to hold his hand, on doing so she started feeling weightless, and was told to lean forwards to launch upwards much like the manner of Superman. This helps give you balance but Paula says you can just launch into the sky like Peter Pan if you have the confidence.

Paula keeping her eyes closed, could feel her feet were off the ground and the wind blowing her hair. In the distance she could hear cars and the nearby beach party. Opening her eyes she could see that they were at about the height of the streetlights, and she began enjoying the warmth of this summer night. Then she saw that the man she was holding hands with had turned into a grey. Her heart felt as if it had dropped to her stomach. She was horrified and confused. She was asked, "Did you like that?" At that moment she woke up in her bed. From the last question she deduced that these beings have limited feelings, and they have to learn them from us.

The Crocodile

One of my contacts with a reptilian was in early 2021, not sure about the date. I don't like putting a label on it. Before this time, I never believed in reptilians and if anyone spoke about them, I said, "no they don't exist."

I went to bed at about 11.30 p.m. switching the downstairs lights off. All I remember, I'm standing in my bedroom with a coffee in my hand, then it is like a switch, I'm downstairs in the front room. It is dark and I'm in my pyjamas. I am normally scared of the dark and would normally switch the lights on. There was just the orange glow of the streetlight outside, and it gave just about enough illumination. I don't know where my cup of coffee went! I had the urge to get the door key and open the front door.

Outside at the top of the road was a group of lads, in their teens or twenties, four were in a group and one near them leaning against a wall. I kept gazing around from the doorway, then one of the lads shouted "lights gone out" or "lights going out". The lights are still on but the lad is adamant, just as I'm thinking "no they haven't" the power goes and the streetlights go out.

I then see a figure between my doorway and the tree next door. It is very tall, seven feet (2.1m) I would say and broad, about three feet (0.9m) wide. I could not see much detail, and considering it was so close I was not fazed by it. It just did not register with me. I wonder why I had no urge to go? I'm still baffled.

Thinking back on it, the lads were probably not human either. The shout seemed to be directed at me. I felt nothing, no emotions at all, yet I'm normally scared of the dark. As the door was still gaping open I went to lock it when something forcefully grabbed me by the top of my left arm, and I was led four paces onto the living room rug. I was facing the wall and seeing a circular, pale blue light coming down from above. It was big enough for three people to fit in this beam. Every emotion was numb. I looked up the wall, I see in the light a crocodile face, it has yellowing teeth beyond its mouth it is too dark to see anything else. Then as it leans down there are two little black eyes that are hard to look at. Its short snout came within inches of my nose. Its skin was leathery and lumpy giving the impression of scales. The skin had an iridescent purple hue, then a brownish colour or grey; it changed when I moved my head even by just a few millimetres. Then I woke up in my bed in the morning. That was it. I describe it as a crocodile-like thing with teeth and fangs, but others think it was what is called a reptilian.

To this day she still does not know where her coffee went!

Pixelated Eyes

Another time Paula saw a strangely dressed being who wore a purple robe with gold sleeves and a huge collar. On its head it wore a very tight-fitting helmet like a skull cap. Her eyes zoomed into his eyes as if she was looking through a telescope. She could see that the eyes consisted of different hued blue brick-shaped pixels that moved around all the time, in an agitated fashion. Her eyes zoomed back to normal and when the being touched her on her forehead, she immediately went back to sleep.

Not a Gift

Regarding her lifetime of experiences, Paula has this to say:

Would anyone want a gift like this? I have it. PTSD caused by aliens; it is a burden. It drains me. It is not something you'd want to keep. Love to give it away. It is not a gift.

It affects millions of people throughout the world. It depends on the psychological make-up of people. Just in the U.K. there could be thousands. Many cannot speak up because of religion, work and fear of ridicule. They want to cry out, but they can't.

I'm a lone person. Abductee groups might help people even if it is only on Facebook, but there are people who take the piss. Groups get infiltrated and people call you deluded. I know it sounds insane but how do we know it is not real? Bruises do not prove anything, and it's the same with the U.S. government, they cannot prove anything. Too many people are reliant on the government for answers, but they are corrupt organisations.

There are millions of encounters yet we are still stuck in the Roswell and the Betty and Barney Hill era.

Greys can move through walls, and they have taken me through a glass window. So why do they need spaceships? I don't get it. They can come and go without them; they can get in your mind.

She acknowledges,

It is ironic I have seen greys, tall blonds and reptilians but I did not believe in them. I was very sceptical about them.

They could be visiting our planet for hundreds of years; I think as we advance, they advance as well. I can understand ETs visiting our planet as it is so beautiful. Why wouldn't they want to visit us? What I and others experience I don't know for certain. I'm in the middle ground between sceptics and those who believe in aliens.

Since 2021 she has not seen a grey or a blond being and feels like this is the end of those type of encounters. But as she says, "who can tell?" Those experiences could often be traumatic: "I thought I'd never get over it. If I see another grey, I'll go back to square one."

Notes and References

Based on interviews with Paula Green,11 and 18 May 2021, 8 April 2024 and Facebook exchanges.

"Brit gran says she's been abducted by – aliens 50 times – and has bruises to prove it," *Daily Star*, 8 May 2021, at: https://www.dailystar.co.uk/news/weird-news/brit-gran-says-shes-been-24068073

"Abductee Claims Aliens Gave Her Warnings and Bruises," *Mysterious Universe*, 10 May 2021, at: https://mysteriousuniverse.org/2021/05/abductee-claims-aliens-gave-her-warnings-and-bruises/

"Alien Abductee Sets the Record Straight About Her Amazing Encounters," *Mysterious Universe*, 17 May 2021, at: https://mysteriousuniverse.org/2021/05/alien-abductee-sets-the-record-straight-about-her-amazing-encounters/

"Hell Fire Corner and the Wyke Woods Flap," by Kia Roberts, *Ghosts and Legends of the Lower Calder Valley*, blog at: https://lowercalderlegends.wordpress.com/2010/03/26/hell-fire-corner-and-the-wyke-woods-flap/

Mortimer, Nigel. "Three On Line: Part One," *UFO Brigantia*, No. 22, Sept.–Oct. 1986, pp. 29–30.

Mortimer, Nigel. "Three On Line: Part Two," *UFO Brigantia*, No. 23, Nov.–Dec. 1986, pp. 29–30.

Chapter Ten

Nocturnal Invaders

In the "Stranger in the City" chapter we speculated that Norman Harrison's experiences were a genuine cry for help, and the only way he could deal with his mental instability was to project his beliefs and values via the aliens. The aliens were a psychological mask which he could hide behind, and this subterfuge protected him from the harsh reality of his own mental vulnerability to disintegration and disorder.

Norman Harrison is an extreme example, but unless we have some outlet for our feelings, we are all vulnerable to mental eruptions of frustration and anger. The belief in UFOs and visitors from elsewhere is a kind of psychological placebo. When our planet is threatened by so many dangers of a global nature, it is not surprising that the UFOs are a powerful symbol of salvation, utopia and planetary freedom.

Mental Contact

In *MUFOB*, New Series, No.15, Dirk Van Der Werff reports on the experiences of Rodney Stewart, a young man in his early twenties who lived in a terraced house in South Sheilds, Tyne and Wear.

In the summer of 1976, Rodney decided to concentrate on trying to mentally contact the space people. His method was to use the symbol of the Space Committee shown in George Hunt Williamson's book *Other Tongues – Other Flesh* as a mandala.

The mandala can be found throughout the Eastern religious systems, who regard it as an instrument of contemplation. Jung regarded the mandala as a depiction of psychic unity. Significantly, Rodney was experiencing a great deal of emotional upheaval within his home, and so he needed something to resolve his troubles. At night in his bedroom before going to bed, Rodney intensely meditated on his mandala. "I asked if I might be privileged enough to see their sign in the sky someday," he said. The next night he went through the same ritual of intense meditation. On the third night he did the same, and then he saw a light which caught his attention. It disappeared from view after 40 seconds, and Rodney said: "I was sceptical to the last but I suppose I was quite willing to believe that was a UFO and that it was in connection with my mental efforts to communicate with them."

For the next three nights he carried on his 15-minute meditation sessions. On the third night he felt disillusioned, and as he lay in bed, he commented: "I suppose I began to moan to myself, thinking that I had been witness to something very privileged, and that now I was asking too much. Who do I think I am?" Those were his thoughts when he saw through his bedroom window a bright light explode high in the sky. Rodney said:

> I had absolutely no doubt that I was witnessing a display of a craft piloted by intelligent beings. This was it, I must have been near to tears as it put on an amazing aerodynamical display moving in an exaggerated wave motion often stopping momentarily and then continuing its course until it disappeared from sight. It was a roundish very bright golden orb with a halo around it, it stayed still for a few seconds, then began to move from right to left, straight along, then down to start the wave-like motion gradually growing smaller as it moved away from me. I really don't know how long it was in view, probably thirty or forty seconds.

Rodney was in a highly suggestive state of mind and he could well have misinterpreted a normal celestial or aerial object for a

UFO. It is worth noting here that there is such a psychological phenomenon as the autokinetic effect. Experiments have been carried out to show that if a person is put into a dark room, with a single point of light facing them, after a few seconds they will see the light moving about.

In the case of Rodney Stewart, it should be added that after this second UFO sighting, he returned to bed and thanked the space people for their display, and he said, "I've never again asked, or for that matter, sent any further thoughts out into space for evidence in the sky. The two incidents have been totally amazing, and I consider myself very lucky to have had the honour to have witnessed them. What more can I say? I am by no means a sensationalist or a liar... the account is the truth."

Later in January 1978, he saw another UFO following an aircraft. The UFO was seen for a while until it altered direction and flew away into the distance.

Dirk Van Der Werff noted that Rodney had read and thought a lot about UFOs and felt that other kinds of phenomena were linked to ufology. Rodney said, "It is not what you see that is suspect, but how you interpret what you see." He interprets the UFOs as solid spacecraft and believes that there are good and bad UFO forces.

As if to show that Rodney is not alone in believing that UFOs are of some profound value and inspiration, a friend of mine who is an amateur writer, wrote in a recent letter to me:

> I had an idea for one story where a man is praying for something – a sign? – and then – by coincidence – he sees a UFO light and then a UFO, and this he takes to be symbolic. Although I didn't know how to a) begin this, and b) wind it up; it was to have two mingled themes, i) the propensity of people to read things which aren't there, i.e. the "sign" and ii) the mystical regard of UFOs people have nowadays.

Perhaps as John Rimmer has pointed out in his article "Facts, Fraud, and Fairytales", the person who is unable to express their feelings through normal creative channels, has no alternative but to project them into reality via unconventional channels, for example, by becoming a UFO percipient, and that such outlets have a symbiotic relationship.

It is worth recounting that as a small boy, Rodney often dreamt of seeing flying saucer shapes flying about, and so we can deduct that the symbol of the UFO had a powerful guiding influence throughout his life. Also, he has reported that he has experienced a few paranormal events.

One day when he was five years old, he was playing darts when the dart he was about to throw suddenly disappeared. Despite a thorough search of the room, the dart was never seen again.

In the autumn of 1975, just a few months before his meditation sessions, he had a peculiar experience. He was in bed and the time was about 12.30 a.m., he had been having difficulty in getting to sleep when he heard a buzzing sound. The sound was all around him, and his body felt very torpid to the extent that he was unable to move.

He tried to shout but no sound left his lips. Then his head moved involuntarily to the left. He saw the curtains of a window, which he knew couldn't be opened, being blown by the wind. Then a skinny-legged Victorian looking table appeared, which held a vase of wilting, dead flowers. "Slowly I saw the flowers come back to life," said Rodney, "they changed from a withered bunch to being in full bloom. It disappeared, the sound stopped, and I ran from that room as fast as I could."

Rodney also claims to have had out-of-the-body experiences (OOBEs) which are usually associated with sleep or deep relaxation. OOBEs are commonly called astral projections and are mainly an involuntary phenomenon.

On several occasions Rodney has felt himself being dragged down a tunnel at a tremendous speed, when on the borderline between sleep and wakefulness. He said, "When I have met people in this state they have just laughed at me when I asked where I was." He believed that on such trips he was on the astral plane or was on a different level of consciousness. During one trip he said that, "I once walked out of a window down to a churchyard where I saw people walking and chatting but they were oblivious to my presence, I was conscious that I was in the middle of a projection at the time and got onto a bus and sat down, a young boy spotted me and said that he knew I was a ghost."

Can You Fix It?

An interesting case that seems to combine some hallucinations and OOBEs was revealed in the *Northern UFO News*. The case came to light after an appeal for sightings by the newly formed West Yorkshire Research group. The percipient was interviewed by Mr Graham Barker of the West Yorkshire Research group along with a colleague. Also, Trevor Whitaker of the BUFORA Yorkshire branch, accompanied by a psychiatrist, visited and interviewed the percipient. The percipient was very wary of any form of publicity and shall thus be called Mr L to protect his anonymity.

All that can be given is that he lives in West Yorkshire. He is a respected man, has a highly regarded position in the local authority and has the good fortune of having reasonable intelligence and financial resources.

Mr L's first encounter occurred around 1974. A being between six feet and seven feet (1.8m to 2.1m) tall came to him as he was lying in bed. The being wore a one-piece suit with a high collar. Mr L says he had an intense feeling of great joy. Then it just said "hello" and disappeared. He had a second similar meeting at an unremembered date, when the being stayed a bit longer.

Mr L was visited again around February 1976. This time the first being was accompanied by a colleague who was similarly dressed but was a few inches shorter in height. According to Mr L's testimony, the beings had ashen grey-coloured faces which were longer and larger than a normal face. They both had a long nose along with long thin lips. The narrow eyes of the beings had pupils like those of a cat and they only had four digits on each hand.

Mr L felt the same feeling of intense joy and warmth but this time something seemed to be troubling the beings. He asked what was the matter. In response they showed him a piece of U-tubing six inches (15cm) by a quarter inch (0.6cm) wide. As it was only a piece of plastic hosing he said that he thought it would be easy to repair. In many contact cases a UFO is seen being repaired by aliens, and of course there are plenty of stories of UFOs crashing to Earth.

They then asked him if he would like to see their craft. He replied in the positive and was asked to lay flat on his bed. One of the beings knelt beside the bed and told Mr L that he should relax and that he would be able to move after a few seconds. Mr L experienced a tingling feeling all over his body and then found he could not move. After that, he found himself floating up into space. However, he felt that his physical body was still on the bed.

A few seconds later he discovered that he was underneath the craft of his two visitors. He described the craft as looking like an inverted bathtub enveloped in a golden glow, like that created by a fluorescent light tube which doesn't spark properly. His entry into the craft was through the middle of its underside.

The next thing he knew he was on a table in a large room. He felt anaesthetised. Above him was a large eye-like structure, which was coloured red/purple. This structure appeared to be examining him. Around him stood eight beings in groups of two.

At this point in his story the investigators found that Mr L became vague. He could not recall what occurred with any great clarity, and the witness himself felt that hypnosis might help his memory. He did remember asking them questions, such as who are they, why they were here, and why he was chosen? He could only remember one answer to his questions. His question was "Who was the Alpha and Omega in the Bible?" The beings replied by saying something like: "An insignificant being such as a worm should not ask such questions. A thousand of your years are but a day to us."

Mr L then found himself back on his bed. Beside him were the same two beings as before. Again, they said he would not be able to move. The tingling or pins and needles sensation returned to him. At this juncture the two beings said "goodbye" and suddenly disappeared. Gradually the tingling feeling wore off and in five minutes he was able to move again. Since that date he had no more contacts.

After this experience, Mr L became nervous and he thought that parts of the event were absent from his memory. He also experienced some physical after-effects. He had a pain in his abdomen and a pain at the base of his skull just behind his right ear. He also had hot flushes. When asked how he felt inside the craft, he said that he was terribly frightened. He wanted to return home, but instead he told the beings "I want to stay". Mr L had no known psychiatric history. The psychiatrist (who accompanied Trevor Whitaker on a visit to Mr L) thought that he had been experiencing hypnogogic hallucinations. This was partly based on the testimony of Mr L's wife who was present during these alleged events and confirmed that he appeared to be asleep during his "contacts". This type of experience is known as an abduction by ufologists, but it is more reasonable to regard it as an example of sleep paralysis.

Aveley

A similar case is the Aveley encounter incident experienced by Mr John Avis, and his wife, Mrs Elaine Avis, (both pseudonyms) and their three children. On 27 October 1974, they had been driving home when at approximately 10 p.m. they saw a UFO following their car. On the road that goes to Aveley, Essex, they encountered a dense green coloured patch of fog. The occupants of the car became unconscious and when they awoke, they found that they had "lost" something like two hours 40 minutes. Over the next few months, the two adults (nothing was reported about the children's reactions to the encounter) kept having strange dreams, which seemed to indicate what had happened when they had been in the green mist.

Eventually John Avis was hypnotically regressed, and a story about them being inside a UFO and meeting with the UFO occupants emerged. Whilst inside the UFO, John recalled how he looked down from a balcony at his car which contained himself and his family. The details of the case are too numerous to describe here but the whole experience seems subjective in nature.

I know one ufologist who totally believed this encounter was an objective meeting with space people of a highly evolved species; and the creatures he attributed to being the "missing links" of human evolution. When I pointed out that the whole story came from no more than dreams and the result of hypnotic regression, he became evasive and angry. Indeed, the encounter with the green mist might not have been an objective experience, but an integral part of their dreams.

The Avises admitted that they had seen a TV programme featuring Joyce Bowles and Ted Pratt, who were driving along the A752 on 14 November 1976, when their car veered to a halt. They saw three entities looking at them through the window of a cigar-shaped object, followed by the exit of a silver suited humanoid from the craft. The bearded entity with long blond hair looked inside their car and then disappeared, after which they were able to drive off. Joyce claimed that she was psychic, had poltergeist activity in the home and suffered a rash on her face after the encounter.

Miss Z

Another case that fits the hallucinatory mould, and has elements which compare with the Aveley story, is the account given by a 16-year-old girl who went under the pseudonym of Miss Z. Peter Rogerson and John Rimmer, both on the editorial team of *Magonia* magazine, interviewed Miss Z and her family in October 1973.

All the incidents took place in the home of Miss Z and her family: a terraced house located in a suburb of a town near Manchester. On the night of the 4 October 1968, Miss Z retired to bed at about 11 p.m. In the early hours of the morning of the fifth she awoke with a strange feeling. After looking about her bedroom and finding no reason for her feeling, she heard a high-pitched whirring sound. She tried to get back to sleep and apparently succeeded. However, she awoke again to find herself paralysed. Naturally she was alarmed, and a few moments later she heard the whirring sound again. This time she was confronted by three figures in shiny silver suits.

The figures had no eyes or mouth or any normal facial features. Instead, their faces were covered completely with shapeless lumps which tended to indicate a sort of face. They were about normal human height, but she couldn't recollect seeing any arms or legs. The three figures were just a general humanoid shape.

Her paralysis vanished after seeing the figures. Two of the figures moved towards her bed and this was when she noticed the lumps on their faces. She thought that one of the lumps corresponded to the position of the human nose, otherwise the lumps were quite random in distribution.

After a few moments, the two figures beside the bed turned around and walked to a craft which Miss Z now observed in the corner of her room.

This craft, however, appeared to be too large for the space it could realistically occupy. The craft was bell or circular shaped and glowed. This illumination shone some light onto the suits of the figures, but it didn't lighten the gloomy bedroom.

Steps led up to an opening in the side of the craft and the two figures joined their colleague who had remained at the bottom of the steps during the encounter. Then the three beings climbed the steps to the craft. There was no doorway in the side of the craft, so when the figures reached the top of the steps, they literally shrunk from view at a fast rate down a long corridor into the UFO.

Once the figures had entered the craft, it simply went upwards, disappearing through the ceiling of the bedroom. During her encounter, Miss Z had the feeling that the beings wanted her to come with them, but she felt no compulsion to go along with this desire. After the craft had gone, she shouted for her mother and told her what occurred.

Besides this meeting, Miss Z also had several OOBEs. During these experiences she felt that part of her was travelling elsewhere. A few months after being interviewed in October 1973, Miss Z woke to the sound of a buzzing noise which grew louder, went away, and then came back. Then she found herself paralysed and she saw the apparition of a young man's face which vanished like the picture on a television set.

Other experiences described by Miss Z include a precognitive dream and an early (pre-1968) experience of waking up in bed and seeing a glowing cross above her. Miss Z's mother revealed that on several occasions whilst awake in bed, she has seen a series of old wrinkled faces. These were presented to her like projected slides. The faces appeared very old, and their lips moved as if they were trying to speak.

The father of Miss Z also reported having had some strange experiences. On one occasion he awoke to find tiny midgets with patchy faces riding about his bedroom on tiny horses. Another time he awoke and saw about a dozen silver-suited, normal looking men in the bedroom.

Miss Z, her father and her grandmother have also seen various other apparitions. In the early 1950s Miss Z's brother, whom we shall call Mr Z, saw a UFO. As a boy he was walking down the alley next to the Z family's house when he saw a white object cross the sky at a low altitude.

In the August and September of 1968 Mr Z, who was by now married and had moved from the Z family's terraced house, wrote several letters to the national press about UFOs. Not long afterwards in late September Mr Z's milkman reported that he had been approached by a man with an Irish accent who made enquiries about Mr Z and his wife. The man drove a large red car which he had parked at the end of the road.

Two weeks later the milkman saw the same car parked at the end of the road, but this time no approach was made. Mr Z and his wife were worried by this as there was no reason for such enquiries. This implied alien Men in Black or government agents were keeping an eye on them.

Last of all Mr Z answered his telephone one Sunday lunch time in 1971, when for ten seconds he heard two women having an angry exchange in an unknown language, then the voices cut-out.

We can explain the main events in the Z story as the perception of little understood hallucinatory experiences, but the addition of strange visitors and telephone callers introduces a sinister twist to these stories.

The percipients involved in the Aveley incident also reported seeing strange visitors who followed them constantly in three different cars for a period of about nine months after their encounter with the green mist.

From the kind of evidence accumulated it is not surprising that many ufologists believe that there is some kind of Government cover-up of the answer to the UFO puzzle. The stories of mysterious strangers and general harassment might reinforce this viewpoint, but if such activities were being carried out, surely the Government would pursue them in a more subtle manner. Probably the answer lies in the fact that these witnesses are being plagued by cranks or that they are interpreting too much into nothing more than coincidental events.

Notes and References

Rodney Stewart's story is contained in: Werff, Dirk Van Der, "UFOs... By Appointment!" *MUFOB*, New Series, No. 15, Summer 1979, pp. 14–15.

Williamson, George Hunt. *Other Tongues – Other Flesh*, Neville Spearman, London, 1969 (orig. Pub. 1953).

Rimmer, John. "Facts, Fraud and Fairytales," *MUFOB*, New Series No. 9, Winter 1977–1978, pp. 3–6.

The experiences of Mr L are featured in: "Contact Experience Claimed in West Yorkshire," *Northern UFO News*, No. 27, August 1976, pp. 7–8.

Collins, Andrew. "The Aveley Abduction: Part 1 and Part 2," *Flying Saucer Review*, Vol. 23, No. 6, April 1978, pp. 13–25. Part 3 is contained in *Flying Saucer Review*, Vol. 24, No 1., June 1978, pp. 5–15.

Rogerson, Peter and Rimmer, John. "Visions of the Night," *MUFOB*, New Series, No. 4, Autumn 1976, pp. 3–6 and p. 2.

Basterfield, Keith. "Strange Awakenings," *MUFOB*, New Series, No. 13, Winter 1978–79, pp. 3–7.

Chapter Eleven

Angelic Visions

There is a reflective element to Paul Bennett's sighting of the Sigma angel-type phenomenon. In 1976, *MUFOB* published an article of mine on the very subject of winged creatures. It is very doubtful indeed that Paul has ever seen this article, and other than talking about his own observations, I have not discussed the subject of winged beings with Paul at all.

Just before, and not long after Paul's series of Sigma angel observations at the end of 1977 early 1978, I dealt with several cases which involved this kind of phenomenon.

On 1 August 1977, Roger Hebb and I interviewed Roger's maternal grandmother. We found out that she has long been a member of the Spiritualist Church and throughout the years she has observed and experienced many aspects of the unknown. The transcript of the relevant part of our dialogue with her is as follows (note: G. = Roger's grandmother, who prefers to remain anonymous):

R.H. "What's this you were telling me once, you reckoned you saw an angel."

G. "Oh, yes, I did. I did actually see that. It was one of our neighbours and they were real chapel people, well of course chapel people don't believe in Spiritualism at all. And so of course I wouldn't say anything to her but anyway I went up to see her husband and I saw this angel dangling just about that (she indicated a height of about 2 feet [0.6m.] with her hands – N.W.) from his head."

N.W. "And was he ill?"

G. "Yes."

R.H. "He was on his deathbed or something?"

G. "Yes, and, well they didn't know that. And anyway, I went downstairs and I said, 'if I was you I don't think I should leave your husband for tonight' you see, but I daren't tell them I'd seen this angel. And he was a really religious man, like. I mean he was really a good chapel man; he wouldn't miss a service or anything and he passed away at two o'clock."

N.W. "In the morning?"

G. "Yes, and I couldn't settle down. I got my thoughts with him all the time, because I had been in and sat with him sometimes you see, to let her go or anything."

R.H. "What did it look like, did it look like an angel?"

G. "Oh yes, it was all in white with wings you know."

In an earlier chapter, Norman Harrison mentions having powerful mental impressions from an extraterrestrial who is associated with the name MIK-AEL or MICHAEL. He wears chain mail and a white tunic which has a red cross on it, and Norman believes he is some kind of guardian angel. It is worth repeating that he said: "He's like a Crusader but the helmet is rather strange it's a funny helmet it completely conceals the features, you can't make out the face it's like a – its [sic] not an ordinary visor – but its [sic] a solid, transparent sort of a plate with a division in the middle..."

This can be compared to Paul's description of his angel's helmet which "had two large vertical slits in it and these gave the impression of eyes".

It is interesting that the two archetypal figures, the Crusader and Angel, should be given astronautical connections. Many UFO writers have speculated that biblical angels were in fact extraterrestrials and a Canadian, the Reverend Wipprecht, has claimed that "the Bible's description of angels fits 'intelligent beings' from other planets". Both Norman and Paul have read the Bible and are familiar with such books as Erich von Daniken's *Miracles of the Gods*, which promote astronaut/angel theories.

Traditionally angels are regarded as personal guardians, and important message carriers between God and mankind, so it is not too surprising they are now placed into the context of alien visitations today.

The highly respected UFO researcher Hilary Evans, in the 1980s, investigated the case of 12-year-old Glenda who lived in Dagenham. Besides having a number of paranormal experiences, she met an extravagantly dressed, humanoid "spacewoman" in her bedroom, that she described as being "like something you see on television". The woman appeared to her over the next five years, either as an unseen presence or in her dreams. None of her family saw the being, and it seemed to take an intense interest in her well-being and gave her advice. Hilary could only compare it with, if we forget the stereotypical images of an angel, with a benevolent form of Guardian Angel. We should note that when Paul Bennett had his bicycle accident, he felt that the presence of UFOs had helped him quickly recover, and had acted like his own personal guardians.

To add one more "coincidence" to this section, I should mention a UFO report I received on 8 April 1978. From Great Coates Road, Grimsby, a person saw, on the nights of the 21 and 29 March 1978, a light at a great distance hovering not far above the horizon. The most interesting aspect of this sighting being that the witness was located on both occasions close to St Michael's Church, Grimsby. This report came quite unexpectedly from somebody unknown to me, who must have obtained my address from a UFO magazine or local newspaper.

On the very day I typed this section, a colleague of mine at work told me how he had come into conversation, the day before, with a blind man who had served in World War I and World War II. During the conversation the man told my colleague, Robin Witting, that he had actually seen the Angels of Mons whilst fighting in World War I.

An angelic type, male alien called Parz, who wore "wings" on his shoulder visited the family in north Wales, It is significant that exactly one year after Paul Bennett's Sigma sightings, on 4 January 1979, a witness in Rowley Regis, near Birmingham, saw a landed UFO in her backyard. Three beings with wings appeared from the direction of the craft. Like Paul's sightings of the angel, these beings were silver-coloured and had lines of light projecting from them. The witness, Mrs Jean Hingley, offered them mince pies that were left over from the Christmas celebrations, which they took back with them to their craft.

At this time Paul's experiences had not been published, and were not widely known, so Mrs Hingley could not possibly have invented her story to match Paul's angelic encounters. To further complicate matters, Whitley Strieber, in his book *Transformation*, describes an encounter with an angelic being on the night of 30 May 1986. All he can remember of the being was that it was dressed in white and had piercing blue eyes – like Paul, he could not remember any other facial characteristics of the being. The visitor told Whitley not to eat sweets and predicted that in three months' time he would take one journey that would lead to death or another that would secure his survival. Four months later he faced having to take such a journey and he, like Paul, survived the ordeal.

Rocketing forwards a few decades, Dr D.W. Pasulka, who is professor of religious studies at the University of North Carolina, in her book *Encounters: Experiences with Nonhuman Intelligences*, notes even more St Michael experiences, encounters and coincidences that mirror those I mention above.

She tells the story of scientist "Gray Man" who woke up to see a powerful male figure with long shining yellow hair a few inches above him. He said it was almost like coming face-to-face with an angel or God. Time became blurred and he found himself outside his bed in a place where the angel gave him weapons and armour to fight a shape-changing black figure shrouded in thick dark smoke. Using a sword, he defeated the figure, and the angel was happy. After this, he woke up and felt the whole experience was very real, and it gave him great comfort.

Pasulka immediately identified this angel as Saint Michael and told him that this angel is known for being the guardian of children and helps lead souls to the afterlife. Then the coincidences started. A week after interviewing the Gray Man, Pasulka received a set of paintings of Saint Michael from another scientist, and in the same week her local church erected a statue of Saint Michael in their garden. On going to a meeting in a child therapist's office, she saw another statue of Saint Michael on a shelf behind the desk. The therapist said she often spoke to the statue, and it guided her in her work.

Although being aware of philosopher Friedrich Nietzsche's view that such coincidences are just striking plays of chance rather than the act of God or any other form of divine entity, Pasulka notes: "Synchronicity is often the engine of spiritual and religious belief as it seems to confirm (the) practitioner's own religious or spiritual tendencies." Yet, she is drawn to the view that they are a strong component of "everyone's reality" especially to those who are open-minded.

Believing in UFOs is, according to Pasulka, a "nascent religiosity".

Just to add to the Michael factor, in her 2024 book, *Mystic Visions*, the Rev Alyson Dunlop Shanes mentions encountering him and that he is a powerful protective force. On one occasion she called upon him for help when she could not fix her smoke alarm, and in response he physically guided her to fix it. She suggests using St Michael's Prayer as protection if you are confronted by the powers of darkness:

"St. Michael the Archangel, defend us in battle.

Be our protection against the wickedness and snares of the Devil.

May God rebuke him we humbly pray;

and do thou, O Prince of the Heavenly host,

by the power of God, cast into Hell Satan and all the evil spirits who prowl about the world seeking the ruin of souls. Amen."

We Are Doomed?

In the accounts of alien encounters in this book, it is apparent that the percipients involved hold the view that something dramatic in the future will occur which will profoundly affect the whole of humanity. The collection of quotes below emphasises this point:

Sooner or later someone must hand in, the true piece of evidence to show the world that UFOs actually do exist.

The ufonauts are much too clever and sensible to land en masse. Maybe they will appear in the skies in massive numbers, or do something outrageous like kidnapping the Whitehouse!

Paul Bennett

I am notified that a final terrible war will definitely take place... and pollution poisoning will soon endanger all vegetation and animal species of the globe.

Norman Harrison

We will no longer need the habitation of this planet, but will be free to come and go as we choose, pure in Spirit and Mind. This will be the future of mankind, when all will exist peaceably.

Josephine Elissah

All these statements indicate an idealistic desire for the destruction of the evil and corrupt elements of humanity, and a wish for a new beginning. Indeed, they indicate that chaos and destruction is the ultimate fate for most of us, though the UFO pilots represent the heavenly saviours who offer salvation to the chosen few. As a consequence, it is not surprising that such percipients are attracted to the millennial visions of the Book of Revelations. Despite this the philosophy of these percipients, particularly Josephine Elissah's, are like those of the heretical Christian Gnostics, whose texts were widely circulated in the first and second centuries AD.

One such gnostic text, the Gospel of Thomas, contains the enigmatic statement that: "Jesus said, 'If you bring forth what is within you, what you bring forth will save you. If you do not bring forth what is within you, what you do not bring forth will destroy you.'"

The decline of the power of Christianity in the twentieth century, has meant that the spiritual needs of man have been neglected, and the unorthodox beliefs have been able to emerge.

The unconscious, spontaneous images of our minds reveal fantastic allegorical visions which have a powerful influence on our lives. But is this enough to explain why we have close encounters and UFO related experiences?

Notes and References

Watson, Nigel. "Winged Creatures," *MUFOB*, New Series, No. 4, Autumn 1976, p. 11.

Evans, Hilary. *From Other Worlds*, Carlton, London, 1998, p. 185.

Strieber, Whitley. *Transformation: The Breakthrough*, William Morrow & Co, New York, 1988.

Pasulka, D.W. *Encounters: Experiences with Nonhuman Intelligences*, St Martin's Essentials, New York, 2023, pp. 62–76.

Shanes, Rev. Alyson Dunlop. *Mystic Visions: Spontaneous Supernatural Visions*, Flying Disk Press, West Yorkshire, 2024, p. 142.

Pagels, Dr Elaine, *The Gnostic Gospels*, Weidenfeld and Nicolson, London, 1980.

Fletcher, John. "Lo! He Comes in Clouds Descending," *Magonia*, No. 1, Autumn 1979, pp. 3–8.

Cohn, Norman. *The Pursuit of the Millennium*, Granada, St. Albans, 1970.

Chapter Twelve

A Combination of Factors

To some ufologists who have abandoned the extraterrestrial hypothesis, the realms of the parapsychological have become a haven. Parapsychological evidence is reinforced by reference to poltergeist phenomena which is alleged to occur through the subconscious agency of adolescent children or emotionally disturbed people, who use this outlet to vent their pent-up desires and frustrations.

Almost invariably, witnesses to a close encounter report experiencing paranormal events after their primary close encounter. The psychoanalyst Carl Jung was one of the first to delve into the mysteries of our hidden nature and discovered the concept of the archetype. He found that the themes of worldwide myths, legends and fairy tales, which also relate to UFO encounters, were similar in nature, and that the same motifs emerged in the dreams and fantasies of modern-day humanity. This could explain how the individuals examined in this book could experience, independently, visions which relate to each other and to millennial and gnostic belief systems.

Fantasy Proneness

More down-to-earth theories have included the concept of fantasy proneness. This asserts that some people are more prone to confusing what is real with their own private fantasies. In a 1983 study by Wilson and Barber they noted that fantasy prone people:

> As children, they interacted with fantasised people or animals, clearly seeing, hearing and feeling them in the same way as they perceived living people and animals.

They see (imagined) sights equally well with their eyes open or closed, imagined aromas are sensed, imagined sounds are heard, imagined tactile sensations are felt convincingly. Almost all have vivid sexual fantasies that they experience 'as real as real' with all the sights, sounds, smells, emotions, feelings, and physical sensations, so realistic that 75% report that they have had orgasms produced solely by sexual fantasies.

Those who have alleged UFO experiences and abductions have been found to be easily suggestible and the late Dr Alvin Lawson pointed out that people can easily fantasise under hypnosis. In Britain BUFORA banned the use of hypnosis as it was felt it is an unethical method that does not necessarily recall real events. Nonetheless, some ufologists seem to regard hypnosis as the ultimate interrogation technique. Charles Bowen the editor of *Flying Saucer Review*, for example, defended such methods because such fantasy might be part of a "planned deception".

However, if we accept this kind of criteria, anything which is disagreeable or contrary to the UFO doctrine, can be dismissed as being part of their deception tactics.

False Memories

A University of Washington study showed that our memories of past events are incredibly malleable and highly unreliable. At a presentation of the findings at Glasgow University it was noted that: "In some sense, life is a continual memory alteration experiment where memories are continually shaped by new incoming information."

To prove this hypothesis Jacquie Pickrell, a doctoral candidate in psychology, and Elizabeth Loftus, a professor of psychology, presented a group with an advert showing Bugs Bunny shaking hands with visitors to Disney World. Later 30%

of the viewers remembered meeting Bugs Bunny at Disney World when they were children. As anyone with any knowledge of animation knows Bugs Bunny is not a Disney character and has never appeared in a Disney theme park. Pickrell concluded: "You can truly implant a memory for an entire event that never happened."

This work shows that people can be convinced (some would say tricked) into believing they experienced something in childhood or in the past that did not really happen. In terms of ufology the implications of this work are profound. In the literature there are hundreds of accounts of people who remember UFO sightings and alien encounters in childhood or many years ago, but never reported such experiences at the time.

Sleep Paralysis

Rather than being the product of false memories Dr Susan Blackmore regards sleep paralysis as the main explanation for alien abductions. This experience can occur in the stage between wakefulness and sleep and is a self-generated hypnogogic hallucination. A hypnopompic hallucination is of a similar nature but is experienced in the intermediate state between sleep and wakefulness. These types of sleep paralysis hallucinations are quite common.

This concept was first highlighted by David Hufford in his book *The Terror that Comes in the Night* when he found that people in different geographical, historical and cultural settings have experienced something called the "Old Hag" or "bedroom invader". It has been given different names, and today in our culture it usually involves alien entities.

Blackmore describes typical sleep paralysis as "waking up" to find yourself as the name suggests paralyzed. You might hear strange buzzing sounds, see strange lights and feel terrified about an undefined presence. An entity might appear, sometimes it might be invisible, to sit on your chest or to strangle and prod you. It is even more frightening because it is very difficult to fight the paralysis and the experiences are very intense and realistic.

If the person is not aware that they are undergoing a sleep paralysis experience the perceptions of lights, buzzing and the appearance of an entity can be interpreted in the form of an alien abduction encounter. In this state, knowledge of aliens from TV, films and other media can help shape their recollection of the experience. When the person is hypnotised, their experience is more likely to fit the expected abduction scenario.

These experiences have been interpreted differently throughout history and in different cultural contexts. The perception of demons and the incubus and succubus that have sexual intercourse with their victims are regarded as classic examples of sleep paralysis.

The argument against this and similar psychological explanations is that abductions do not just take place in homes, they occur whilst people are awake driving on highways or whilst taking part in other outside pursuits. Sleep paralysis does not have the sequence of events reported by abductees nor do they have the same sense of realism or emotional charge.

Undermining this argument is the study by Spanos et al. that found many abduction experiences occurred at night, and of these 60 per cent were sleep related. Almost a quarter of them could be regarded as symptomatic of sleep paralysis. In a group of six abductees Cox found that they experienced more sleep paralysis than the control groups. These studies involve only a few subjects, but it is clear that most abduction experiences that occur in the bedrooms or homes of abductees are triggered by sleep paralysis.

The work of Dr Jorge Conesa confirms that sleep paralysis (SP) can involve vividly experiencing floating, going through tunnels, seeing lights and hearing noises. Furthermore, these types of experiences can be triggered by anxiety, tiredness and sleep deprivation making it common in shift workers, truck drivers, hospital workers and other people who work long and odd hours. Conesa also suggests that geomagnetic activity might trigger SP experiences, and that birth trauma memories might shape the imagery of those who interpret their SP experience in terms of an alien abduction. He also indicates that these experiences run through families and that people can learn to use SP to have out of the body experiences, lucid dreams and shamanic journeys.

Additional Factors

In addition to fantasy proneness, false memories and sleep paralysis, other psychological factors have been considered, these include: Mental Illness, Psychological trauma, Abuse, Masochism, Birth trauma, Misperception and Misinterpretation, Sensory Deprivation, Hallucinations, Auto Hypnosis, Subliminal Peripheral Vision Psychosis, Fabrication and Exaggerations, Temporal Lobe Epilepsy, Electronic Pollution and Exposure to Earthlight plasma. These factors are also conditioned by our culture, society, myths, beliefs, peer pressures, and preconceptions.

What lends credence to the importance of these psychological factors is that there is a distinct lack of objective physical evidence.

In the face of these complex interactions ufologists easily dismiss them as attempts at sceptical debunking that spoils their belief in UFOs as spaceships, non-terrestrial craft, inter-dimensional vehicles, mental projections, time machines or some other science-fiction themed concept with little or no proof. Who cares when countless TV documentaries are willing to promote such ideas?

Instead of this gung-ho approach, each case should be examined on its own merits. Only when or if plausible explanations are exhausted should parapsychological, extraterrestrial or any of the other exotic paradigms be considered.

Trigger Points

The following points have a bearing on how and why UFO experiences might be caused, experienced and reported:

1. Misinterpretation of normal celestial or aerial phenomena, and psychological embellishment.
2. Rare meteorological or geophysical phenomena.
3. Percipient expectations and illusions.
4. The preconceptions and prejudices of UFO investigators.
5. Alien abduction experiences recalled under hypnotic regression.
6. False memories.
7. Hallucinatory experiences and states of altered consciousness which can be induced by meditation, lack of stimulation, hunger, illness and drugs.
8. Sleep paralysis.
9. Neurosis and other pathological states of mind.
10. Delusions, caused by the percipient's need to externalise their feelings into the real world.
11. Pure invention, as a means of gaining status and attention for one's own views.
12. Fantasy proneness.
13. The influence of the media, science fiction and other UFO reports and stories.
14. Personal trauma and stress.
15. The social context where outside events can seem overwhelming and threatening, requiring the need for extraterrestrial salvation.
16. Physical evidence is "found" by the process of attributing meaning to coincidental phenomena or by parapsychological means.

17. Aliens, time travellers or visitors from other dimensions could be responsible if all other factors are eliminated.

A combination in varying degrees, of the above causes is evident in nearly all the cases we have examined, and this has led to the apparent complexity of the UFO subject. The list is by no means exhaustive, but it is a fair indication of the areas we should be studying if we are to achieve a greater understanding of what we collectively term the UFO experience.

It should be noted, however, that UFO percipients and witnesses even if given a very plausible and mundane explanation for their experience are not always convinced. Susan Clancey author of *Abducted: How People Come to Believe They Were Kidnapped by Aliens*, said:

> I can tell you most of them that have read the book are upset. I have to be honest with that. And I understand why, because what's happening in the book is I am presenting my own opinion, but I'm challenging their deeply held beliefs, beliefs that are very important to them. So they're angry, and I feel terribly about it.

Genesis of a Percipient

From what we have studied so far, we can demonstrate the genesis of a UFO percipient. The following listing is skeletal because of the many varying factors involved in a person's life, but it does give an indication of the primary factors which contribute towards UFO experiences.

1. The percipient experiences often at an early age a UFO sighting, a sighting of an apparition or has a similar kind of unusual encounter, caused by the trigger points noted in the previous section.

2. The percipient because of an initial experience reads a great deal and seeks information about UFOs and the paranormal.
3. After a suitable gestation period the percipient has a close encounter experience or similar kind of dramatic experience, which has a profound effect on their life.
4. After the prime encounter, the percipient might not have any more UFO or paranormal experiences.
5. After the prime encounter, the percipient begins to have more encounters and paranormal experiences which are even more subjective in nature.
6. The percipient receives a cosmic philosophy and new concepts.
7. The percipient starts to collect a cult following, as in the case of Adamski and many other contactees.
8. The percipient carries on having experiences and becomes a UFO investigator or a silent contactee who does not look for publicity or followers.
9. The percipient stops taking any interest in UFOs or related subjects because of a fear of insanity or mental instability, or fears the experiences are of an evil origin.

The cases examined in this book do not supply any objective proof for the existence of any kind of physical extra-mundane vehicles darting about in our skies, but they do prove the fundamental influence and impact this phenomenon has on us.

Rather than manipulate the evidence to support any hypothesis, I've attempted to illustrate the many hidden facets of the UFO experience, and I've considered some rationalistic psychological and sociological explanations along the way. Such speculation is not as exciting as a contemplation of the wonders of the Universe and the millions of life forms living within it, but considering the bizarre nature of the UFO phenomenon, a pragmatic approach based on the merits of each individual case is perhaps the safest and wisest way to avoid the pitfalls which can cloud our understanding of this phenomena.

Notes and References

J Jung, Carl Gustav, *Flying Saucers: A Modern Myth Things Seen in the Sky*, Routledge & Kegan Paul, Oxon, 2002; (orig. pub. 1958).

Jung, Carl Gustav. *Memories, Dreams, Reflections*, Collins and Routledge & Kegan Paul, London, 1963.

Wilson, S. C., and Barber, T. X. "The fantasy-prone personality: Implications for understanding imagery, hypnosis, and parapsychological phenomena," in A. A. Sheikh (Ed.), *Imagery: Current theory, research, and application*, New York, Wiley, 1983, pp. 340–390.

Lawson, Alvin H. "What Can We Learn from Hypnosis of Imaginary 'Abductees?'" California State University, English Dept., May 1977.

Bowen, Charles, "The Validity of Investigations Under Hypnosis," *Flying Saucer Review*, Vol. 24, No. 1, June 1978, p. 2.

"False-memory study recruits Bugs," UPI Archives, 11 June 2001, at: https://www.upi.com/Archives/2001/06/11/False-memory-study-recruits-Bugs/7823992232000/

Blackmore, Susan. "Abduction by Aliens or Sleep Paralysis?" *Skeptical Inquirer*, Vol.22, No. 3, May/June 1998, pp. 23–28, at: https://skepticalinquirer.org/1998/05/abduction-by-aliens-or-sleep-paralysis/

Hufford, David J. *The Terror that Comes in the Night: An Experience-Centered Study of Supernatural Assault Traditions*, University of Pennsylvania Press, Philadelphia, 1982.

Spanos, N. P. Cross, P.A., Dickson, K. and DuBreuil, S. C. "Close encounters: An examination of UFO experiences," *Journal of Abnormal Psychology*, No. 102, 1993, pp. 624–632.

Cox, M. *The prevalence of sleep paralysis and temporal lobe lability in persons who report alien abduction,* Unpublished thesis, University of the West of England, Department of Psychology, 1995.

Conesa, Dr. Jorge. *Wrestling with Ghosts: A Personal and Scientific Account of Sleep Paralysis,* Xlibris Corporation, Bloomington, Indiana, 2004.

Clancy, Susan. *Abducted: How People Come to Believe They Were Kidnapped by Aliens,* Harvard University Press, Cambridge, Mass., 2005.

Author Biography

Nigel Watson has researched and investigated historical and contemporary reports of UFO sightings since the 1970s.

He writes a monthly column "Saucers of the Damned" about UFOs for *Fortean Times* and regularly writes book reviews for the *pelicanist* blogspot. He has regularly contributed to *Magonia, All About Space, Starburst, Aquila, History Today, Fate, Flying Saucer Review, UFO Brigantia, Northern UFO News, The Unexplained, Paranormal Magazine, UFO Magazine* and *Outer Limits Magazine*. He has contributed to the *Darklore* anthology series and to several books edited by the late Timothy Green Beckley. For *The Reliability of UFO Witness Testimony*, edited by V.J. Ballester-Olmos and Richard W. Heiden, (UPIAR Publisher, Italy, 2023) he contributed a chapter on the Betty and Barney Hill abduction case, available at:

https://www.academia.edu/101922617/The_Reliability_of_UFO_Witness_Testimony

He has a degree in film and literature from the University of Warwick and a degree in psychology from the Open University.

Nigel worked as a copywriter in London and now lives in Plymouth, UK.

Previous Titles

Phantom Aerial Flaps and Waves, Magonia, London, 1987.

The 1912–1913 British Phantom Airship Scare with Granville Oldroyd and David Clarke, Fund for UFO Research, Mount Rainier, Washington, D.C., 1988.

The 1912–1913 British Phantom Airship Scare Catalogue with Granville Oldroyd and David Clarke, Fund for UFO Research, Mount Rainier, Washington, D.C., 1988.

Phantom Helicopters over Britain. A Review of the 1973-1974 Scare and an Overview of the Phantom Helicopter Phenomena, with David Clarke, Fund for UFO Research, Mount Rainier, Washington, D.C., 1990.

Portraits of Alien Encounters, VALIS Books, London, 1990.

Seeing and Believing: UFOs and Aliens in Film and TV, VALIS Books, London, 1991.

Supernatural Spielberg, VALIS Books, London, 1992.

The Scareship Mystery, editor, DOMRA publications, Corby, 2000.

Flying Saucer Cinema, Selfhelpguides.com, 2007.

The Origin of UFOs: Phantom Airships 1807 to 1917, Selfhelpguides.com, 2007.

The Alien Deception, YouWriteOn.com, UK, 2009.

UFO Investigations Manual: UFO Investigations from 1892 to the Present Day, Haynes, Yeovil, UK, 2013.

The Great UFO Cover-Up, UneXplained Rapid Reads, Windmill Books, London, 2015.

UFO Government Secrets, UneXplained Rapid Reads, Windmill Books, London, 2015.

UFOs: The Nazi Connection, UneXplained Rapid Reads, Windmill Books, London, 2015.

Ghostships of the Skies, UneXplained Rapid Reads, Windmill Books, London, 2015.

Spontaneous Human Combustion, UneXplained Rapid Reads, Windmill Books, 2015.

UFOs of the First World War: Phantom Airships, Balloons, Aircraft and Other Mysterious Aerial Phenomena, History Press, Stroud, Gloucestershire, 2015.

Captured by Aliens? A History and Analysis of American Abduction Claims, McFarland, Jefferson, North Carolina, 2020. dedicated to the memory of Peter Rogerson and has a foreword by him. It looks at the Betty and Barney Hill case in the context of other abductions and factors that might have caused it.

Fortean Times Presents: The UFO Files, with Jenny Randles, Diamond Publishing, London, 2024.

Note to the Reader

I can be contacted at NigelwatsonXL5@gmail.com

Or see my Facebook page: https://www.facebook.com/UFOInvestigationsManual

Appendices

Appendix 1

A Safe Home for UFO Files

In the past nearly everyone who had more than a superficial interest in UFOs collected UFO, astronomy, space exploration and paranormal books, magazines, videos, audio cassettes and document files. Such collections have the sneaky ability to find room in any unoccupied space until they take over your home if you're not careful.

I'm not as bad as some ufologists who have accumulated thousands of books, but it is still a problem. The thought of letting these hard-won collections go is difficult, but if we don't do something with them, they are likely to end up in a skip after we've met the grim reaper. A fate that has already happened to many collections.

The answer is to donate to a UFO archive. One of the biggest in Europe is the Archives for the Unexplained (AFU) based in Norrköping, Sweden. Clas Svahn and his team of helpers regularly visit ufologists all over Europe to collect and preserve their works for future generations of ufologists and academics. The objective of this non-profit foundation is also to support, promote and conduct UFO research, and to stimulate a critical, scientific discussion about UFOs.

Using twelve locations in Norrköping, the archive houses over 30,000 books and as many periodicals. The library includes 2,000 cases collected by the Swedish armed forces since 1946, and collections of the late Hilary Evans, William Corliss and Gordon Creighton the former editor of *Flying Saucer Review*, and literally boxes of books provided by Peter Rogerson in Manchester and the founding father of *Fortean Times*, Bob Rickard. They have also obtained material from the USA and have shipped three pallets of material obtained from the California based Borderland Sciences Research Associates, who took an early occultist interest in flying saucers. A large quantity of archive material from BUFORA and of the British Contact International group have also been collected and digitised.

When the truck loads of boxes arrive in Sweden, a team of volunteers painstakingly sorts and catalogues it. This is an amazing project that has managed to preserve huge chunks of ufological history and research that provides a valuable resource for anyone interested in UFOs and all aspects of the paranormal.

A few years back I gave copies of my Scunthorpe UFO files to the local library, which I thought was safe until someone told me that the library had been flooded and the files were destroyed. So, I decided to donate most of my files to AFU. In 2016, Carl-Anton and Clas Svahn came to Plymouth to collect my files, unfortunately their car broke down a few miles away and I ended up taking them back to Bob Rickard's home in London. It took Clas a lot of sorting out with his insurance company and the necessity to buy a new car, but at least we had a good chat about UFOs, and I got the chance to meet up with Bob after many years.

Clas chronicles his trip to Plymouth here:
http://csblogg.ufo.se/csblogg3/?m=20160922
and
http://csblogg.ufo.se/csblogg3/?m=20160923

They are always on the lookout for more donations of UFO material and anything else related to paranormal and Fortean topics, and are worth supporting.

More details about their activities, and access to their digitised files can be found on the *Archives for the Unexplained* website:

https://www.afu.se/

Appendix 2

UFO Databases

In contrast to large, unwieldy organisations that can be hard to maintain, barrister Isaac Koi has over the past few years coordinated with individuals and groups to scan a vast amount of UFO literature. Much of this material has been scanned and made available by the Archives For the Unexplained (AFU) and are easily available through Isaac's blog page.

Besides long runs of scanned UFO magazines from throughout the world, Isaac is currently uploading UFO articles from mainstream UK and USA magazines of the late 1940s to 1960s. Having made hundreds of these documents available online, he is now going on to tackle UFO databases and software that can be used to study and make sense of all these archived files. He quotes from the chapter "Computers in Ufology" in *UFOs: 1947–1987*, edited by Hilary Evans John Spencer, Fortean Tomes/BUFORA, London, 1987, p. 245:

> Computers are a powerful tool which properly used will give enormous assistance to ufologists the world over... but it should be recognised from the outset that they alone will not answer the questions. [T]he UFO enigma will not be answered by computers but by the talented and intuitive thinking of human minds.

Since the late 1980s numerous databases and lists of databases have been created. Isaac notes that new database projects often do not take into consideration previous projects and there is the danger of people wasting time reinventing the wheel. Fortunately, many published or online databases do not overlap as much as we might expect, and Isaac intends to create an extensive listing of them. Notable projects in this area is the International Committee for UFO Research database of international UFO reports and Larry Hatch's UFOCAT.

Isaac also notes other databases have been created that could usefully be expanded. These include lists/databases/indexes of different types of Identified Flying Objects (IFOs), bibliographies, government documents, SETI projects, and UFO/ET themed science fiction. Also, there are expert resources, like image analysis software, scanning and digitising software.

So that we can make greater use and sense of all the information that has been exhaustively collected by researchers over several decades, Isaac has created a new UFO database blog to discuss all the issues involved in this ambitious project, including the use of AI software.

Isaac Koi – New Uploads blog at:
https://isaackoiup.blogspot.com
Isaac Koi – UFO Databases blog at:
https://isaackoidata.blogspot.com/

Appendix 3

The Great British UFO Learning Centre

Retired West Midlands police officer John Hanson has spent an enormous amount of time and effort publishing his series of *Haunted Skies* books that cover the history of ufology from 1939 to 1990. The early volumes are a comprehensive review of British UFO cases, which include John's own investigations, news reports and statements from witnesses. The latter volumes feature global sightings, and he has published separate volumes on Wiltshire cases, the Rendlesham Forest Incident and three volumes involving UFOs seen by police officers.

The information for these books has been gathered from ufologists throughout the UK and is all collected in chronological order in 200 files which each contain 200 A4 pages covering the period 1950 to 2017. The archive holds letters; hundreds of photographs; newspaper clippings; scrapbooks and collections from Ron West; Brenda Butler; Isle of Wight UFO information supplied by Kath Smith; and Kent and Staffordshire UFO Group files. With the help of archivist Shirley Edwards, they are still filing papers up to the present date chronologically.

John, in his 20 plus years of UFO research, has also accumulated a good collection of journals, periodicals and correspondence.

All this material is being put together in an accessible manner to form an archive available to UFO researchers.

The Haunted Skies website is at:
https://www.hauntedskies.co.uk/

Magazines and Websites

Magazines

Most print magazines and newsletters are no longer produced or have gone online.

Regular e-magazines are the *Outer Limits Magazine* (OLM) and *Phenomena Magazine*.

Some organisations like ASSAP and BUFORA do produce a few print publications, but the only regular print newsstand magazines are the monthly *Fortean Times* and the quarterly *Haunted Magazine*.

Websites

Here is a selection of websites and blogs that are devoted to UK UFO reports and offer excellent starting points for further reading and research.

The Association for the Scientific Study of Anomalous Phenomena

ASSAP is a British scientifically orientated organisation that investigates all types of anomalies.

https://www.assap.ac.uk/

Birmingham UFO Group

Hosts skywatches, meetings and their website features numerous case investigations and useful links.

https://www.bufog.com/

British UFO Research Association

Has lots of useful links on how to investigate UFO sightings, UFO reports and BUFORA publications.

https://www.bufora.org.uk/

Dr David Clarke: Folklore and Journalism
Contains links to his own UFO reports and to the National Archives UFO Files:
https://drdavidclarke.co.uk/

Flying Saucer Review
This is mainly a site for selling back issues.
http://www.fsr.org.uk/

Fortean Times
Mainly a site for subscribing to the printed *Fortean Times* magazine.
https://subscribe.forteantimes.com/

Haunted Magazine
Contains information about the latest contents and how to subscribe.
https://www.haunteddigitalmagazine.com/2022/11/blog-post.html

The Haunted Skies
News and information about the Haunted Skies books that chronicle the history of British UFO sightings.
https://www.hauntedskies.co.uk/

Ian Ridpath's UFO skeptic pages
Links to classic cases like the Rendlesham Forest Incident and the general state of UFO research.
http://www.ianridpath.com/ufo/ufoindex.html

Lancashire Anomalous Phenomena Investigation Society
Investigates sightings in northwest Britain. The site contains reports on UFOs and other anomalous incidents.
https://www.lapisparanormal.com/

Magonia
The *Magonia* website carries regular book reviews and has links to the *MUFOB* and *Magonia* archives and Peter Rogerson's INTCAT report listing worldwide contact cases.
https://pelicanist.blogspot.com/

Northern UFO News
Gives a history of NUFON and British UFO cases and research.
http://www.ozfactorbooks.com/northern-ufo-news-january-2019.html

Outer Limits Magazine
A monthly e-magazine edited by Chris Evers that covers UFOs and other anomalous phenomena.
https://olmmag.wordpress.com/

Phenomena Magazine
A free monthly e-magazine edited by Steve Mera; the site carries an archive of all their editions in pdf format to download.
https://www.phenomenamagazine.co.uk/

UFO Identified
Contains a database of the latest British UFO sightings, articles and several detailed case reports. The group holds meetings and intends to set up a network of investigators.
https://ufoidentified.co.uk/

UFO reports in the UK
UFO reports 1997 to 2009, showing dates and times, location and a brief description of the sighting.
https://www.gov.uk/government/publications/ufo-reports-in-the-uk

Bibliography

Allingham, Cedric. *Flying Saucer from Mars. The Facts*. Frederick Muller, London, 1954.

Andrews, Ann and Ritchie, Jean. *Abducted: The True Story of Alien Abduction in Rural England*, Headline, London, 1998.

Chapman, Robert. *Unidentified Flying Objects*, Arthur Barker, London, 1969.

Bowen, Charles (ed.). *The Humanoids*, Neville Spearman, London, 1969.

Briggs, Katherine, *A Dictionary of Fairies*, Allen Lane, London, 1976.

Clark, Jerome and Coleman, Loren. *The Unidentified*, Warner, New York, 1975.

Clark, Jerome and Coleman, Loren. *Creatures of the Outer Edge*. Warner, New York, 1978.

Clarke, David and Roberts, Andy. *Phantoms of the Sky*, Robert Hale, London, 1990

Clarke, David. *How UFOs Conquered the World*, Aurum, London, 2015.

Clarke, David. *The UFO Files, The Inside Story of Real-life Sightings*, Bloomsbury, London, 2012.

Devereux, Paul. *Earthlights Revelation*, Blandford, London, 1989.

Dewey, Steve and Ries, John. *In Alien Heat: The Warminster Mystery Revisited*, Anomalist Books, New York, 2005.

Dodd, Tony. *Alien Investigator: The Case Files of Britain's Leading UFO Detective*, Headline, London, 1999.

Downes, Jonathan and Wright, Nigel. *The Rising of the Moon: The Devonshire U.F.O. Triangle*, DOMRA Books, Corby, 1999.

Evans, Hilary. *Visions, Apparitions, Alien Visitors*, Aquarian, Wellingborough, 1984.

Evans, Hilary. *Gods, Spirits, Cosmic Guardians*, Aquarian, Wellingborough, 1987.

Evans, Hilary and Spencer, John (eds). *UFOs 1947–1987*, Fortean Tomes/BUFORA, London, 1987.

Fort, Charles Hoy, *The Complete Books of Charles Fort*, Dover, New York, 1974 (orig. pub. 1919-1932).

Gleaves, Jason (ed.). *UFO Encounters: Up Close & Personal*, Flying Disk Press, West Yorkshire, 2022.

Godfrey, Alan. *Who or What were They?* CMP Digital Print Solution, UK, 2017.

Goodman, Kevin and Dewey, Steve. *UFO Warminster: Cradle of Contact*, Fortean Words, 2012.

Hanson, John and Holloway, Dawn. *Haunted Skies: The History of British UFOs*, several volumes covering the chronology of reports from 1939 onwards, Haunted Skies Publishing, Stratford-on-Avon.

Harold, Clive. *The Uninvited*, Star, London, 1979.

Hendry, Allan. *The UFO Handbook*, Doubleday, New York, 1979.

Hynek, J. Allen. *The UFO Experience*, Regnery, Chicago, 1972.

Jenkins, Stephen. *The Undiscovered Country*, Neville Spearman, Sudbury, 1976.

Kameron, Michael. *High Strangeness: A Lifetime of Alien and Paranormal Experiences*, Flying Disk Press, West Yorkshire, 2023.

Keel, John A. *UFOs: Operation Trojan Horse*, Putnam, New York, 1970.

Keel, John A. *The Cosmic Question*, Panther, London, 1978.

Keyhoe, Donald E. *The Flying Saucers Are Real*, Fawcett, New York, 1950.

Leslie, Desmond, and Adamski, George. *Flying Saucers Have Landed*, Futura, London, revised edition 1977 (orig. pub. 1953).

Michell, John. *The Flying Saucer Vision*, Sidgwick & Jackson, London, 1967.

Mantel, Philip and Nagatis, Carl. *Without Consent, Missing Time and Abduction Phenomena*, Ringpull Press, Poynton, Greater Manchester, U.K., 1994.

Mantel, Philip. *UFO Landings UK*, Flying Disk Press, West Yorkshire, 2020.

Oliver, Norman. *The Isle of Wight Entity Case. AFU Special Case Report Number One*, Flying Disk Press, West Yorkshire, 2024.

Olly, Mark. *Europe's Roswell: 40 Years Since Impact*, Flying Disk Press, West Yorkshire, 2023.

Pugh, Randall Jones and Holiday, Frank. *The Dyfed Enigma*, Faber, London, 1979.

Randles, Jenny and Warrington, Peter. *UFOs, a British Viewpoint*, Robert Hale, London, 1979.

Randles, Jenny. *The Pennine UFO Mystery*, Granada, London, 1983.

Sanderson, Ivan. *Uninvited Visitors*, Tandem, London, 1974.

Saunders, Colin. *Triangular UFOs of the United Kingdom*, Flying Disk Press, West Yorkshire, 2023.

Shanes, Rev. Alyson Dunlop. *Mystic Visions: Spontaneous Supernatural Visions*, Flying Disk Press, West Yorkshire, 2024.

Shuttlewood, Arthur. *The Warminster Mystery*, Neville Spearman, London, 1967.

Stanway, Roger H. and Pace, Anthony. *UFOs, Unidentified - Undeniable*, Newchapel Observatory, Staffordshire, 1968.

Vallée, Jacques. *UFOs: The Psychic Solution*, Panther, London, 1977.

Glossary

Abductee: Person who is involuntarily abducted by aliens.

Ancient Astronaut Theory: Belief that extraterrestrials visited Earth in the past.

Astral Travel: A non-physical form of travel unlimited by time and space.

Channeller: Person who uses paranormal means to contact aliens.

Contactee: Person who voluntarily meets aliens.

Close Encounter. Dr. Allen Hynek's classification system used to catalogue UFO reports.

Cultural Tracking: Concept that UFOs mimic our social and cultural expectations.

Direct Contactee: Contactee who has face-to-face encounters with aliens.

Earthlights: Rare luminous aerial phenomena associated with earthquakes and tremors.

Experiencer: A person who has contact or communications with UFOs or aliens.

Flap: An intense period of UFO activity, usually in one specific geographic area.

Flying Saucer: An aerial craft presumably operated by aliens.

Fortean: A person interested in the philosophy, and curiosities collected by, Charles Fort.

Grey: Large headed, small-bodied alien.

Implant: Object inserted into the body of an abductee.

Indirect Contactee: Person who does not meet aliens face-to-face but via astral travel, dreams or mediumship.

Ley Lines: Lines linking ancient sites and buildings. Claimed to be conduits of magical or electromagnetic energy along their pathways or at strategic points.

Leys: See Ley Lines.

Magonia: Alleged historical home of alien beings, and name of British UFO magazine/website.

Mothership: Large alien spaceship that does not land on Earth. It dispatches scoutcraft to Earth.

Nuts and bolts: Physically and literally real spacecraft or aliens.

Oz Factor: Time and reality seems frozen when a UFO is encountered.

Pelicanist: Usually a derogatory term for a UFO sceptic.

Percipient: A person who has had a UFO or alien encounter.

Project Blue Book: United States Air Force project to investigate UFO reports. It ran from 1953 to 1969.

Scoutcraft: Small flying saucer that is dispatched from a mothership.

Screen Memory: Aliens distort our perceptions to present themselves as animals or people.

Silent Contactee: Person who does not make public their voluntary contact with aliens.

Sleep Paralysis. Occurs in stage between waking or going to sleep, causing realistic seeming alien experiences.

Spooklights: Apparently intelligent or intelligently controlled balls of light.

Switched off: Whilst an abductee encounters aliens, the people around them seem to go into some form of trance state.

Telepathy: Mental communication between people and/or aliens.

Trigger Event: Something that causes a person to believe they have had a UFO close encounter.

Ufologist: Person who studies the subject of UFOs.

Ufology: The study of UFOs.

Ufonaut: Alien associated with a UFO encounter.

Ultraterrestrials: Intelligent alien beings who secretly seek to control human society.

Wave: UFO activity over a period of days, weeks or months over a wide area.

Window Area: A location where UFOs and other phenomena are seen on a regular basis.

Index

Abduction, 17, 183-184, 190, 192, 200-201, 214, 229-234
Accidents, 14, 54, 67-70, 161, 222
Adamski, George, 9, 11, 14, 27, 51-52, 235
Addinall, Robert, 165, 167
Aetherius Society, 30, 80
Alpha, 214
Angels, 63-66, 130, 133, 187, 220-225
Angels of Mons, 223
Anlaby, 101-102
Archives for the Unexplained, 245-246
Aroniel, 157
Arna, 99-100
Atlantis, 141-142, 148, 160, 166, 178
Autokinetic effect, 210
Automatic writing, 144, 152
Aveley encounter, 215, 219

Babylon, 160
Backstone Circle, 83-84
Barker, Graham, 212
Beeston, Leeds, 153
Bellis, Terry, 97
Bennett, Paul, 21- 86, 144, 196, 220, 222, 223, 226

Bennett, Phillip, 63-66, 74
Bible, 21, 80, 132-134, 166, 214, 221
Birth, 173, 176-177, 232
Black entity, 43-46
Black magic, 28
Bolton, Martin, 165-182
Book of Revelations, 21, 226
Bowen, Charles, 4, 229
Bowles, Joyce, 215-216
Bradford, 30, 49, 57, 60, 69, 72, 81, 194-197
Bradford Astronomical Society, 24
Brain implants, 178
Briefing For The Landing On Planet Earth, 178
Brighton Triangle, 26
BRUFORP, 26
Buddha, 159
BUFORA, 90, 212, 229, 246

Callaghan, Andrew, 31, 48
Caswell, Harvey, 60
Chariots of the Gods, 9, 21
Clark, Jerome, 23
Clark, Phillip, 24
Clarke, David, 17, 180
Cleckheaton, 66-67

Close Encounters of the Third Kind, 5, 16, 71, 74, 96, 133, 175
Coleman, Loren, 23
Collins, Andrew, 102, 105
Condon, Edward, 24
Contactee, 3, 5, 9, 14, 22, 51, 76-77, 79-80, 82, 131, 163, 181, 235
Contactee Syndrome, 76
Cottingley fairies, 52
Cresswell, Ian, 63, 119
Cup and ring markings, 49-50

Davis, Paul, 58, 64-65, 67
Doyle, Sir Arthur Conan, 51,

Edmundson, Neil 43
Elissah, Josephine, 135-148, 226
Evans, Hilary, 6, 130, 222

Fairies, 50-53, 118-119
Fantasy, 77, 91, 96, 106, 118, 184, 229
Fantasy proneness, 228, 232, 233
Forbes, John Foster, 50
Force Fields, 151
Freud, Sigmund, 118, 177

Goole, 171-172
Gorbals vampire, 117-118

Green, Paula, 190-207
Grimsby, 223
Grinsell, Leslie V., 60
Grove, Carl, 17, 179

Hale, Richard, 58
Hammond, Andrew, 32, 35-39, 47, 75
Harrison, Norman, 147, 150-163, 178, 208, 221, 226
Hebb, Roger, 34, 56, 94, 220
Holiday, F. W., 50
Hollow Earth Theory, 51-52
Holroyd, Stuart, 178
Hopkins, Budd, 192, 200
Hopkins, Robert, 31, 56
Hull, 94, 102, 135, 165
Humber, Jane, 135
Hypnogogic hallucinations, 214
Hypnotic regression, 175, 181, 215, 233

Idle Hill Reservoir, 29, 31-32, 41, 73-74
Idle Moor, 53, 73
Ilkley Moor, 48-50, 52-53
Invisible car, 171
Invisible hand, 172
Invisible walkers, 57-58, 60-61

JASON, 25, 27
Jones, Brian (BAS), 24

Index

Jones Brian, 111-113, 117, 120
Judy Woods, 194-196
Jung, Carl, 18, 228

Kay, David, 26
Keel, John, 10-11, 17, 23-24, 85
King, Barry, 102
King, George, 79
Klass, Phillip, 24
Kraspedon, Dino, 80

L, Mr, 212-214
Lawson, Dr Alvin, 229
Lawson, Brian, 58
Lawson, David, 27, 70
Leeds, 81, 153, 161-162
Leeds-Bradford Airport, 57, 81,
Ley Lines, 48-49
Liverpool Echo, 110-111, 114
Lobuczek, Stefan, 183-188
London Triangle, 24
Lyon, France, 135-136

Magonia, 10, 17, 119, 121, 150, 216
Manchester, 40, 216, 245
McDermott, Michael, 45
McIver, Shirley, 16,
Meditation, 138, 143, 154, 165, 167, 172, 209, 211, 233
Men In Black (MIB), 22, 46-47, 56, 74, 218

Metro Triangle, 24-26, 73
Michael/Mik-ael, 157, 221-225
Missing time, 187, 194
Moon, 15, 31, 47-48, 97, 127-128, 130, 140, 194
Movos, 144
MUFOB, 10, 16, 208, 220
Mystery man, 55

National UFO Research, 26
Newcastle, 115
Nightmares, 60, 63, 65, 183, 186
Northern UFO News, 13, 15-16.
Northern UFO Skywatch Organisation, 27

O'Connell, Vincent, 27
OOBEs, 188, 211-212, 217
Omega, 214
Operation Trojan Horse, 22, 28
Oron, 166, 168

Pateley Bridge, 67
Pendleton, Dave, 47
Phillips, Graham, 102
Phillips, Ken, 90
Physical traces, 36, 93-94, 172
Pratt, Ted, 215
Pregnancy (phantom), 199-200
Premonitions, 69, 132, 143, 161-162

Psychic phenomena, 55, 74, 165, 197
Psychic powers, 26. 77-78, 100, 167, 208, 216
Psychic questing, 100

Rampa, Lobsang, 166
Randles, Jenny, 13-14, 16, 21, 82, 94, 100, 174
Ravenscliffe Woods, 43
Rimmer, John, 119, 150, 154, 211, 216
Robot, 32-40, 75-77, 144, 147, 203
Rogerson, Peter, 6, 76, 216

Sapphire and Steel, 100
Schreber, Dr Daniel, 176-177
Schwarz, Berthold, 56
Sheffield, 14, 17, 82, 92, 150, 155, 162
Shuttlewood, Arthur, 21, 26, 75
Sigma (angel), 63-66, 220, 223
Sleep paralysis, 192, 214, 230-233
Spielberg, Steven, 5, 16, 74
Spiritualist Church, 155, 220
Stead, Susan, 69-70, 77,
Stewart, Rodney, 208, 210
Swastika Stone, 52, 83

Tate, Darryl, 26, 30, 49
Telegraph & Argus, 68

Telepathic voices, 168, 173
Telepathy, 74, 137, 143, 160, 184
Telephone troubles, 55-57, 180, 218
Through the Minds of Others, 135
Tilleard, Jon, 31, 40-41, 46, 48, 53-54, 56, 58, 60, 64, 66, 71
Time travel, 203, 234
Trench, Brinsley Le Poer, 30, 75
Trench, Mrs, 125-134

UFOs: A British Viewpoint, 174,
UFO Brigantia, 16
UFO combat, 57
UFOIN, 16
Unidentified, The, 23
Uranus, 144
Uriel, 157-158

Vallee, Jacques, 21, 110
Venus, 29, 71, 129

Warminster, 11-12, 26, 30, 75
Warrington, Peter, 174
Watkins, Alfred, 25
Wawne, 94-95, 101
Weber, Dr, 176-177
Werff, Dirk Van Der, 208, 210
West Yorkshire Research group, 212
Whetnall, Paul, 100

Index

Whitaker, Trevor, 212, 214
Whiting, Sarah, 72
Willerby, Hull, 135
Williamson, George Hunt, 9, 208
Wilson, Don, 48
Wipprecht, Reverend, 221
Witting, Robin, 223
Wollaton Park, 105-106

Wood Lane House, 57
Wright, Elsie, 29, 50-51
Wrose, 21, 36
Wyke Woods, 196-197

Yeadon, 28, 81
Yoga, 138, 167, 169

Z, Miss, 216-219

6TH
BOOKS

ALL THINGS PARANORMAL

Investigations, explanations and deliberations on the paranormal, supernatural, explainable or unexplainable. 6th Books seeks to give answers while nourishing the soul: whether making use of the scientific model or anecdotal and fun, but always beautifully written.
Titles cover everything within parapsychology: how to, lifestyles, alternative medicine, beliefs, myths and theories.
If you have enjoyed this book, why not tell other readers by posting a review on your preferred book site?

Recent bestsellers from 6th Books are:

The Scars of Eden
Paul Wallis
How do we distinguish between our ancestors' ideas of God and close encounters of an extraterrestrial kind?
Paperback: 978-1-78904-852-0 ebook: 978-1-78904-853-7

The Afterlife Unveiled
What the dead are telling us about their world!
Stafford Betty
What happens after we die? Spirits speaking through mediums know, and they want us to know. This book unveils their world...
Paperback: 978-1-84694-496-3 ebook: 978-1-84694-926-5

Harvest: The True Story of Alien Abduction
G. L. Davies
G. L. Davies's most-terrifying investigation yet reveals one woman's terrifying ordeal of alien visitation, nightmarish visions and a prophecy of destruction on a scale never before seen in Pembrokeshire's peaceful history.
Paperback: 978-1-78904-385-3 ebook: 978-1-78904-386-0

Wisdom from the Spirit World
Carole J. Obley
What can those in spirit teach us about the enduring bond of love, the immense power of forgiveness, discovering our life's purpose and finding peace in a frantic world?
Paperback: 978-1-78904-302-0 ebook: 978-1-78904-303-7

Spirit Release
Sue Allen
A guide to psychic attack, curses, witchcraft, spirit attachment, possession, soul retrieval, haunting, deliverance, exorcism and more, as taught at the College of Psychic Studies.
Paperback: 978-1-84694-033-0 ebook: 978-1-84694-651-6

Advanced Psychic Development
Becky Walsh
Learn how to practise as a professional, contemporary spiritual medium.
Paperback: 978-1-84694-062-0 ebook: 978-1-78099-941-8

Where After
Mariel Forde Clarke
A journey that will compel readers to view life after death in a completely different way.
Paperback: 978-1-78904-617-5 ebook: 978-1-78904-618-2

Poltergeist! A New Investigation into Destructive Haunting
John Fraser
Is the Poltergeist "syndrome" the only type of paranormal phenomena that can really be proven?
Paperback: 978-1-78904-397-6 ebook: 978-1-78904-398-3

A Little Bigfoot: On the Hunt in Sumatra
Pat Spain
Pat Spain lost a layer of skin, pulled leeches off his nether regions, and was violated by an Orangutan for this book
Paperback: 978-1-78904-605-2 ebook: 978-1-78904-606-9

Astral Projection Made Easy
and overcoming the fear of death
Stephanie June Sorrell
From the popular Made Easy series, Astral Projection Made Easy helps to eliminate the fear of death through discussion of life beyond the physical body.
Paperback: 978-1-84694-611-0 ebook: 978-1-78099-225-9

Haunted: Horror of Haverfordwest
G. L. Davies
Blissful beginnings for a young couple turn into a nightmare after purchasing their dream home in Wales in 1989.
Paperback: 978-1-78535-843-2 ebook: 978-1-78535-844-9

Readers of ebooks can buy or view any of these bestsellers by clicking on the live link in the title. Most titles are published in paperback and as an ebook. Paperbacks are available in traditional bookshops. Both print and ebook formats are available online.

Find more titles and sign up to our readers' newsletter at
www.6th-books.com

Join the 6th books Facebook group at
6th Books The world of the Paranormal